MICHIGAN DUI LAW
The Citizen's Guide to the Laws Against Intoxicated Driving

By
Patrick T. Barone

© 2013 by Patrick T. Barone

All rights reserved. Except where otherwise provided in the text of this publication and except as provided by law, no portion of this publication may be reproduced, copied, or transmitted in any form without the written permission of Patrick T. Barone (author). No copyright is claimed in any statutes, rules, or official forms contained in this publication. Copyright is also claimed under the Berne Copyright Convention, Universal Copyright Convention, and Pan American Copyright Convention. No part of this book may be reproduced, scanned, stored in a retrieval system, or transmitted in any form, or by any means, digital, electronic, mechanical, photocopying, recording, or otherwise, without prior permission of the publisher. Notwithstanding the foregoing, for the limited purpose of use in their business, journalists and students may quote from passages in this book (giving full attribution to this book and the author) without charge and without obtaining prior written permission, so long as the cumulative total of such quotations are less than 200 words in length in any single work, web site (URL) or article. The permission granted hereunder does not permit any party to copy any forms, charts, driver's rights cards, or other parts of this book for the purpose of reproducing same for resale, use in a business or office, or for commercial exploitation of same. Other use of this book, its forms, or any other part hereof must be made only with written permission from the publisher. The authors do not claim a copyright in works of other writers and sources, which are shown throughout this book by means of a footnote or credit line. Requests for permission to use portions of the book should be e-mailed to Mr. Barone at: pbarone@baronedefensefirm.com.

Copyright by Patrick T. Barone ©2013

Published and Distributed by

Barone Defense Firm

280 N. Old Woodward Ave., Suite 200

Birmingham, MI 48009

Table Of Contents

Dedication 5

Acknowledgements 7

Introduction 9

Chapter 1: Introduction To Michigan DUI Law 15

Chapter 2: Police Confrontation and Becoming an OWI Suspect 21

Chapter 3: Avoiding Mistakes While In Jail or After Your Arrest 51

Chapter 4: How to Find, Interview and Hire a Top DUI Defense Law Firm 59

Chapter 5: How to Prepare For Your Legal Defense and Can You Drive After Your Arrest? 75

Chapter 6: How to Use Strategies and Defense Tactics to Unshackle the Prosecutor's Case 85

Chapter 7: Specific Challenges and Issues that Can Force Complete Dismissal of Your Case 119

Chapter 8: The "Discovery" Process: How Your Attorney Learns What Evidence The Prosecutor Has And Decides How To Challenge Or Explain It 127

Chapter 9: Understanding Michigan's Implied Consent Laws ... 141

Chapter 10: Understanding and Defending Breath and Blood Tests 157

Chapter 11: Understanding Michigan's License Suspension and Revocation Laws 175

Chapter 12: Your Attorney's Pre-Trial Activities 185

Chapter 13: Should You Have a Trial or Negotiate a Plea Bargain? 201

Chapter 14: Using Motions Practice to Handicap the Prosecutor and Possibly Win in Court 215

Chapter 15: Bench Verses Jury Trials 231

Chapter 16: The Verdict: Acquittal or Conviction? Issues Related to Jail, Probation and Loss of License 263

Chapter 17: Appeals and New Trials 283

Chapter 18: Michigan Driver License Restoration 297

Chapter 19: Boating Under The Influence And Other Related "Impaired Operation" Laws 309

Chapter 20: Snowmobiling And Off-Roading Under The Influence 317

Chapter 21: Enhanced Intoxicated Driving Cases and Those Involving Injury or Death 325

Bonus *Champion Reprint:* — Independent Juries: Liberty's Last Defense 337

Index of Authorities 349

About the Author 370

DEDICATION

Michigan DUI Law - A Citizen's Guide is dedicated to the many Michigan citizens, past and future, who have placed their confidence and trust in me and the Barone Defense Firm, and in doing so have expressed their ultimate belief in and respect for our system of self-government.

I would also like to thank William C. Head; a true champion of justice, whose leadership, support and confidence continues to inspire me as we fight our mutual battle, despite the considerable odds, for the rights of our clients, and for his overriding belief that it is still possible to obtain justice in our courts.

I also dedicate this book to my two wonderful daughters, Madeline and Olivia, who even as teenagers remain a constant source of fascination and joy. Most importantly I dedicate this book to, and thank my wife Elizabeth. Over the last many years she has demonstrated considerable patience, support and understanding as to why I am so driven to assist my clients in finding answers to their legal problems. Based on this understanding, she agreed to limit both our time together, as well as our family time, so that I could spend this time writing while still maintaining a busy law practice.

P.T.B.
May 8, 2013

ACKNOWLEDGEMENTS

I want to thank my office staff, associate and senior trial attorneys for their patience and understanding during my absence from the office department and for assisting me with my research, thereby freeing up the necessary time for me to devote to this important project.

I also want to thank paralegal Greg Guro, who greatly assisted me in both researching Michigan law and creating the edited final draft of this 2013 Edition; particularly as it relates to driver license restoration cases, an area of particular specialization for him. This edited edition would never have reached publication without his help

Patrick T. Barone
Birmingham, Michigan
May 8, 2013

INTRODUCTION

Nearly every day I see Michigan citizens accused of intoxicated driving being poorly represented by their attorneys in courts throughout the State. My hope is that this 2013 update to the original book will have the continuing effect of raising the level of advocacy in Michigan by better informing the accused about how the criminal justice system works. My belief is that better informed clients spur attorneys to work harder and more to become more effective lawyers. The ultimate goal of course is to improve justice for those accused of what is perhaps the most politically unpopular crime of the 21st Century.

Each year my Firm interviews several hundred potential clients. All of them have been accused of intoxicated driving caused by drugs, alcohol or any number of intoxicating substances, or what Michigan now calls "OWI" (operating while intoxicated). Many of these citizens have never had any contact with lawyers, let alone the criminal justice system. It seems that persons accused of this crime, as well as those whose lifestyles place them in jeopardy of becoming the "accused," have similar questions about the "system." In particular, those who are already facing OWI charges have two questions foremost on their minds: (1) what's the "worst case scenario" if I am convicted, **and** (2) how "defendable" is my case. They want to know the specifics of what will happen to their driver's license, whether they would go to jail, and how an OWI conviction might impact their jobs, their ability to travel, or their ability to maintain or pay for automobile insurance. *Michigan DUI Law - A Citizen's Guide* addresses those issues as well as hundreds of other issues relating to how to choose a qualified, experienced trial attorney to handle your Michigan case. This new edition also explains what to expect from each stage of your OWI case in Michigan as it proceeds to trial and even beyond trial.

A person charged with a drunk or drugged driving offense in Michigan faces an assortment of sanctions, but these can be placed into three broad categories: (1) the criminal sanctions imposed by the judge, (2) the driver license sanctions imposed by the Department of State, and; (3) the non-judicial "sanctions" or collateral consequences that occur simply from having a permanent, alcohol related, criminal conviction on your driving history and criminal record. Each of these categories is discussed in detail in this new edition of the book.

The Michigan crime of OWI can be proved through the traditional intoxicated driving offense (OUIL/OUID) and possibly also by proving the so-called "per se" alcohol or zero-tolerance drug offense [UBAL/OWPD which means driving while having an illegal amount of alcohol or any zero tolerance drug in the driver's breath blood or urine]. For a "per se" alcohol or zero tolerance drug prosecution to be pursued by the State, it is not necessary for the prosecutor to prove that you were affected or influenced by the alcohol or drugs you consumed.

Michigan drivers are required to provide a sample of their breath, blood or urine (very rare) for testing by the police. Based on 2003 changes to the law the administrative penalties for refusing a chemical test have been made more severe. Now, persons who refuse to submit to implied consent testing (that has been legally and properly requested by a police officer) will have their driver's license suspended for one year. If there has been a prior refusal within 7 years, then the sanction imposed is a two year license suspension with no right to appeal.

Also, in the 2003 legislation, a new "bad driver tax" was also added. Drivers who are convicted in Michigan are now required to pay the Department of State up to $1,000.00 per year for two years. This type of assessment is clearly designed to bolster sagging tax revenues in

Michigan, as federal funds become more and more limited. Consider it as a "surcharge for losing" an OWI case in Michigan.

Many of these increased sanctions for Michigan drivers are the result of public campaigns pursued and financed by MADD and other political activists. These activists seek to wipe out drunk driving and drugged driving, or (as some writers have stated) possibly seek to reinstitute Prohibition. These efforts have caused Michigan's legislators to write and rewrite laws that persistently become more and more punitive. In addition, Michigan's judges, from the Michigan Supreme Court down, are generally unsympathetic to those accused of drinking and driving (or accused of drugged driving). Because Michigan's laws change constantly, the reader will need to go on-line to get current information about the State's laws on drinking and driving and drugged driving. Within this book, a summary on Michigan law can be found.

Michigan has historically been somewhat behind other states in its efforts to have law enforcement officers specially trained in the detection and arrest of drunk drivers and now to become drug recognition "experts." Nevertheless, nearly all State Troopers have now received SFST specialized field sobriety training, and many members of the "local" law enforcement are similarly trained. Another recent trend is for more officers to obtain training to become so called "drug recognition experts." These officers purport the ability to determine if a driver is on drugs and if so, what class or category of drug they have consumed. This information is used to provide probable cause for the arrest, and also, to provide a starting point for blood testing to confirm (or not) the officer's suspicions.

It is also becoming more common to confront Michigan prosecutors who have taken special training courses developed to increase the likelihood of conviction. Unfortunately, obtaining convictions has become an increasingly simplistic task because many courts (and just as often many jurors) assume that the breath or blood test evidence is irrefutable. Prosecutors also benefit from the State's judiciary who is often either wholly unsympathetic or perhaps even openly hostile to a well-defended intoxicated driving case. Without question these facts complicate the aggressive intoxicated driving defense and they have an unfair impact on the OWI trial. They also make the job of the criminal defense lawyer who undertakes the defense of these cases particularly challenging.

The main purpose of this book is to provide an authoritative guide and to inform and assist citizens accused of drunk or drugged driving about what to expect as their case moves through the court. The information provided is also intended to help the accused better prepare for what lies ahead. The detailed information provided in this new edition of the book should significantly decrease the levels of stress and anxiety felt by the citizen accused of OWI. This is because understanding how things work within the court system generally has a therapeutic and calming effect on otherwise frazzled nerves.

This 2013 edition should also assist Michigan's criminal defense attorneys who defend OWI cases. *However, this book is written primarily for the non-lawyer. My two-volume treatise "Defending Drinking Drivers" (James Publishing) is written as a definitive guide for the DUI defense lawyer and the subject matter in this treatise goes well beyond what appears in "Michigan DUI Law – A Citizen's Guide."*

Nevertheless, attorneys may find it useful to offer this book to their clients who have not already read it. For those clients that have read the book, it should assist in making better use of the various interviews and briefings that their attorney and his or her staff provide to their clients. Either way as it becomes a useful source of authoritative information this book should help ease the time constraints on the OWI practitioner and the members of his or her staff. This new edition might also act as a surrogate for answering the many questions common to all who are accused of OWI.

This book is accurate and current regarding the applicability of laws and statutes as of this date of publication. However, laws are fluid and constantly evolving, ending, and starting from scratch. It is important to do your due diligence to make sure what is stated in this text is still valid in your situation and at a later time.

Also, *Michigan DUI Law - A Citizen's Guide* was never intended to be a compendium of the Michigan law of intoxicated driving and yet readers will find that many of the State's most important legal authorities are included as footnotes, and included in the "index of authorities." Nevertheless, a written work can never replace the personal advice and counsel from a well informed and experienced attorney. This 2013 edition should also not be thought of as a "do it yourself" book. The law and practice of intoxicated driving defense is far too complex for such a thing. This book should however increase the overall quality of representation of the intoxicated driving accused in Michigan, and it is my hope that this book will reach this goal very well.

Patrick T. Barone

Chapter 1:
Introduction to Michigan DUI Law.

Tens of thousands of Americans will go out this evening, just to have a drink or two with friends or with dinner, or possibly even drink more than that, then get into their vehicles and drive on public roads. In Michigan, these actions by themselves are not necessarily illegal for persons age 21 and over, although the police may use the odor of alcohol on their breath as a part of their justification for the arrest. A number of these people will be stopped by the police and arrested for operating while intoxicated (OWI). Since 2003, OWI has been the general term covering each of the intoxicated driving criminal offenses recognized in Michigan (discussed in greater detail in Chapter 2). Since 2010 if their bodily alcohol content was above .17, then the crime is called "high BAC/OWI" or super-drunk[1].

Certain factors may exist that make it much more likely that you will be stopped. After living in a region for any period of time, you may recognize that because of an area's high concentration of late-night drinking establishments, certain sections of town will be more prone to a heavy police presence. Similarly, certain main business highways are traffic arteries leading to and from "party areas" of towns or cities. It is common knowledge that the police are more likely to be present on or near such roads.

If you drive through these areas after 10 PM, you are much more likely to be stopped by the police than if you drive in these areas while the sun is out. Likewise, your chances of encountering the police in these areas at 2:00 A.M. are 100 times more likely than they are at 2:00 P.M. If you routinely place yourself in these situations, or if you have already gone through an incident where the police have arrested you for an OWI, then in order to assist you and your OWI criminal defense specialist in preparing your best defense, you should read this book. Each chapter will help you to build a factual foundation for use by your attorney, and this foundation can assist him or her in formulating and building your defense. By understanding the legal process, you will also be better equipped to assist in your own defense.

Michigan OWI law evolves every day. There are new laws constantly arriving effecting where the lines are drawn, and how to prove it. There are just as constantly new court decisions interpreting those laws, and determining their effects, and sometimes, their validity. Not to be overlooked, there is also a constant evolution of knowledge in numerous scientific fields that effects the determination of the guilt or innocence of those accused of OWI.

The author will strive to explain the current state of affairs in each of these areas through the course of this book. However, this book is not written as a treatise or encyclopedia of OWI law for the benefit of OWI lawyers, whether they work as prosecutors or defenders. Likewise, this book is not intended to evaluate the efforts and research of the many scientists and others who study matters related to the prosecution and defense of these cases.

This book is intended to help those people whose lives have been, or are now being, affected by a prosecution for the offense of OWI in Michigan. Whether the reader is the person accused, or perhaps a loved one, or maybe a witness to or victim of, a possibly impaired driver, this book should help to explain what has happened, what is happening, what happens next, and how certain actions by certain people involved might affect the direction of the events, and the ultimate outcome.

In 1933, Congress ended a decade of Prohibition. Automobiles were becoming abundant and alcohol became even more widely available. The combination had predictable results: an increase in car accidents attributed to alcohol-impaired drivers. As early as 1917 in Michigan, there have been some criminal offenses to operating a moving conveyance of one type or another while under the influence of alcohol, with marked changes commencing in 1948.[2] The first per se limit was 0.10 grams. (*Per se* meaning you are automatically breaking the law if your blood alcohol level is above this limit, even if you show no signs of any impairment.) This was revised to the current 0.08 limit in 2003.[3] The first forms of the implied consent law were also passed in 1948.[4]

Since those first laws were passed, OWI arrests and convictions have radically changed hundreds of thousands of lives in Michigan. It is one of the most common misdemeanors prosecuted throughout the Michigan court system, and it remains a hot-button issue for advocates on both sides. The organization of Mothers Against Drunk Driving (M.A.D.D.) has led to at least a dozen other groups being formed with similar public awareness or political influence agendas relating directly to drinking and driving (such as R.I.D., S.A.D.D.,[5] and R.A.D.D.).

The purposes of this book are many. If you have been arrested and charged with one or more of the many forms of OWI, your attorney may recommend you buy and read this book (may have even given you a copy to read). One purpose of this book is to help you better understand what is a confusing and, at times, brutal legal process once you are involved in an OWI situation. You should begin planning for several months or more of meetings with your attorney and others involved in your defense, court hearings and possibly a trial, a year or more of possible punishment (jail time and probation); tens of thousands of dollars in possible costs, and having the government more in charge of your life than you are at times. This book takes you through the entire process, from before your initial stop until your life might be considered normal again.

Second, this book explores your legal rights under Michigan law. If you ever drink any alcohol then drive, it is critical that you understand your constitutionally guaranteed rights and the protections they afford you. In a system which is set up to assist the police and the prosecution in most ways, it is vital that you do not give up any of your rights unless and until they are taken from you properly. A significant portion of this book tries to take you through these rights, as interpreted through federal and Michigan law.

Last, this book is meant to educate you as a driver, as an adult, as someone who may drink alcohol or use prescription medicines or even herbal remedies. It is a book for parents to share with their teenagers who may be starting out on their own, driving and possibly drinking. This book is not meant to teach anyone the law or to make you a lawyer. OWI law is a rapidly changing kaleidoscope of many laws, best handled by a seasoned criminal defense attorney. However, this book is meant to better prepare you to make hard life decisions at 2:00 in the morning when you see flashing blue lights in your rearview mirror.

If you have any questions, or if you have been arrested and charged with an OWI offense, this book is no substitute for the advice of a well-seasoned OWI attorney. The last purpose of this book is meant to supplement that advice.

Chapter 2:
Police Confrontation and Becoming an OWI Suspect

2.0. Purpose of this Chapter. The primary purpose of this chapter is to explain *when, where* and *how* you are most likely to be confronted by police in situations where you may be suspected of impaired driving and be asked to submit to an implied consent chemical testing of your breath, blood or urine. If you were already arrested for OWI it is critical you are aware of these factors. This chapter will then discuss which factors are most crucial for your possible defense, how to recognize them and how to help your attorney gather them.

2.1. The Two General Types of OWI - Alcohol. In Michigan, if you have been charged with drunk driving, then you are specifically charged with violating the law by operating a motor vehicle while you were either intoxicated or impaired by alcohol. The principal, or more serious, crime of drunk driving is known by the acronym "OWI," standing for Operating While Intoxicated.

Regarding alcohol, this more serious charge can be proved in two ways. The first way is for the prosecutor to show you were OUIL, which stands for Operating a vehicle while Under the Influence of Liquor. To prove this crime, the prosecutor needs to prove beyond a reasonable doubt that your ability to operate a motor vehicle was substantially lessened because of drinking alcohol. This is known as the common law offense of drunk driving. The specific *elements* of OUIL (essential parts of a crime that must be proven by the prosecutor to get a conviction) are: (a) operating or being in actual physical control of a "vehicle"; (b) on a roadway, public way or other place prohibited by Michigan's laws (sometimes any place within the state); (c) while under the influence of an intoxicating beverage, substance, vapor or chemical, or some combination of these chemicals and substances.[6] A breath or blood test result can be used by the judge or jury to determine if you have committed this crime, but a CHEMICAL TEST RESULT IS NOT REQUIRED TO PROVE THIS CRIME.

The second form of OWI is known as UBAL. This means that at the time you were operating your vehicle you had an Unlawful Blood Alcohol Level. As you are undoubtedly aware, for adults who are not driving commercial vehicles, the legal limit in Michigan is 0.08. So, if the prosecutor can prove beyond a reasonable doubt that your blood alcohol level at the time you were driving was 0.08 or greater, then you can be found guilty of drunk driving. This is known as a "per se" offense, meaning there is *NO REQUIREMENT FOR PROVING IMPAIRMENT* of the driver. The prosecutor does, however, have to prove that the chemical test result is both admissible and reliable. In Michigan, we do not have "trial by number," and the jury must decide what meaning or what "weight" to give the chemical test evidence. Just because there is a breath or blood test result in your case does not automatically mean that the jury must or even will find you guilty.

You can be found guilty of UBAL based on different "legal" limits so long as you have consumed enough alcohol to exceed the applicable legal limit for your age group and vehicle type.[7] Presently, Michigan the following laws covering these various situations:

"Super Drunk"	0.17%
Drivers age 21 and over, in a non-commercial vehicle	0.08%
Drivers under age 21 [ZERO TOLERANCE *]	>0.02%
Any driver of a commercial motor vehicle	0.04%
Under 21. Commercial vehicle.	>.02%

For those who take the state's test and render a sample with an alcohol level at or over Michigan's legal limit, this alone (assuming the test result gets into evidence and is believed by the jury or judge hearing your case) constitutes the separate offense of OWI "*per se*"). Note that "per se" limits for contraband drugs have not YET been "established" by the federal government, but that this legislation will be enacted within the next 2 to 5 years. Hence, today in Michigan, only ALCOHOL has "per se" limits for *Driving with an Unlawful Bodily Alcohol Level UBAL*. These two alcohol offenses cover 95% of all active OWI cases.

2.2. The Many Kinds of OWI - Drugs. As OWI alcohol cases continue to decline in Michigan, law enforcement is making up for the lost revenue by arresting ever increasing numbers of OWI drug cases. The legislature is obliging this effort by broadening the definition of "drug" making more and more people subject to potentially violating the new law.

This is all possible because the Michigan crime of "OWI" can be proven based on the presence of a drug in your system, or a combination of drugs and alcohol at the time you were operating a motor vehicle.[8] If the drug in question is a prescribed or over-the-counter drug (having a potentially medicinal purpose), then the prosecutor must show that this drug or combination of this drug and alcohol caused your ability to operate the motor vehicle to be "substantially lessened." This is essentially the same as the common law OUIL except the impairing or intoxicating substance in this case is a non-schedule 1 drug. The acronym for this crime is OUID (Operating Under the Influence of Drugs).

On the other hand, if the drug in question is a recreation drug (having no generally recognized medicinal purpose), then the acronym for the intoxicated driving offense is OWPD, which stands for Operating With the Presence of Drugs. This crime is "zero tolerance," meaning if the drug is present in your system while you are driving, then you are guilty regardless of if the drug impacted your ability to drive. The zero tolerance drugs are set forth in "Schedule 1" of the Michigan statutes.[9]

Additionally, on January 2, 2013, Governor Snyder signed into law Public Act 543 which broadly expands the legal definition of "drug" to include "intoxicating substances." The effective date is March 31, 2013.

As used in this the new law[10] "intoxicating substance" still embraces the old definition of "drug," but significantly expands it to include any substance recognized as a drug in the official United States Pharmacopoeia (USP), Homeopathic Pharmacopoeia (HPUS) or the National Formulary. Although likely to be litigated due to the law's ambiguity, it appears that these drugs do not require any intent on the part of the driver. If the prosecution can prove that these drugs are in the driver's body, and the driver is impaired or intoxicated, then he/she has violated this law.

The law further defines intoxicating substance to include anything, other than food, that is taken into a person's body that is used in a manner or for a purpose for which it was not intended, and that may result in a condition of intoxication. This subsection appears to require the further element of intent.

In reading the law it is important to understand the difference between USP and HPUS in order to fully appreciate just how broad this proposed definition really is. The USP lists and monitors those substances that are commonly thought of as medicines; the kinds of things your medical doctor might prescribe or recommend. On the other hand, an osteopathic doctor, or a holistic healer might engage in homeopathy, which favors the use of herbal medicines; and it is in this arena that the proposed real expansion of the drug definition takes place. These herbal medicines are the province of the HPUS.

According to the HPUS web site[11] "any substance may be considered a homeopathic medicine if it has known "homeopathic provings" and/or known effects which mimic the symptoms, syndromes or conditions which it is administered to treat, and is manufactured according to the specifications of the Homeopathic Pharmacopoeia of the United States (HPUS). Official homeopathic drugs are those that have been monographed and accepted for inclusion in the HPUS." Alternative medicine websites as well as stores indicate a product is listed in the HPUS as a kind of selling point. Such medicines include: Chamomile, Bitter Cucumber, Yellow Jasmine, Tobacco, and Red Onion.[12, 13] Therefore, certain teas and food ingested not even as a "drug" can get one arrested if an officer so deems fit.

Closely related is the "National Formulary." This compendium was "established in 1888 by the American Pharmaceutical Association and includes standards for excipients, botanicals, and other similar products." The VA National Formulary as of October 2012 includes the following: Insulin, Lithium, Multivitamins, and Amino Acids.[14]

2.2.1 Drug Recognition "Experts". Based on the enactment of Public Act 543 (see section 2.2 above), and more generally the overall law enforcement environment in Michigan, increased emphasis is now being placed on law enforcement officers to find and arrest drivers who are impaired by any intoxicating substance. Beginning in 2012 officers from local and county police agencies and the Michigan State Police (MSP) began participating in an intensive three-week drug recognition course. The class also includes Michigan prosecutors. Upon graduating from this training the officers now carry the moniker of "Drug Recognition Expert" or DRE.

This DRE training program was developed in Los Angeles during the 1970s. In 1979 the drug recognition program received official recognition of the LAPD.[i] The program itself is based on a three step process:

Step One: Verify that the subject is impaired, and verify that the subjects' blood alcohol concentration is not consistent with the degree of impairment.

Step Two: Determine whether the impairment is drug or medically related (injury or illness).

Step Three: Use proven diagnostic procedures to determine the category (or combination of categories) of drugs that are likely the cause of impairment.[ii]

The ostensible purpose of the program is to provide "the strongest articulable evidence" that drugs are the cause of impairment, as opposed to something else, to obtain probable cause for a driver who refuses a blood test and to show that the drug is psychoactive (as opposed to merely present).[iii]

While based on a three step process, the drug influence evaluation procedure includes the following twelve steps:

a. The breath test (machine number, time of test, test administrator, etc.)
b. DRE interview with arresting officer
c. Preliminary examination by DRE (determination whether suspect has suffered from any injury or illness or some other condition other than drugs)
d. Eye examination (horizontal gaze nystagmus, vertical nystagmus and lack of convergence)
e. Divided attention psycho-physical tests (Romberg balance, walk-and-turn, one-leg stand and finger-to-nose)
f. Dark room examination (check for pupil dilation under three different lighting conditions: near total darkness, indirect light and direct light)
g. Vital sign examination (pulse, blood pressure and temperature; certain drugs elevate vital signs while others lower them)

h. Muscle tone examination (certain drugs may cause muscles to become tense while others produce flaccidity)
i. Examination for any injection sights (evidence of hypodermic needles, fresh needle marks, scars or tracks)
j. Review of suspect statements and other observations (Miranda invocation, implied consent rights, warnings, etc.)
k. DRE opinion (suspect's state of impairment in category or categories of drugs involved)

> Note: "The DRE must document this opinion in a formal report that specifies the basis for it." *Id* at 40

l. Toxicological examination (a chemical test or urine or blood corroborate the DRE opinion into obtainable admissible scientific evidence)[iv]

As part of the evaluation, the DRE will prepare a drug influence evaluation form or "Face Sheet" that will contain his or her observations made while or after conducting the above twelve steps. Then, pursuant to step twelve, the blood (or urine) is then sent to the state lab for testing. This twelve step examination takes about 45 minutes to one hour to complete.

As indicated the process suggests that a DRE is able to use this twelve step evaluation to determine the "category or combination of categories of drugs" causing the impairment. There are seven categories, which include:

- CNS Depressants: examples include alcohol, barbiturates and valium;
- CNS Stimulants: examples include cocaine, crystal "meth," Ritalin and amphetamines;
- Hallucinogens: examples include LSD, peyote; mushrooms, ecstasy (MDMA), toad licking and nutmeg;

- Inhalants: examples include glue, gasoline, paint thinner, spray paint, nitrous oxide, Scotch guard and Freon;
- Cannabis: examples include marijuana, hashish, hash oil, Thai sticks, marinol and dronabinol;
- Narcotic Analgesics: examples include heroin, morphine, codeine and synthetic opiates (e.g., Demerol, methadone);
- Phencyclidine (PCP): examples include PCP, angel dust, dust, super kools, sherm, ketamine (special k) and vetelar.

The possible mixture of drugs and wide possible variance within one single category (LSD vs. nutmeg for example) leaves doubt that anybody within a forty five minute period can accurately know any one drug or all drugs present in one's system. How can one seriously know the difference between a single heroin needle injection or if one donated blood earlier that day?

2.2.2 Top Five Ways to Avoid a DRE Arrest or Conviction. There are many ways to avoid being arrested for drugged driving, and many more ways to avoid being convicted. Here are the top five:

1. **Don't carry any medications or pill bottles with you in your car.** If the police spot such a container or find medications on you then you run the risk of the officer putting two and two together and getting a wrong answer: namely that the medications have caused you to be impaired.
2. **Don't admit to taking any drugs.** A typical DRE arrest begins with the roadside officer's investigation. Once the DRE gets called in he/she will ask the roadside officer if any admissions were made. The DRE will also ask you once more if not twice more if you are taking any medications or drugs. Just politely decline to answer these questions. You have no legal obligation to answer these questions from any police officer.
3. **Refuse to take any roadside tests and refuse also to participate in the DRE evaluation.** Again, the roadside

officer will be asking you questions and asking you to submit to "field sobriety evaluations." Just politely say no. As of the date of this publication, as a Michigan driver you have no obligation legally to take these "tests." Also, refuse to submit to any tests back at the station from the DRE officer. In other words, decline to submit to the DRE 12 step process.

4. (After you've taken the breath test at the station) - **Refuse to provide a blood sample.** A DRE evaluation requires that you be given an evidentiary breath test first. This is the one at the station not the one at the side of the road. After you've taken the station breath test (on the DataMaster) you can refuse any further testing without violating Michigan's implied consent law or otherwise placing your license in jeopardy. If you blow all zeros or a low number, the DRE will ask for a blood test to "confirm" his "opinion" about the drugs you've taken. You can "just say no" to this request. (While this is true as of date of this book, the implied consent law is very likely subject to interpretation and change so as to make it mandatory to give a subsequent blood test! See section 2.9 for further details.)

5. **Find a DRE trained defense attorney.** If you follow the above advice and are arrested anyway, or don't read this until after you've been arrested for drugged driving, make sure you find the best lawyer you can afford. Only a very small number of Michigan DUI lawyers have DRE training. If you're charged with drugged driving, and don't hire one of these lawyers, you're chances of a favorable outcome will be significantly limited.

2.3. Remain Silent — It Is Your Right! The Fifth Amendment to the United States Constitution[15] has been found to include that you have an absolute right to remain silent and not incriminate yourself during your arrest and booking process.[16] This right applies to everyone once invoked by the suspect,[17] is true in nearly every state,[18] is true in Michigan and it is true even if you are an alien or an illegal alien.[19] Once the arresting officer has read you your Miranda warnings, this silence cannot be used against you in court.[20] In order to "activate" this right, you must tell the officer(s) you have made the choice to remain silent.[21] This does not mean that you should not be appropriately polite with the law enforcement officers, using such terms as "please," and "thank you." Beyond providing the police identification information such as your name, address and showing them your driver's license, you do not have to answer any questions relating to why you were arrested.

If your stop was based on the officer's "reasonable suspicion," the police officer has the right to expect you to identify yourself,[22] and to have you produce your driver's license.[23] Police officers receive training, including mock trial practice, during which they must recite sufficient information to support their decision to arrest a suspect. The training has led to officers spouting off a litany of these "common" symptoms of apparent intoxication so that the officer can survive a pre-trial motion to suppress the arrest decision, due to lack of clear evidence of impairment. One handbook for prosecutors and police officers provides this partial list: smell of alcohol; impaired muscle (gross and fine motor) control; slurred speech; flushed face, bloodshot eyes; and other physical symptoms.[24] Officers are also taught a list of explanations (excuses) that officers sometimes ask the driver about so as to eliminate these alternative reasons for the bad driving that has been observed. Remember that an officer WANTS to hear your speech patterns to determine if your speech is slurred or otherwise "impaired" sounding. Certain drugs will cause thick-tongued or very slow, halting speech patterns. If an officer can address any possible excuses immediately, it is more likely that the driver he or she is dealing with will not be able to find a viable explanation of the errant driving.

When the officer approaches your window, after asking for your license and possibly other documents, a question will usually start off the encounter. The *content* of your answer is relatively unimportant to the officer. The *manner* of speech is what is being observed. Unfortunately, even those with extensive training can be fooled, falsely leading officers to believe they can predict how much alcohol you have in your system through your speech patterns.[25] Engaging in lengthy excuses does nothing to improve the chances that you will be allowed to leave the scene, if the smell of alcohol or of contraband drugs is present. If the officer smells or suspects that he or she smells anything that might impair you, the next step is usually to ask you to step out of the vehicle. Each part of this maneuver will be noted by the officer in detail later, from how quickly you exit, whether you use the side or frame of the car, whether you fumble with items in your hands, such as keys or wallet, whether you drop anything, how you balance yourself or possibly sway —*anything and everything.*

2.4. Assume that Everything is Being Recorded. A large number of police vehicles have the capability for either video or audio recording (or both) of everything that occurs in the general vicinity of the officer manning the vehicle. The camera usually is positioned to catch the scene in front of the vehicle, often next to the interior rearview mirror. That is why the officer usually does any field sobriety testing or questioning in front of his or her car. Most modern cameras can be rotated by the police officer 360 degrees to focus on you sitting in the backseat of the car while you are being transported to jail.

Audio microphones are located both on the officer's shirt or vest and inside his or her vehicle. The officer often has the capability to turn these microphones on and off individually, so that he or she can have private conversations with other officers, their dispatcher or supervisor, yet catch any and every word you say on tape. **Remember: remain silent even when you think you are alone and in a "private" place.** It is safest for you to assume that everything from the time the officer first stops your vehicle through being delivered to the jail is being recorded. This is especially true of anything you say, since the microphone in the back of the officer's patrol car can pick even a whisper that you utter under your breath.

2.5. Why The Police Stop You. The first interaction with a police officer usually occurs when errant driving conduct or some defective item of equipment or expired tags draws the officer's attention to your vehicle. Sometimes the "thing" that leads to your pullover may be unrelated to your driving actions, such as when an obvious equipment defect exists or an expired registration or inspection sticker is visible on your car.

However, the NHTSA (the National Highway Traffic Safety Administration, an arm of the federal Department of Transportation) has identified a number of visual driving cues (or clues, as they are sometimes referred to by officers) that the NHTSA suggests police officers use to identify possible alcohol-impaired driving. The list of clues or cues, as originally published, included weaving and swerving, following too closely, driving erratically or with your headlights off, or driving too slowly and signally inconsistently.[26] For an up-to-date list of factors, check a recent pamphlet from the NHTSA.[27] The two things that should immediately come to every reader's mind are **(1)** everyone has done these things, almost on a daily basis, especially in the era of the hand-held cell phone, and **(2)** that the most common traffic offense, ***speedi*ng**, is <u>not</u> on the list. ANY driving behavior, vehicle deficiency or activity that looks the slightest bit suspicious will usually result in an officer coming in contact with you, just to see if you display any signs of drinking or using drugs.

2.6. Driving a Vehicle that Invites Being Pulled Over. Equipment defects or vehicle safety problems sometimes provide the basis for an officer to pull you over. Examples include: tires with insufficient tread; a damaged windshield; dim or burned out headlights or brake lights;

someone in the vehicle not wearing a seatbelt; or smoke emerging from the vehicle.

These correctable items (which likely would never merit a pullover during morning rush hour) have led to many traffic stops that ultimately resulted in OWI arrests. Remember, the officer only needs a single REASON for coming in contact with your vehicle. His or her REAL purpose in stopping you is to see if you are impaired or have other smells, visible or audible evidence of possible impairment. If this sounds "unconstitutional" to you, it does NOT sound unconstitutional to the United States Supreme Court! The high court *UNANIMOUSLY* approved of this tactic in a decision that drastically reduced our legal and privacy rights as Americans.[28]

2.7. When Being Followed by Police, Don't Pull Over Before Being Required to do so. Intelligent people should not engage in conduct to "waive" or give up constitutional protections. One of the most basic of these constitutional protections is the right to be free from arbitrary traffic stops.

A driver that sees a police car following his or her car may instinctively think that pulling over is the correct thing to do. *WRONG!* Keep proceeding within the speed limit, obey all traffic laws, stay entirely within your lane and make sure that no "outward" (visible) problems exist with your vehicle. Use turn signals to make any lane changes or turns, no matter how minor. Stay off the cell phone and do nothing to distract your attention from the roadway.

Court cases across the USA have consistently upheld the right of police to come in contact with you when you are on foot, *or* if you pull over and stop your vehicle. A legal farce that has helped perpetuate this practice is a doctrine known as the "community caretaking" doctrine. The theory goes, if an officer sees anything amiss in his or her community, he or she can and should investigate the "problem" area or suspicious behavior to clear up any problems.

If an officer sees you pull into a shopping center parking lot in an effort to get him or her to quit following you, the officer is hoping that you will come to a stop. Then, he or she is going to be able to legitimately come in contact with your car (and your face) without any legal basis to suspect a crime has been committed or is about to be committed. If you kept moving, and never pulled over until signaled to do so by the blue or red lights of the patrol car (or the siren or hand signals to stop), then any encounter created by the use of "color of law" (using the emergency equipment to force you to stop your vehicle) is called a "tier one Terry stop".[29]

The *Terry* decision embodies the Fourth Amendment's protection against stopping a vehicle without a legal justification for doing so. Beyond the protections of *Terry* in prohibiting use of police power to stop a vehicle on a mere hunch, and for no real traffic violation (tier one stops), *Terry* further outlines the illegality of an officer fulfilling the original purpose of the stop and then (with no justifiable belief that criminal activity is afoot) start investigating for further potential crimes. This is a tier two detention.

Thousands of legal decisions have interpreted and made rulings on both tier one and tier two *Terry* issues. A recent case from Utah states that any further temporary detention for investigative questioning after fulfilling the purpose for initial traffic stop constitutes an illegal seizure, unless an officer has probable cause or a reasonable suspicion of a further illegality.[30]

2.8. If You Don't Take Field Tests, Will You Lose Your License?
In Michigan, there is no requirement for you to take any of the field sobriety tests, and if you politely refuse, there is no automatic license suspension. A roadside portable breath test or Preliminary Breath Test "PBT" is one type of field sobriety test. You may also refuse this test, but if you do, you will be charged with a civil infraction and receive a fine.[31] However, there is no mandatory driver license sanction for refusing a roadside breath test. This is a significant

difference between the refusal of any of the field sobriety tests and the refusal of a blood, breath or urine test at the station house or jail where there is a mechanism for the police to automatically take your driver's license. Having a driver's license is a qualified right for you, one that can and is continuously reviewed by the State of Michigan. That means Michigan can take your license away, but only with an adequate reason, and only with notice to you and an opportunity to be heard.[32]

Now, if you do not take the field sobriety tests, and you are eventually convicted of an OWI offense, you will lose your license as a part of that proceeding. However, that is likely months away from your stop, and may never occur if an experienced OWI attorney helps you with your case.

2.9. If You Refuse to be Tested at the Station House or Jail, Will You Lose Your License? Following your refusal to take the offered state testing of your blood, breath or urine, unless you are then able to get your driver's license back at an administrative hearing, your driver's license is automatically suspended for a year for a first refusal within 7 years, 2 years if a second refusal within 7 years.[33]

If you refuse the blood, breath or urine tests asked of you by the police, and the police take your plastic driver's license, you will be given a paper license that will allow you to remain driving until either you fail to make a request for an "implied consent" hearing within 14 days of your arrest, or you lose the administrative hearing when it is scheduled. This paper license is called a "DI-93," and also includes instructions on how to schedule your hearing. Your OWI specialist can better advise you of your rights with this temporary license, and can request the hearing for you, that is so long as you retain him or her prior to the 14 day deadline.

2.10. If You Take the State's "Chemical" Test(s), Will You Get to Keep Your License? In Michigan, your license will not be suspended or revoked unless and until you are found guilty of an alcohol related traffic offense.[34] Upon learning of this conviction, the Michigan Department of State will take the appropriate licensing action, and will notify you of this sanction by mail. It is the court's responsibility to notify the Department of State.

2.11. If You Refuse the State's Tests, Can You Obtain a "Work" Permit? If you have lost your license because of an implied consent refusal, and you have no prior implied consent refusals, then you may appeal the one year suspension to the circuit court. Under these circumstances, this is called a "hardship" appeal, and is for the purpose of obtaining a restricted driving privilege. You may also file a legal appeal if you believe the hearing officer was wrong in his or her determination that you inappropriately refused the chemical test. If the legal appeal is successful, then you will obtain a full restoration of your driving privileges, but these appeals are rarely granted.

In order to obtain limited or restricted driver's license privileges, you must meet certain statutory criteria such as true necessity, no other travel sources available to you, and no family members who can provide transportation for you.[35] This is at the discretion of the court, not your choice and not the choice of your attorney. Certainly, the basic requirements are that you have a job which requires you to drive and that you have no other reasonable way to get around without a driver's license. It is also likely that the circuit court judge will want to see a substance abuse evaluation showing that you are at low risk of repeat behavior. Even if your hardship appeal is successful such a license typically severely restricts your ability to drive, determining where and when you can operate a vehicle.[36]

2.12. Who <u>Can</u> Refuse to be Tested? Unless someone was serious injured or killed as a result of an accident related to your OWI arrest, you have the right to refuse to allow the police to take a blood, breath or urine sample from you.[37] In other words, the drawing of your blood, or the taking of a urine or a breath sample by the police must typically be voluntary.[38] However, if incapacitated, either because you are unconscious, incoherent or unable to consent for whatever reason (including being too intoxicated), you lose your right to refuse.[39]

In almost all circumstances, however, if you are arrested in Michigan, and you refuse a chemical test, the arresting officer will obtain a warrant to draw your blood. Thus, instead of a breath test result, you will be faced with a more accurate blood test and automatic license sanctions. Not only that, but the results of your independent test are also admissible at your trial.[40] If your independent test confirms the State's test, then your attorney will have two tests to confront and overcome at trial.

An increasing trend, now seen in more than a dozen states including Michigan, is a situation where a person who refuses breath testing to be restrained or even physically harmed to have their blood forcibly drawn, or have a catheter inserted in the person for a urine sample, if the officer gets a warrant.[41] Typically, this occurs when another person (as a result of your alleged bad driving) has been seriously injured or killed as a result of your accident.[42]

2.13. Who <u>Should</u> Refuse to be Tested? Perhaps because of prior OWI convictions, or because even a single OWI conviction on your criminal record would be devastating to your life, the punishment for any OWI conviction may be significantly worse than anything you face as a penalty from the refusal to be tested. It is certainly more difficult for the police to prove most OWI charges against you when there is no scientific testing of any kind which the prosecution can use as evidence.

Also, keep in mind that the punishment against you for a refusal (an administrative loss of your driver's license of a year for a first refusal in seven years) is automatic,[43] while the punishment against you for the criminal charges of OWI must be subsequently proven in court beyond a reasonable doubt. Many other reasons may exist for the criminal charges against you to be dropped or reduced, or you might win at trial. Some case facts are so favorable that it is best for you to fight the charges against you, accepting no punishment for the OWI, while giving a blood, breath or urine sample as requested by the police.

Thus, if you are someone for whom even a single OWI on your record might be devastating, or if you have prior OWI convictions on your criminal record, especially if there is a chance you may place yourself or be placed in a position where you may be stopped and questioned regarding a subsequent OWI charge, it is a good idea to sit down beforehand with a well-seasoned OWI specialist and figure out what is best for you to do in these situations. Each circumstance and every client is different, and these sometimes subtle variances may make all the difference in your future. If you refuse to consent, however, understand that as indicated in § 2.12 above, the police are likely to get a warrant. If you continue to refuse, force may be used to extract your blood.

2.14. Will Your "Refusal" be Used Against You in Court? Your refusal can typically be used against you in some way in your criminal OWI trial. The admission into evidence by the prosecution of your chemical test refusal is invariably detrimental and this admission has been held to be constitutional. Unless satisfactorily explained, the jury will normally assume that you refused to be tested because you had consumed too much alcohol and were afraid of failing the test, an assumption that the prosecutor seldom fails to bring to the jury's attention. In Michigan, though, there is a standard jury instruction that they not consider the refusal in any way, and that the only reason it came into evidence is to prove that a test was offered.

Nevertheless, as a practical matter when evidence of a refusal is admitted during the prosecution's case, it is often necessary for you to have to testify in order to effectively explain your reasons for refusing to submit. If your attorney gets to question you on all the things that may help your case, the prosecution gets to question you on all the things that may harm it. Obviously then, the admission into evidence of a chemical test refusal should be avoided, if at all possible. Most experienced trial lawyers prefer to NOT put their clients on the witness stand.

2.15. *Never* Attempt to Perform the SFST's or Other Voluntary Field Tests. Police officers usually ask drivers whom they suspect of driving under the influence of either drugs or alcohol to perform "standard field sobriety tests." Exactly what tests you are asked to perform varies, but may include the horizontal gaze nystagmus, a nine-step walk and turn, and a straight leg raise. Other tests often include giving parts of the alphabet (without singing), adding or subtracting numbers in your mind, or giving a breath sample into a handheld alcohol device.

The field sobriety tests are, without a doubt, the greatest source of bad arrests and faulty convictions in OWI cases in this nation. Virtually no American is aware that they have an absolute right to NOT attempt to perform these agility and medically-created evaluations that are being offered by an officer who may even have an arrest quota to fill. They are all subjective. If you attempt any of them and fail in any small portion, the officer is going to testify to this at your trial. Your failures may also be caught and recorded on any video or audio recordings. Judges and juries find such evidence very strong in their decision whether or not to convict you of OWI.

In the end, the chances of a field sobriety test helping you are so slight, and the chances of them hurting you so great, few situations exist where you should agree to performing the tests. Just say no - politely.

2.16. Avoid "Verbal Gymnastics" or Police Officers' "Catch-22's." If you are stopped by the police, be polite and respond appropriately. You cannot and will not win in a battle of mental or verbal gymnastics with a law enforcement officer. He or she is not interested so much in your answers as the manner in which you give them.

The more you talk, no matter what you say, the worse the situation is likely to become. You are not in charge of the situation. The officer is. Most officers take formal training on how to use questioning to keep you "off balance." One such course is called "verbal judo." Remember, that the officer is going to go home at the end of their shift, while you are trying to stay out of jail. Your adherence to these guidelines could prevent you from spending the next several years of your life straightening out a life-changing and job-ending nightmare.

2.17. Don't Lose Your Composure or use Bad Language. Police officers are in charge when they stop you and start an evaluation for OWI. Most stops are in the middle of the night, when you are already tired. It is very easy to lose your composure or use harsh or bad language if you are stopped, especially if you think you have done nothing wrong.

Take a deep breath. Remember that everything you say or do is likely to be recorded. You may be technically correct that the officer is not treating you well. However, the jury or the judge is not going to think highly of your bad language or of you if you lose your composure. In their eyes, that is another sign that you may have been intoxicated. In the brief minutes of your traffic stop, or the hours during the processing of your arrest, you **MUST** be on your best behavior. Think always of how you will appear to a jury.

2.18. Politely Attempt to Leave by Cab, on Foot or with a Friend Even if Your Car is Towed. If you have been drinking **any** alcohol, or done **any** illegal drugs on the day before you have an accident, after you have traded insurance information with any other driver involved in the accident and before the police show up to investigate, politely attempt to leave the scene. Try walking away, call a cab, or use your cell phone to have a friend come and get you. If you have traded insurance and license information with the other drivers, you are not leaving the scene of the accident. This assumes that no one is injured and needs medical assistance.

If you have been stopped by an officer who is asking you questions about drinking or the use of drugs, make no admission of any usage. If you are not detained by the officer after your refusal to perform any field sobriety tests, attempt to call a cab, call a friend to come get you, or start walking home. State to the officer that you are willing to satisfy his or her concerns for safety by handing him or her the keys to your ignition and taking a cab home, but that you will not submit to testing that you do not trust to be reliable or accurate.

If the officer responds by challenging your awareness that you are unsafe to be driving or something similar, be sure to respond, *"Absolutely not true. I am merely trying to satisfy you that I am cooperative in every way, even if I believe your concerns are not reasonable."* If taking the cab results in your car being towed, that is a small price to pay to avoid being arrested and possibly convicted of OWI.

2.19. You are Being Arrested Anyway — Why is That? Under the "police" power inherent in the authority given to the States, the police officer has the right to arrest you if he or she feels they have an articulable suspicion that you are committing a crime or have recently committed one. Please understand that you can be arrested for a routine traffic offense like speeding, a lane violation, or aggressive driving.[44] While such minor offenses do not usually lead to an arrest, it is within the officer's power to arrest someone rather than just give them a ticket at the scene.

Certain conduct by you or items observed by the officer will almost always get you arrested for OWI. First, if you admit you have been drinking, even one or two drinks, the officer is going to believe you have been driving with lessened ability or that you are under the influence. Second, if the officer can smell what he or she believes is alcohol on your breath, then he or she will likely arrest you whether or not you perform any field tests. The police are going to ask you to provide a blood or breath sample if they suspect the tests will reveal alcohol in your system. If they have any evidence of drug usage, blood or a urine samples will be requested. In Michigan, you can be forced to give a sample.

2.20. You Were Given an Advisement, and it was not the *Miranda* Warning. What is it? The *Miranda* warnings are statements of your rights the police have to give you when they arrest you.[45] If you have ever heard these from a police officer before you were being arrested for some criminal offense, that offense is likely OWI if you are reading this book.

By driving your vehicle on a public road in Michigan, you have given your implied consent to have your blood, breath or urine tested to assure you are not impaired by some chemical substance (legal or illegal drugs, or alcohol).[46] By law, before the police officer can ask you for a sample based on your "implied consent" associated with your operating a vehicle on a public road, he or she must inform you of your rights. In Michigan, you need to be arrested before being informed of these rights.[47] Your implied consent rights will be further discussed in Chapter 9. If your rights were violated, any results from these tests could be deemed inadmissible against you, leading to the OWI charges against you being dismissed or reduced.[48] That is why it is critical for you to remember everything the officer told you (as close to word-for-word as possible).

2.21. Can You Obtain Your Own Test(s)? If so, When and Who Pays? The Michigan implied consent statute provides that a person who submits to the requested chemical testing of the state may, at his or her own expense, have an additional "independent" blood, breath or urine test performed.[49] If you request an independent test, the law enforcement officer must do what he or she reasonably can to accommodate that request, including taking you to a hospital of your choice, if your choice of hospital is reasonable.[50] If you are denied your right of an independent chemical test the first test is still applicable, but a jury instruction shall be given that the police violated your statutory right to a reasonable opportunity for an independent chemical test.[51]

2.22. Here Are Some Precautions You Can Take if You are Going Out this Evening and May have Anything Alcoholic at all to Drink. Most people are so certain that being confronted by a police officer investigating a possible OWI offense will not happen to them that they make little or no preparation for the possibility. About one million people made that error last year, and not a single one thought it could happen to him or her either. Before you head out, make sure you have the following:

1. The name and phone number for the top OWI attorney in your area.

2. The "hard line" phone number for a person who will be willing and able to bail you out of jail. Many jails only allow "collect" calls to be made, and cell phones can't take collect calls. Don't plan on using stored numbers on your cell phone, because it will be confiscated.

3. The phone number of someone who can remove your vehicle from the roadway.

4. Clean your vehicle totally of any alcoholic beverage containers, including empties.

5. $500 cash or more to cover your bond, more if you have a criminal record.

6. Take a credit card *and* a debit card. You may be forced to use one or the other to pay for bond fees or an independent test, if one is available.

7. Because police have an unbelievable amount of latitude about towing your vehicle, do NOT have even the slightest amount (this includes ashes in the ash tray) of contraband drugs or any other medications in your vehicle that: (a) are not prescribed to you; (b) are not in their individual, proper containers (original

pill bottles from the pharmacy); and (c) be sure to remove all paraphernalia (pipes, wrapping papers, bongs, clips, etc.).

8. Keep in your possession the phone numbers of a co-worker who can cover for you if you do not get bonded out of jail in time for the next work day.

9. Get the red out. Take Visine® with you to use after being in the smoky rooms and harsh lights. Red eyes are a symptom of a long day. Don't let the police use this against you.

10. Use gum or mints, or even brush and floss your teeth before leaving to drive home. Take steps to freshen your breath before getting in your vehicle and remove that alcohol odor.

2.23. Summary - What Do I Say and do if I am Confronted by a Police Officer and Suspected of OWI? No single answer will suffice for all people in all situations. For example, if an accident has occurred involving serious bodily injury or death of another person, you may have no choice but to either voluntarily submit to testing or suffer forcible blood or urine extraction if the police get a court order for this testing.[52] Here are five universally sound things to do, if stopped by the police:

1. If asked (or told) about an alleged traffic violation, do not try to appease the officer by agreeing with him or her that you committed some traffic offense. Don't get belligerent. Remember, everything you are saying is likely being recorded, and your OWI attorney may be able to use the favorable things said by you in your favor.

2. If asked about alcohol use or drugs, either admit nothing, or blame it on your bottle of mouthwash.

3. If asked for your license or any documents, have them ready to show the officer. Stay inside the vehicle, seated, with your hands visible on the steering wheel. If the officer asks you to step out of the vehicle, explain that you prefer to not get out,

due to safety concerns. If the officer claims to smell or detect alcohol or drugs, do not admit to having consumed anything. Only when he or she ORDERS you to get out, and physically opens your door should you reluctantly leave your car.

4. Once out of the car, *do nothing* and *walk no place other than where he or she insists, or forces you to go.* Explain your desire to not get out of the car at the roadside, and your desire to not be asked to walk, balance, count or perform any voluntary roadside evaluations of any type. If offered a hand-held breath analyzer, decline doing it, if you can.

5. Ask to call your attorney on your cell phone as soon as the officer starts getting "pushy". Tell the officer that you are willing to satisfy his or her concerns for safety by handing your keys to him or her and taking a cab home.

2.24. Are Penalties Worse for a Second Offense? Yes. The lookback period for criminal enhancement to a second offense penalty is 7 years.[53] The calculation goes from date of arrest to date of arrest. The penalty for a second offense is enhanced to 5 days to one year in jail, and also carries with it a one year license revocation, provided the conviction for the second offense is within 7 years of the prior conviction. The fine is $200.00 to $1,000.00.

2.25. What is Felony OWI / DUI Intoxicated Driving? On January 3, 2007 Governor Granholm signed into law legislation that removes the 10 year "look back" period for all intoxicated driving offenses. Under prior law, a third offense would be considered a felony only if it occurred within a prior 10-year time period. With this new amendment a driver arrested for intoxicated driving with two prior offenses, regardless of their age, will face felony charges.[54]

The law was championed by the parents of Heidi Steiner, a northern Michigan high school senior who was killed by Danny Buffman. Mr. Buffman plead no contest to the charge of intoxicated driving causing death, and was sentenced to ten years in prison. Then, in 2005, he was arrested again and charged with a first offense intoxicated driving because the prior offense, committed in 1991, was more than 10 years old. A first offense intoxicated driving is a misdemeanor punishable by up to 93 days. The new law would have allowed him to be charged with felony intoxicated driving punishable by 1-5 years in the state prison.

Other changes to the law include a relaxing of the proof necessary to prove a defendant's prior record. This was necessary because very old convictions were sometimes difficult to prove because under the old there were only three ways to establish the record in court.

The new law expands the options available to prosecutors to seven. These include a copy of the court's register of actions and information contained in pre-sentencing reports or the defendant's driving record. The Michigan Secretary of State will also now maintain records of intoxicated driving convictions for the life of the driver.

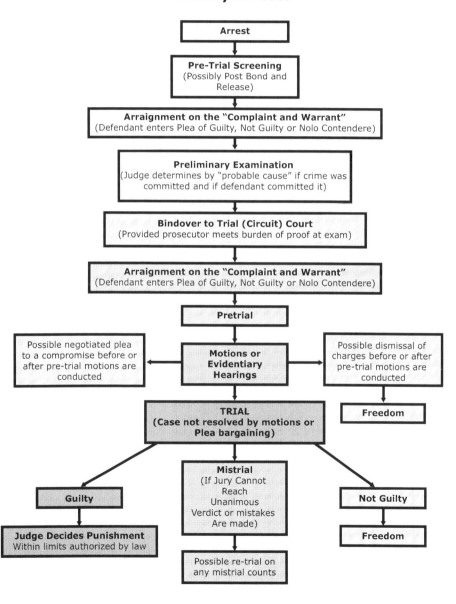

Michigan Criminal Justice System Overview for Misdemeanor Arrests

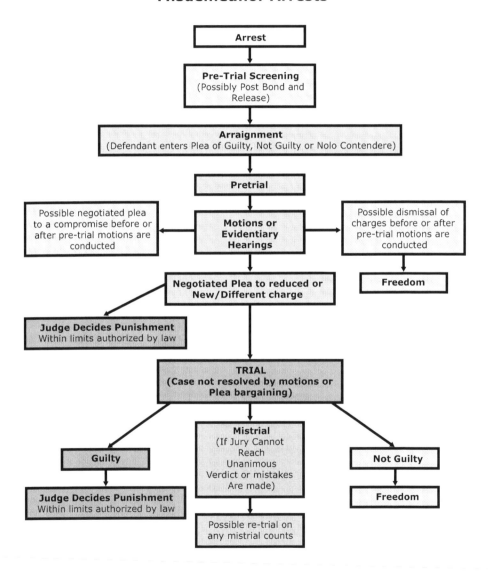

Chapter 3:
Avoiding Mistakes While In Jail or After Your Arrest

3.1. Overview of this Chapter's Purpose. Whatever the reason, the police officer has just made the decision to arrest you for OWI and has placed you in the back of his vehicle. This chapter covers what you should do at this point. Presumably, if you are reading this, it is because you have already gone through this experience, or because your lifestyle may place you in this situation in the future. If certain steps to start building a defense have not already been done, it is important to do them as soon as possible.

3.2. In the Process of Being Arrested. In reviewing and evaluating your OWI case, your skilled attorney will review several distinct time periods during your arrest process: your time with the arresting officer(s); your time at the jail with other officers including the administration of any chemical tests; and your time at the jail with anyone else. Although not as critical as the foregoing three time periods, the bonding process and your release from jail may also be important.

3.2.1. In the Police Vehicle and Your Time with the Arresting Officer(s). Once the arresting officer has placed you in his or her vehicle, and you are on the way to the jail for processing or further testing, the officer may attempt to strike up a "friendly conversation" or ask you further questions about your arrest. At this point, it is best not to answer these questions or speak further with the officer. Anything you say is likely being recorded, and possibly videotaped.

Anything you say can and will be used against you in the prosecution of your case.

You should pay close attention to what is happening because there may be some helpful details that you can discuss later with your criminal defense attorney, and these details may bolster your case. Write down everything as soon as you can about the circumstances that arose during this time period.

3.2.2. Be Polite with the Jail Personnel, but Remain Silent about Your Case Facts. What you will endure during this entire arrest and jail process is rude, hurtful and embarrassing. You are not in charge. However, the Fifth Amendment to the United States Constitution[55] provides that you have an absolute right to remain silent and not incriminate yourself during your arrest and booking process.[56] This right applies to everyone,[57] is true everywhere,[58] and it is true even if you are an alien or an illegal alien.[59] Once the arresting officer has read you your *Miranda* warnings, your silence cannot be used against you in court.[60] You need to tell the officers unambiguously that you have made the choice to remain silent.[61]

Remaining silent does not mean that you should not be appropriately polite with the law enforcement officers, using such terms as "please," and "thank you." Beyond providing the police identification information such as your name, address and turning over your driver's license, insurance and registration papers, you do not have to answer any questions relating to what you did, where you were going or why you were arrested. Just as importantly, do not talk to anyone else you meet in jail or at the testing facility about anything that happened related to your arrest. Whether talking about your case facts to a cellmate, by telephone to a friend or your spouse and are overheard by the police keep in mind this information likely can be used against you by the prosecutor and police in court.

3.2.3. Note the Names of Every Jail Person You See as well as Sober and Credible Cellmates. It is often true that a significant part of the prosecutor's case will come down to the word of the police against yours. Your side of the story gains credibility with every witness and every single piece of evidence you can gather for your defense. Even if someone you met with or saw in jail will not be able to add anything to your defense directly, they might be able to help.

Any person at the scene of your accident or your arrest may be a potential witness. This not only includes those in your favor, but those looking to make a deal for themselves and testify against you. Be sure to mention NOTHING to anyone that may harm you later. In certain instances police have been known to put a suspect in jail with another individual for purposes of gathering statements for later use. Get their names and numbers immediately after you are released from jail. This applies to anyone you met at the jail, including guards, janitors, nurses, other people being processed for offenses while you were at the jail. Obtain telephone numbers or the names of their place of business. If necessary, write down names and contact information on your arm or hand.

3.2.4. If "Stonewalled" or Ignored, Use "911" to Record Your Message. The law enforcement officers who are holding you may be too busy, or may claim they are too busy, and consequently, may deny you access to your friends or family via telephone. Your jailers have different priorities than you when you ask for a telephone. If you have tried to get someone at the jail to help you obtain an independent test, or if you need to give immediate information to someone to establish an indisputable time line, dial "911." Your conversation will be recorded once the operator takes your call. Remember, that anything you say will be accessible and useable by the prosecutor as well. Speak clearly, precisely and be careful what you say.

3.2.5. Get Bond Posted and get out of Jail ASAP. Nothing productive happens while you are in jail. Anyone who might be a witness in your favor is already forgetting details of what happened. Any physical evidence at the scene of your arrest is being rained on, driven over or otherwise altered by nature. Your car may be sitting unguarded by itself wherever you were stopped, and at least until you get out of jail is accessible to anyone but you. The police have already completed their investigation and have collected most if not all of their claimed evidence of impairment. You, on the other hand, are wasting time gathering dust in jail.

3.3. What to do as Soon as You are Out of Jail. Once you are out of jail, it is critical that you do several critical things as soon as possible. Most important among these is to write down all the details of your arrest, detention, testing and jailing. Waiting even an extra day will possibly cause you to forget important details. Besides contacting a lawyer to help you, you need to record your side of the story as completely as possible and take pictures of your vehicle, both inside and out. This is particularly crucial whenever any relevant evidence (e.g., open container inside the vehicle; deployed air bags) is in danger of being altered or lost.

Important details to record and give to your attorney include **any** details you can remember about your day immediately preceding your arrest, and anyone you met during your arrest and any time you spent in custody. Regain possession of your vehicle by either getting it from where it was left at the time of your arrest, or from where the police had it towed as soon as possible. If your license has been suspended, do not drive your vehicle yourself. You need to have a friend who might make a good witness for you photograph the insides of your car, the scene of your arrest, anything that was in your car at the time of your arrest.

3.4. What to do After this. After having been arrested, booked, tested (or have refused to be tested), you have likely posted a bond to get out of jail. You have written down as much of the detail surrounding your arrest as you can remember. You have put together a list of everyone you met during your arrest and your time in jail, what they said to you, and what you told them. You may even have taken pictures or video footage of your car. Possibly, you have spoken to an attorney and taken care of some preliminary matters. What should you do next?

3.4.1. Keep Your Arrest Details to Yourself. *Arrested* does not mean *__convicted.__* While being convicted of an OWI offense can affect your job, your insurance rates, and on the rest of your life, simply being arrested for OWI should not. In fact, if you are eventually found not guilty, or if the charges are significantly reduced or dropped, the impact on your life should be minimal. Minimizing the impact of your arrest should be your goal and that of your attorney.

The best general rule to follow is to only discuss your case with people (such as your attorney's staff) who have a "need to know" these details. Because your arrest for OWI is public knowledge in Michigan, your employer may learn of your arrest because you cannot avoid telling them, as for example when you miss work the day after your arrest. If you believe that you do have an obligation to report your arrest to your employer, then speak with your attorney first. Your attorney can help you devise a plan of disclosure that can help lessen the impact that this information may have on your employment situation.

3.4.2. Staying Out of Trouble While the Case is Pending. As will be discussed elsewhere in this book, once arrested for OWI, you face a legal process that could be over in as little as a few days (unlikely) to as long as a year or more. However, in Michigan, there is increasing pressure on the district courts to complete intoxicated driving cases as quickly as possible, even if such speed adversely impacts your ability to present a defense. In fact, effective January 2006, two new court rules have significantly changed the time limits applicable to these cases. The new rules require that intoxicated driving misdemeanor cases (first and second offenses) be totally completed, trial and all, within 91 days. If the case is not finished this quickly, the district court judge must file a monthly report with the Michigan Supreme Court explaining the delay. For felonies, this time limit is 151 days.[62]

Such time limits often help prosecutors and hurt you. These time limits also make your choice of counsel all the more important, and make it critical to find the best possible lawyer in the shortest period of time after your arrest. Also, while your case is still active and pending, you do not need to add to your problems. Any new infractions or legal problems can be disastrous, especially if it is a similar new offense. Do not drink any alcohol, or take any illegal substances and drive. A second OWI charge on top of the first will be disastrous for you. Until your OWI case is resolved, consider yourself always under the watchful eye of the prosecution, who will use anything wrong you do against you. The good news is that this harsh part of your life will eventually be over.

3.4.3. Once You Have Hired a Lawyer, Get Busy. Despite it being very easy for an OWI arrest to take over your life, don't let it. You need to concentrate on the other issues identified in this book to maximize your chances of winning your case or achieving a plea reduction. As your case progresses, your life must go on. Staying employed is critical. Besides maintaining a sense of normalcy for your life, hiring a top OWI attorney is costly, plus court expenses, expert witness costs and other expenses add to the financial burden.

Appearing for your court hearings and your trial will likely require taking time off from work so you can attend and assist your lawyer in his or her preparation. Such preparation might take place anytime in the days and weeks before your court appearances. Be flexible with meetings and agree to telephone consultations when he or she suggests that a face-to-face meeting is not feasible.

Start taking positive steps in your life such as becoming more active in religious endeavors or performing volunteer work. If you believe that you may have an alcohol or drug abuse or dependency problem, then you may also decide to become involved in treatment.

You may also begin treatment because of a recommendation from your lawyer. Being involved with treatment is often the best thing you can do to help your lawyer obtain the best possible plea or sentence If you do begin attending a program like Alcoholics Anonymous stay with it and attend a minimum of two to three times per week. Keep a record of every meeting you attend, and have your sponsor or chair sign off on your attendance sheet every time you attend a meeting. Your attorney can provide you with a "sign-in" sheet that you can use to keep track of your attendance. These steps provide your lawyer and yourself some positive "evidence in mitigation" if your case is lost at trial.

Chapter 4:
How to Find, Interview and Hire a Top DUI Defense Law Firm

4.1. Overview of this Chapter. If you have been arrested and charged with OWI, then it is important for you to contact and retain the best available lawyer to represent you. You should act quickly to retain counsel, but only make a hiring decision after looking at all of your options. By the time you have been arrested, the legal process has already started and the prosecution has already begun to organize its case against you. The purpose of this chapter is to show you how to find not only the best possible OWI lawyer to represent you at this stressful time in your life, but to also advise you how to deal with the lawyer and his or her staff during the legal journey that you will need to take over the next year or so.

4.2. Top OWI Lawyers Nine Times More Effective Than Average. Studies have shown[63] that when it comes to individual differences at all levels at all types of employment, the difference between the best and the rest is enormous. Among knowledge workers such as lawyers the difference between the average and top performers is six times or more. For example, "before becoming chief justice of the U.S. Supreme Court, John Roberts prevailed in 25 of the 39 cases he argued before the court. That record is almost nine times better than the average record of other winning attorneys."

To see the difference in other fields of work, here are some documented examples. The best developer at Apple is at least nine times as productive as the average software engineer at other technology companies. This might explain why it took Apple only two years to produce OS X, whereas it took Microsoft five years to develop Vista. The best blackjack dealer at Caesars Palace keeps his table playing at least five times as long as the average dealer, and the best sales associate at Nordstrom sells at least eight times as much as the average sales associate at other department stores. Even the best surgeons have dramatically better results. The best transplant surgeon at a top-notch medical clinic has a success rate at least six times that of the average transplant surgeon.[64]

There are no studies related to DUI/OWI lawyers, but based on the Harvard Business Review research, it stands to reason that the same would be true in this highly specialized field. Why would top OWI lawyers obtain results that are any different than top heart surgeons or engineers?

4.2.1. Understanding Lawyer Fees. The vast array of fees charged by self-professed intoxicated driving experts can make choosing a lawyer very difficult and confusing. You may be wondering why there is such a large range in the fees charged for the defense of even a first offense OWI case. The short answer is this: it's all about the lawyer's level of training and expertise.

To help you identify a particular lawyer's actual level of true expertise, you may find it helpful to consider role theory. This was developed for psychodrama by J.L. Moreno, who believed that the self emerges from the roles we play. Moreno postulated that when people learn a new role, they follow a particular pattern of role development. The arc of the learning curve begins with role taking and proceeds to role playing and role creating. To hope to obtain a result *up to nine times better than average*, you will want to choose a lawyer who has reached the level of "role creating."

Role Taking - refers to an enactment of the role in a routinized, somewhat stilted way. When a lawyer first decides to become an OWI lawyer, he/she is likely to appear awkward as he tries to cross-examine a police officer during an OWI trial. He may need to practice in several trials before he can get the officer to provide answers that will help him tell his client's story.

Role Playing - as the lawyer progresses with his or her experience, he will gain ease and will be able to move about the courtroom easily and may feel comfortable making spontaneous choices relative the questions he asks potential jurors or the arresting officer. He can begin to incorporate advanced learning in trial skills as well as breath, blood and field sobriety testing, and he will not have to think every minute about the basics of cross-examination, or to refer to a list of pre-written questions.

Role Creating - When an OWI lawyer role-creates, he is able to add new and sometimes unique elements to the courtroom trial and to think beyond the confines of the typical attorney or one in the other two phases of development. He is able to devise unexpected solutions for difficulties that emerge during the OWI trial. At this point the lawyer may create a new and completely novel method of cross-examination, jury selection, opening or closing statement that may become a model for others to follow. He has probably also become a trial skills instructor at seminars or colleges attended by other OWI lawyers.

Having reached the role creating level of experience, what then is the appropriate fee to charge for the defense of an OWI? Fees for the defense of a first offense OWI generally range from a low of about $500.00 to a high of about $25,000.00, with some lawyers in some states charging even more than $25,000.00. Fees for the defense of a felony OWI are generally $2,500.00 to as much as $50,000.00, again with some lawyers in some states charging even more. If death or serious injury is involved, fees can easily be double or triple this amount. You should expect top OWI lawyers, those who have reached the role creating phase of their development, to charge fees at the high end of these estimates, whereas lawyers in the role taking phase are usually those charging fees at the lower end of this range.

When determining what lawyer to retain for your Michigan OWI case you should consider the current phase of development for that particular lawyer. A fee charged might be an indication of this, but you should also ask questions of the OWI lawyer candidate, such as how many OWI jury trials they've conducted as the lead attorney; what scholarly writing(s) they've authored; and find out if they are leaders in any bar organizations. A complete list of criteria follows in the next section.

4.2.2 How to Immediately Identify and Locate a "Top" OWI Attorney. Even if you are a lawyer, because of the constant changes and the hidden secrets that surround Michigan OWI law, you will not get justice unless you locate and contact a top OWI lawyer to take charge of your defense. These offenses carry too much public scrutiny to ask the prosecutor to "give you a break" and drop the charges. In Michigan, this is an even greater concern than in other states due to the intoxicated driving audit. This audit requires tracking of all OWI cases from the moment they are filed until the moment they are fully resolved, and all of this information is public knowledge. The last thing any judge or prosecutor wants is for their opponent in the next election to use this public information against them and make them appear soft on intoxicated driving.

A number of factors need to be considered when hiring your OWI defense lawyer. Only about 500 lawyers in the United States are "the best" in their geographic regions in defending intoxicated driving cases. Hence, you need to eliminate the 99 avowed criminal lawyers to find the ONE "best" attorney for your OWI case. The following list of factors may prove helpful in narrowing the candidates to two or three specialists:

A) **References From Friends or any Lawyer you Might Know Personally.** A strong reference from a friend or colleague who has used or successfully referred the potential OWI attorney is often the best indicator of whether a lawyer is worthy of hire. In lieu of or in concert with this advice there are reputable websites which rank attorneys by various criteria. One such site is www.avvo.com. It separates lawyers by region and categories of expertise. The site also features reviews from past clients as well as peer endorsements.

B) **Community and Courthouse Reputation** — *Checking the attorney's COURTHOUSE Reputation is the Most Direct and Accurate Litmus Test of the GREAT Intoxicated Driving Defense Attorneys.* Go to the courthouse in the county in which you were arrested, not necessarily the county in which you live. Very politely, talk with a person from the clerk of court's office, a bailiff, a deputy who is assigned to that courthouse or to a court reporter who is in court. Ask WHICH one of the lawyers you are considering would he or she hire if they were facing a DUI prosecution and HAD TO TAKE THEIR BEST SHOT AT WINNING. Another good source for a referral is *law enforcement officers* who regularly face these lawyers in court, assuming they will tell you their honest opinion. Be sure to give them any names you might already have in mind, because they may be hesitant to "recommend" or suggest any one attorney or law firm. After you receive the name or names from court personnel, check the Internet or professional listings to further investigate any possible candidates.

C) **Advanced Training.** After you receive the name or names from court personnel, check them out on-line with a Google[65] or Bing[66] search. Search the Internet profiles of any attorney you consider to confirm that he or she actually specializes in "intoxicated driving defense." Advanced training is an excellent way of determining the lawyer's commitment to DUI defense. For example, is the lawyer certified as a participant and/or instructor in the National Highway Administration's Standardized Field Sobriety tests? Has he/she obtained advanced training in infrared spectroscopy (breath testing) and gas chromatography (blood testing), and obtained advanced training in the "DRE" (drug recognition expert) program? Is he or she a graduate of the Gerry Spence Trial Lawyer's College?

D) **Specialized Membership or Professional Affiliations.** Once you have names and have checked their websites, before you call any one attorney, consider their "involvement" and "commitment" to the field of intoxicated driving defense. See if the candidate lawyer associates with the following: The Gerry Spence Trial Lawyer's College (TLC), National College for DUI Defense, Inc.;[67] The National Association of Criminal Defense Lawyers (NACDL),[68] and Martindale-Hubbell[69] (look for a high "AV" rating).

E) **Academic Appointments.** Has the attorney ever obtained any academic appointments to teach at a law school or university? Has the attorney ever been an editor of a publication and is he/she on faculty at any criminal law or trial practice colleges?

F) **Authoritative Authorships.** Another way to determine an attorney's level of knowledge and commitment is to evaluate whether or not the attorney has ever written a book or journal article on the top of DUI defense. The best lawyers are typically those who teach others through these various academic means. Look for publications in the Michigan Bar Journal or the Journal of the National Association for Criminal Defense Attorneys (NACDL) called the "Champion."

G) **Disciplinary Actions.** Has the attorney ever been disciplined by the Board of Professional Responsibility of the State bar of his/her practice location? Contact the American Bar Association on line to find links to all state Bar associations.[70]

Once you have the name of your top choice, and perhaps your number two choice, it is now time to interview them, to see if they fit YOUR needs. The supposed "best" OWI lawyer may not be the best one for you if your personalities clash. Because you will be forging a very personal relationship with your attorney to help you during this stressful time, it is important that you select an attorney who makes you feel comfortable as well as confident. Write your questions down before you even go in and ask them about the following:

H) **Seminar Speaker.** The top attorneys in each state are asked to speak for OWI-DUI seminars in their state and others.

I) **Fees and Fee Structure.** How does the attorney set his or her fees? Most intoxicated driving lawyers work on a ***flat fee basis.*** As you might expect, highly experienced attorneys often charge ***much*** higher fees than younger, less experienced lawyers. For many persons facing the extreme penalties of an OWI conviction, price is secondary to an excellent track record for results. One ex-State trooper turned DUI attorney from Louisiana, Glynn Delatte, ends each e-mail with this maxim: "Good lawyers aren't cheap, and cheap lawyers aren't good."

J) **Focus of Practice** - Most truly great OWI attorneys either restrict their cases to only intoxicated driving or at least stay entirely within the field of criminal law.

K) **Years in Practice** - *There is no substitute for experience.*

L) **Lawyer - Paralegal Ratio** - A busy, experienced DWI-DUI trial attorney will have 1 to 2 paralegals assisting him/her. Trial preparation requires more time than processing guilty pleas. *A knowledgeable paralegal is worth his or her weight in gold.*

M) **Caseload** - A trial attorney may limit his or her caseload to between approximately 40 and 80 cases per year. Some top intoxicated driving lawyers limit their practice to as few as two cases per month. Make sure your attorney will not be too busy to satisfy **YOUR** needs.

N) **Use of Technology** - Technology has revolutionized the practice of OWI law probably as much or more than any other area in the legal profession. Lawyers who master technology deliver legal services with better quality and can often leverage technology to deliver legal services less expensively. Ask how they utilize technology in the courtroom.

O) **Promising Too Much** - *Be skeptical about lawyers who promise or even guarantee success.* In many instances, it can even be unethical to promise a particular result. This is especially true if such promises or guarantees are made during an initial interview before the full facts of your case are known. If such promises are made, you are probably well advised to seek other representation.

P) **Educational Background** - You can go to the ABA web site to look up your attorney's law school.[71] If it is not listed, there could be a problem. Also, look for undergraduate education in a related field, particularly a science background such as biology or chemistry. A science background is of immense value to an attorney trying to understand or to explain infrared breath testing or gas chromatography blood testing to a judge or jury.

Q) **Publications** - Lawyers who write frequently about their area of law practice tend to keep themselves better informed about their area of specialty. Publications also help demonstrate that the lawyer has a great command of the subject matter, but perhaps even more important, is passionate about the work they do. It is also true that publications can help establish the lawyer's reputation among fellow lawyers and judges.

R) **Promotional Materials** - Pay attention to a law firm's client information package, marketing, Internet and promotional materials. Cheesy written materials usually come from sloppy law firms.

S) **Conflicts of Interest** - Ask your attorney if he or she will have any conflicts of interest in regards to your case.

T) **Engagement Letters** - Beware of lawyers who do not put their fee agreements in writing. While this is not an absolute requirement, the rules of professional ethics in Michigan strongly encourage written fee agreements. Also, read the fine print in your engagement letters or "fee agreements." Make sure you understand what is, and what is not, included in the engagement fee. Otherwise, when looking at the fee charged and comparing it with what is charged by other lawyers, you may not be comparing "apples with apples."

U) **Language Skills** - For non-English speakers, a skilled OWI trial attorney who does not speak your language should have staff members available to translate for you or utilize telephone-based translation services. In trial, courts must make translation services available.

V) **Ethics** - Run as fast as you can from lawyers that tell you it is okay to lie or otherwise act dishonestly. Unethical lawyers rarely have good reputations, and this will hurt you in the long run. Lawyers have a nearly absolute duty of candor to the tribunal, and this duty often covers the client's conduct as well. Judges never forget lawyers that try to "pull one over" in their courtroom.

W) **Personality Compatibility** - At the end of the day, a lawyer's "bedside manner" can mean a lot to how the overall relationship goes. Find a lawyer who really cares about winning, and be realistic about your level of need in being "nurtured" (or not being nurtured) by the attorney. In the end, the question to ask yourself, "Is this the attorney I want spearheading my defense?"

X) **Communication** - The ***number one complaint against lawyers*** in this country is not poor work quality. It is failing to communicate with their clients. You are paying a lot of money to hire a lawyer and it is your right to expect to be kept informed of developments and have your calls and e-mails returned in a timely manner.

4.3. What if I Just Cannot Afford the TOP OWI Lawyer in my Area? Many people will not be able to afford the top OWI lawyer in their area due to cost. Many lawyers who are excellent at fighting these difficult cases are ***partners, senior trial lawyers or associates*** in the firm headed up by the top attorney in your market, and they usually charge less than the "top gun."

If you are not able to afford such top representation, you may be better served going with a public defender. Keep in mind that you may need to be screened by the court administrator or a similar organization handling indigent cases and the appointment of public defenders. Their purpose is to determine if your financial resources are low and that you are therefore eligible for a court-appointed lawyer. You may also be screened extensively by your judge or his/her staff to determine whether you truly are unable to pay a fee. Unfortunately, this evaluation by the judge may not take place for months after your arrest, thereby losing you critical time for mounting your defense while evidence is still fresh.

4.4. Don't Expect Your Attorney to be a Magician. Your lawyer can only be your best possible advocate, not a miracle worker. If you decided to drink any alcohol and then drive, you may be held liable for this in the form of a conviction. He or she cannot lie for you, perform some sleight of hand and make the charges against you go away, or make you any guarantees as to the outcome of your case. However, one of the reasons to obtain the best possible legal representation you can afford is that with greater experience and a well established reputation for success, your lawyer may be able to help you through the legal process as smoothly as possible. The best lawyers are also much more likely to meet with success at your trial.

4.5. Don't Ask Your Attorney to be a Crook. A lawyer has two dominant and almost absolute duties. He or she must zealously represent you as your advocate before the court and the rest of the world, and he or she must also uphold the highest ethical standards of the professions. Consequently, your lawyer cannot lie or misrepresent the facts or the law to the court, even if doing so would be in your best interest. If your lawyer lies to the court or misrepresent anything to the court, he or she could face disbarment and criminal charges.

4.6. Treat Your Attorney's Staff Like they are Your Family Members. For approximately the next six months to a year, that is what your attorney's staff will be — a part of your family. This "closeness" or "family connection" does not mean you can abuse them. Remember, people work harder for people they like and respect. The best teams work like a family — with trust and caring tempered with being able to tell the other person honestly that what they are doing is wrong. Treat the other people working in your lawyer's office like you would want to be treated. An experienced trial attorney will know his staff's dedication and support them in any disputes that arise from your boorish or offensive behavior. Don't lose your attorney by acting improperly toward his or her staff.

4.7. Providing Input to Your Attorney, but Don't be a Pest. Your attorney or members of his or her staff are going to ask you a lot of questions. They might ask you to help them contact witnesses, or go to the scene with an investigator. In the search for information, facts and identities of people who might be able to help you in your defense, there must be information flowing both from you and to you.

Your attorney is going to push to get you through the process as soon as possible, but must temper this with a knowledge that court proceedings must also be done at the time that is best for your case. You should resist the urge to "get it over with." The prosecution may be ready the day after your arrest to put you in jail, but your lawyer is going to need months of preparation to help you obtain the most justice.

All of this said, a high quality lawyer keeps you involved when anything changes. You will get copies of all of the paperwork (filings, motions, memorandums of law and judicial rulings) that pass between your lawyer and the court or the prosecution. Some attorneys may have someone on his or her staff contact you once a week or so, even if nothing changes.

However, calling your lawyer on a regular (daily) basis just because you haven't heard anything for a few days only wastes the time of both you and your lawyer. Stop to think about the time it takes to answer your "anxiety" call, and ask yourself whether it is worth interrupting the attorney's staff from the important work that needs to be done on your case and others being handled by your attorney. You may be better served obtaining the services of other professionals to help you deal with the emotions you are feeling.

4.8. After Selecting an Attorney, Follow his or her Advice. If you "second-guess" every step your attorney takes, you either have an incompetent attorney or you have "control" or "trust" issues. Either way, this creates tension in the attorney/client relationship, and this tension will usually result in your attorney withdrawing as your legal counsel. You should listen to and always try to follow your attorney's advice. This does not mean that you should expect your lawyer to tell you what to do with your case, or even if you should plead guilty or go to trial. These are decisions only you can make, and then only after your attorney has provided you with ALL of the important information. You should not attempt to make these critical decisions until AFTER your attorney has completed a thorough investigation of the facts and circumstances of your case. Thereafter, your attorney should expect to provide you with an honest and forthright opinion regarding your chances for success and a detailed explanation of what the likely outcome will be. At this point, and with this information, you will be making a "fully informed" decision regarding the outcome of your case.

4.9. Maintain a File with all Your Papers From Legal Counsel. Right from the start of your arrest, you will have a large amount of paperwork coming your way. Expect to receive forms used by the police, information from the jail, from your bondsman, and from the court hearings in your case. You will also receive written information from your lawyer and his or her support staff. While your lawyer may want the originals or copies of some of the forms, it is critical to your defense that you keep at least a copy of everything, especially the court documents your lawyer sends you. That way, if your lawyer calls you and asks you a question about a specific document, you will be able to quickly give an answer.

Expect copies of all of the legal paperwork that passes between the court and the prosecutor and your attorney, and your attorney to the court or the prosecutor. This may include copies of any motions, filings, memorandums of law and other legal forms. You should be informed of any plea or sentence bargains made to your attorney or from your attorney.

4.10. Let Your Attorney Decide Which Witnesses to Interview. You have hired the best lawyer for your defense based on all the factors listed above. You have hired this highly trained professional who has years of experience with not only OWI charges, but who has also worked in the court where your case will be heard, and likely is very familiar with those who will be prosecuting your case. In preparing your defense, your lawyer will know who the critical witnesses to interview are. Once you have made the overall and critical decision as to who is going to be the best lawyer for you, let this person do their job. Second-guessing only costs you more stress and wastes everyone's time. Your "doubts" about your attorney's strategy may actually be visible on your face, like a deer caught in the headlights.

4.11. Follow Your Attorney's Advice on Securing Help from the Best Available Expert Witness(es) for Your Trial or Motions. Hopefully, you chose your attorney based on all of the factors listed above. In doing so, you have arranged to have the best possible person act as your champion in court. You should understand that the best lawyers have relationships with the best experts and can obtain them to assist in your case. If your lawyer tells you he or she thinks that Expert X rather than Expert Y is best for your case, then you can bet he or she is suggesting this based on years of expertise with OWI trials. Often, one particular expert has unparalleled knowledge and experience on the medical or scientific issue that is the lynchpin of your defense, while another may not. Go with your attorney's choice and **HIRE THE BEST EXPERT AVAILABLE.**

4.12. Assist Your Attorney in Locating & Staying in Touch with Fact Witnesses and Medical or Other Records. Your lawyer is going to ask you to assist in coordinating your defense because you are the best person to handle certain matters. Due to strict federal laws,[72] the process by which your medical records may be procured requires written consent. Hence, you may be asked to go to your doctor's office (or even to the hospital) to procure a copy of your full medical records, particularly those that relate to an issue in your OWI case.

People who have witnessed something, such as all or part of your arrest or booking are much more likely to talk to you than to an attorney whom they do not know. The same may be true for waiters, waitresses and any passengers in your vehicle when you were arrested.

You may need to contact witnesses who may be able to help with your defense. Your attorney may ask you to keep in touch with them. It is your defense. You are the one charged with the crime. If your lawyer asks you to "remain friendly" with these witnesses, please do so. Ultimately as your lawyer begins to prepare for your trial in earnest, he or she will need to contact these witnesses. This contact will be to collect information in preparation for your trial, and also to prepare the witness's testimony. Consequently, you should make sure these witnesses understand that they should expect such contact in the future.

Chapter 5:

How to Prepare For Your Legal Defense and Can You Drive After Your Arrest?

5.0. Purpose of this Chapter. If you have been arrested for an OWI offense, there are things you should be doing to help prepare your legal defense, and things you should certainly avoid doing that will worsen your situation. If you are facing a serious charge such as OWI, the worst thing you can do is to get into additional legal troubles. In some jurisdictions, the prosecutor can **COMBINE** both cases and let one jury hear both at one time if the charges at all relate to one another.[73] While in Michigan, combining charges that occur separately is very unlikely, new charges create an environment that is a losing proposition almost 100% of the time. This chapter discusses these potential helpful and harmful activities, and when you can again expect to be able to drive.

5.1. What Happens if You get Caught Driving on a Suspended License? Simply stated, driving on a suspended license is a new, additional crime.[74] This new offense may well carry a jail sentence, especially if you are a repeat offender or have serious charges pending when you drive while suspended. Driving on a suspended license might also worsen your chances and the likely outcome of your pending OWI case if you end up with the same judge for both charges. This is particularly likely in one of Michigan's smaller, northern communities. Such "repeat" offenses send the judge a message that you are not remorseful for your OWI because you violated an additional state law even before the first case was resolved.

5.2. Is Getting a "Limited Permit" the Solution to Your Problems? In Michigan, no action will be taken against your driver's license (provided you have consented to the chemical test) unless and until you are convicted of OWI or some other crime that carries with it driver's license sanctions as a part of the penalty. For example, if you are convicted of OWI, and you have no prior alcohol convictions within the prior 7 years, then you will have a fairly broadly restricted driver license. However, if you have prior alcohol related offenses within 7 or 10 years, your license may be revoked completely. With a revocation, you will not be able to obtain even restricted driving privileges until after the revocation period has ended and after an administrative hearing.

If your license has been revoked because of multiple convictions one of the most pressing questions to determine is whether you can drive to and from work. Limited driving permits are a creation of Michigan statutes and are not a "right" under any state or federal constitution. Certain drivers may be required to install an ignition interlock device prior to receiving their restricted license or work permit that allows restricted driving privileges.[75]

A restricted or "work" license severely restricts your ability to drive, determining where and when you can operate a vehicle.[76] Thus, a "work" permit may help you with some of the transportation problems you face following your OWI arrest, but is seldom the solution to all of your problems. For example, many rental car companies will not allow you to rent their vehicles without a full driver's license.

5.3. When Can You Get Your License Reinstated? If you are a Michigan driver, and if you were lawfully able to drive when you were arrested, then you may continue to drive with whatever privileges you had prior to your arrest. As a part of the arrest procedure, your plastic Michigan driver's license should have been destroyed, and you should have been issued a "paper license." This is called a "DI-177." Out-of-state licenses are not destroyed, but paper licenses are nevertheless issued. You will remain on this paper license until your case is dismissed or until you are found or plead guilty.

Thus, you may continue to drive until after the Department of State imposes a license sanction. This sanction is usually imposed a couple of weeks after the Department of State receives notice of your conviction and consequently may or may not occur before you are actually sentenced by the court. This notice of conviction is sent to the Department of State by the court clerk. Afterward, you will be notified of the license sanctions by mail, and the driver's license sanction imposed will depend on the crime of which you have been convicted. If your OWI arrest is your first offense, then you may be able to get your full driver's license back after 90 to 180 days.[77] However, if your arrest falls under the "super-drunk" statute, you cannot drive at all for 45 days and if allowed, restricted driving while using an interlock device.[78] After you have completed this mandatory license sanction, then you need only pay a reinstatement fee and your "plastic" photo license will be returned to you.

Things are completely different if after your conviction your license is revoked due to multiple OWI convictions. In these circumstances, you will not be able to obtain even partial driving privileges until after a successful hearing before the administrative hearing office. There is no "due process" during the revocation period, meaning there is no way to even request a hearing regarding your license. You should have been notified how to request a hearing when you received notice of your revocation. See more detail in Chapter 11 of this book.

5.4. Can You Just Obtain a License in Another State? The very short answer is no. Once your plastic license is physically taken from you by the Michigan officer as a part of the OWI arrest process, an administrative license suspension (or revocation) action is started against your license. The notation on your driving record is "625g permit" issued. The 625g permit is your paper license. If any other state licensing office contacts Michigan, a "block" will be in place informing the other state that you have a pending license suspension or revocation driver's license action that is unresolved. As it is in other states, a prerequisite for getting a Michigan driver's license, you must not have your current license suspended or revoked in any other state.[79] Lying on an application form to obtain a driver's license, vehicle certificate of title, vehicle registration, vehicle inspection, self-insurance, personal information, or commercial driver training school, is a felony.[80]

5.5. Can You Drive on an "International" License Here in the USA? If you are from another country and have a legitimate foreign license with an "international" license, you should be able to drive anywhere in Michigan if your country is recognized as such by Michigan.[81] An international license is NOT a standard license. It is merely a translation of your license from one language to the language of the nation where you will be visiting. Michigan will not allow you to drive on their roads if your license is suspended or revoked in any other state. International driver's licenses are a type of scam to take desperate people's money.

5.6. Once You are Permitted to Drive Again, is Everything Back to Normal? It depends on what you mean by normal. If you are convicted of OWI, your license will be suspended for 30 days and restricted for the next 150 days (for a first offense). For a first offense "super-drunk" violation no driving is allowed for 45 days and restricted driving with an interlock device thereafter. If you have two alcohol related convictions within 7 years, then your license will be revoked for at least one full year.[82] This means not being able to drive at all for a full year. If you have 3 prior alcohol convictions your license will be revoked for 5 full years.[83]

In the alternative, for a conviction for operating while visibly impaired first offense, your license will be restricted as to where you can drive for a period of 90 days. After the statutory suspension or revocation period is over, you can take the necessary steps set forth by your state's law to get your FULL license returned to you. Then, no restrictions on location and time of day for your driving remain. However, for the multiple offender situation, a full restoration is rarely granted on the first attempt at an administrative restoration. Usually, the first year following a revocation will be a restricted license with an ignition interlock device. After that, the motorist will be eligible for a full restoration. Thus, for the multiple offender, a one year revocation usually turns into a two year or more license sanction. Bottom line, of course, is to avoid multiple convictions.

Although getting reinstated after a first offense is relatively painless and essentially only requires the payment of a reinstatement fee, the opposite is typically true for second (or subsequent) offenses. Michigan has seven and ten year "look back" periods for prior offenses, for determining when you will be considered to have a second offense or subsequent offenses, thus when you will be put through the ringer in trying to regain your full driving privileges.[84] Multiple offenders rarely get their licenses back without the assistance of an attorney who is well-versed in this area of administrative law.

5.7. Alcohol and Drug Assessment (and Possible Treatment) Prior to Going to Trial. Simply being charged with intoxicated driving does not necessarily mean you are an alcoholic. Research indicates, however, that the probability that you have an alcohol disorder, of which there are several types, increases according to the number of your intoxicated driving arrests. Once arrested for an OWI offense most courts, employers, friends, and even family assume that you may have an alcohol or drug problem. Drug and alcohol evaluation programs are available almost everywhere, and most can be researched on line for information

Your attorney may suggest that you undergo an alcohol and drug assessment, and then to follow through on any recommended treatment plan. The first reason for this suggestion is that if you do have an alcohol or drug problem, the sooner you face the problem, and obtain treatment, the sooner you will be on the road to recovery. Second, even if you do not have a drug or alcohol problem, the sooner you seek a private, independent assessment, the more likely this prompt action will impress your trial judge and, in the event of a conviction, help your OWI attorney arrange a favorable negotiated sentence.

Furthermore, the results of you actions may also be used by your attorney in his or her discussions with the prosecutor. If this substance abuse evaluation shows that you have no drug or alcohol problems, this might give some credence to and is yet another reason why the charges against you might be lessened. In the alternative, if the counselor suggests some educational sessions and it can be shown that you have completed them, this can be a negotiating "chit" for your attorney to use to try to get a negotiated plea in your case.

Michigan has a mandatory provision that all OWI convictions require an evaluation for alcohol and drug dependency prior to sentencing.[85] These evaluations are done by the court's probation department and will help them make a treatment recommendation for use by the judge at sentencing. Be sure that the counselor or treatment center you choose is appropriately qualified, or a state-approved provider of alcohol and drug rehabilitation. Some courts prefer their own approved counselors.

5.8. Cleaning Up Your Driving History Before Your Case Reaches Trial or Final Disposition. As a part of taking on your OWI case, your lawyer will want to know full details about any of your past violations of the law, including any traffic infractions. You must also fully disclose any pending criminal actions or traffic matters against you. This includes any speeding, reckless driving or any other traffic offenses you may have pending.

The reason for "cleaning" up your record is several-fold. First, if you have any other legal matters hanging over your head, it is far less likely your attorney will be able to make any deals with the prosecution regarding your OWI offense. Second, if you are found guilty of your OWI offense, almost anything in your life can be used either for you or against you in your sentencing. Finally, your attorney may be able to work out a "package" deal on all open charges, especially if all are pending within the same jurisdiction.

5.9. Make Certain You Have Funds Available to Cover All Costs. Once you have been arrested for OWI, you face significant expenses throughout the process. Typically, court costs, fee payments and related expenses payable to the court occur over the entire length of your sentence, which may take one or two years or longer.

There are also legal expenses to consider. These expenses may include posting a bond to get out of jail, possible alcohol or drug treatment costs, paying the fees of your attorney and all experts, and the income you will miss from the time when you have to be in court and not working. If convicted, there may be monetary fines and costs that you will have to pay, either directly to the court or through your probation officer. There are also additional expenses such as probation oversight expenses, crime victim's rights fees, screening fees, the fees associated with alcohol monitoring and ignition interlock devices and other "statutory surcharges" or assessments associated with being on probation. Your car insurance will increase dramatically. There is also a "driver responsibility" fee that you will have to pay to the Department of State.[86]

Considering all of the costs and expenses you face, it is best to look seriously at all possible avenues you have for generating the money you will need to cover them. It is best to start exploring all of these possibilities at the beginning of your legal process in order to assure that you will be able to meet these costs and expenses as they occur.

5.10. Keep Your Schedule Flexible for Court Proceedings — Save All Vacation Days. The legal process involves several steps that require you to clear your schedule. Some of these times include appointments when you will meet with your lawyer, your investigator or possibly your expert witnesses. You will likely have to go to the scene of your arrest for several reasons. Usually, these matters can be scheduled at times that will fit both your work schedule and the schedule of the expert witnesses. Other times, you must make your schedule "fit" the court's schedule. You will probably need to be present any time your case is in court. These court days will include your arraignment (where the charges against you are read by the judge and you are asked to plead either guilty, no contest or not guilty), any pretrial motion hearings, your trial and your sentencing.

At your arraignment, the issue of bond will be visited or revisited by the court, and conditions may be added to your bond.[87] These conditions often include alcohol use prevention measures, such as daily or regular random drug or alcohol testing. You may also be required to wear a "SCRAM" bracelet, or have a home alcohol tether installed in your home. Because these conditions can be very imposing, you will NOT want to appear for your arraignment without your attorney present.

You must be ready to proceed to trial at any time your case is scheduled. Your attorney and all of your witnesses must also be ready to attend, and often with very short notice. This means that you must be flexible and make yourself available to be present in court if your lawyer calls. For some types of employment, this is a task that is either impossible or extremely difficult.

It is thus possible that you will need to be able to take up to two weeks off from work during the year after your arrest. For most people, this means possibly giving up your entire paid vacation time for the year. If given the choice between having to take unpaid vacation days off from work and using your paid days, considering the expenses you face, it may be better for you to forego other vacation and use your paid "leave" days to resolve your legal problems.

5.11. Community Service is a Good Thing to do. Michigan OWI statutes require a "minimum" number of hours community service work as a part of their mandatory punishment scheme, depending on whether your offense is a first, second or subsequent offense within the proscribed seven or ten year "look back" periods.[88] If your OWI attorney recommends that you begin doing community service hours, follow his or her advice. You may get to choose the type of service you perform (instead of what the court orders you to perform) and may give your attorney ammunition for mitigating part of your sentence. You may also enjoy helping others.

5.12. Anxiety can be a Killer! Seek Professional Counseling if Needed. Being arrested and charged with OWI is the beginning of a long and often stressful process that can be the worst experience of your life. If you find that you are having a tough time "shaking" your stress, discuss this with your attorney. If you have chosen the right OWI attorney, he or she will understand what you are going through.

5.13. How will the judge or jury perceive you? Often, just having been arrested for OWI is equivalent to being labeled in the minds of both judges and juries as having an alcohol or drug problem. Jurors tend to think that you "must have done something" if you are in court as the defendant.

Almost without exception, your jury "pool" will consist of fairly conservative individuals. Most of these people either work or are retired from an active career. When dressing for the jury, it is best that your clothing and manner of dress be somewhat conservative, to reflect the composition of your likely jury pool. Also, remove any "body jewelry" or other visible symbols that will make an immediate poor impression on a conservative, middle-aged, working-class juror.

The more conservative the hair style, the better. Clean shaven men can expect to be more readily accepted. Similarly, women need to keep any skirt lengths "appropriate" and of course, no low-cut shirts. Remember, you are in a court of law. Listen to your OWI attorney when your "trial appearance" is in question.

Chapter 6:
How to Use Strategies and Defense Tactics to Unshackle the Prosecutor's Case

6.0. Purpose of this Chapter. The prosecution of a typical OWI case involves hundreds of facts and potential legal issues. The cornerstone of a successful defense is a full and open discussion of each aspect of your case with your experienced OWI attorney. What you think are minor factual changes or the discovery of certain "statements" by police during their investigation of a case or your arrest can lead to a favorable outcome. This is why your lawyer may use extensive questionnaires and lengthy interviews at the beginning of your case.

A defense is a general term for the effort of an attorney representing a defendant during trial and in pre-trial maneuvers to defeat the prosecution in a criminal case like an OWI.[89] Broadly speaking, there are two categories of defenses: "legal" and "factual". Legal defenses include things like unlawful stop or arrest issues. Legal defenses are for the judge to decide. A jury cannot dismiss your case because they believe your arrest was unlawful. On the other hand, factual defenses are for the jury to decide, and might include things like a rising blood alcohol defense. Stated somewhat differently, in some cases, your attorney may identify a "complete defense" (a legal excuse) to the alleged OWI charges, called an affirmative defense, to counter, defeat or remove all or a part of the contentions of the state (the prosecution). In other cases, your highly qualified defense attorney will be looking for shortcomings in the police evidence that creates a "failure of proof" on some aspect of the case.

In beginning the evaluation of your case, your attorney will be considering the first of these general considerations, that is, whether or not the prosecution has any evidence at all on all the requisite "elements" of each OWI count. (A count is a legal term for each separate crime the state has charged you with committing).

Another consideration is whether or not the police, in their arrest of you, violated any state statutes, constitutional provisions, regulations or other legal authority (such as decisional law from a court that has ruled on the same evidentiary issue). If they did, was the violation of such a type or "degree" that it will offend the notion of fair play and justice from the point of view of the trial court?

Your lawyer should also consider whether or not the prosecutor can "lay a foundation" for the admission of the breath or blood test. If there are issues with regard to the manner in which the police obtained this evidence, then you lawyer may be able to have it "suppressed" meaning the prosecutor cannot use it at trial. This is sometimes the surest way to obtain a great plea bargain.

This chapter discusses some of these possible defenses, strategies and tactics to the OWI charges against you. The more complete your knowledge of these issues and legal matters, the more helpful you can be to your attorney in fighting for your legal rights in your OWI case. You need to give your attorney ALL the facts so he or she can uncover potential defenses, strategies and legal challenges in your case.

6.1. Defenses Related to the Legality or Sufficiency of the Indictment, Accusation, Complaint, Information, or other Charging Instrument (such as a Uniform Traffic Citation). In a criminal prosecution, you start with a presumption in your favor that you are innocent until and unless proven guilty.[90] You also have the right to be accurately and completely informed precisely what the charges are that the State is bringing against you.[91] Such information is vital to protect your constitutionally guaranteed right to a fair trial.[92]

The paperwork starting an OWI case can be as simple as the citation or ticket that the law enforcement officer gave you at the time of your arrest. The prosecutor is also allowed to draw up more precise (or even additional) criminal charges by way of a typewritten accusation, information or complaint that more clearly states how and when the offense occurred. In such a case, the ticket or citation is "superseded" or replaced by the new formal document. The State has the option of bringing additional (or different) charges against you if their investigation of the facts of the case reveals that amended or alternative counts should be pursued against you. In Michigan, it is typical for a first offense OWI to be charged using only a traffic ticket or citation. Second or subsequent offenses, and all felony intoxicated driving charges including where a death is involved, are commonly charged using a more formal complaint and a warrant.

Because this charging document must inform you adequately of the charges against you, deficiencies in the form of the document or in the contents can be used by your attorney as means to either cause the documents to be redrawn or possibly (in certain circumstances) to completely BAR prosecution in the event that "jeopardy" has attached and the State did not correct the flawed charges. A motion to quash is an attack on the form or the content of the accusatory document. The timing and form of this kind of legal challenge is very important, and requires an extensive knowledge of state law and criminal trial practice to succeed.

6.2. Defenses Relating to an Illegal Search Warrant, if Applicable. In limited circumstances it is possible that you were arrested and have been charged with OWI based on an illegal search warrant for your blood or urine. This is because the Fourth Amendment to the United States Constitution guarantees to everyone the right not to have to defend against an illegal search warrant.[93] If you have refused to consent to a chemical test, or in some situations following a collision causing a death or serious bodily injury, the police in Michigan may seek a court order called a "search warrant" to procure a blood sample from you for suspected drugs or alcohol in your system. An appropriate amount of "probable cause" is required in order for this search warrant to be valid. Michigan law provides that probable cause can be based on the results of a preliminary breath test result alone.[94]

Of course, a successful motion attacking the warrant for blood may not result in the dismissal of the case against you. Evidence unconstitutionally seized by the police cannot be used against you in court, nor can evidence "resulting from or growing out of an illegal search be utilized as evidence."[95] If the blood evidence is thrown out, the question becomes whether or not the prosecutor can prove the OUIL part of the OWI charge, that is, was your ability to operate the vehicle substantially lessened?

6.3. Defenses Related to the Legality of a Roadblock. The police must have a very good legal reason to stop your vehicle as a general rule. This reason can be based upon an observation of a traffic offense, defective equipment, an expired tag or inspection sticker, or some observable evidence that a crime is being committed or is about to be committed. In some states other than Michigan, roadblocks are valid under the ambit of a State's police powers to insure that the roads are safe from drunk drivers. The United States Supreme Court upheld this power under the federal constitution in the case of *Michigan v. Sitz*.[96] However, on return of this case to the Michigan courts, it was decided that such roadblocks violate the Michigan constitution, and are thus unlawful in Michigan.[97] Thus, if you were stopped at an OWI roadblock, your attorney can use this as a defense to the charges against you.

6.4. Defenses Related to the Legality of the Stop of your Vehicle. For any law enforcement officer to have a valid reason to stop you while driving your vehicle, there must be an "articulable and reasonable suspicion" that: (1) you are an unlicensed driver; (2) that your vehicle is not registered; (3) either you or the vehicle you are driving is in violation of the law.[98]

"Articulable" means the law enforcement officer is able to verbalize specific facts and reasons to the court, through testimony, a reason why he or she believed there was a violation of the law justifying the stop of your vehicle. What constitutes "reasonable" is analyzed on a case by case basis,[99] but it typically has to be more than a mere "hunch" or guesswork on the part of the officer.[100] The officers must have some reasonable and articulable suspicion that you are committing a crime before they decide to stop you, not just develop this suspicion after the stop. Most of these challenges are won on extremely minor evidentiary points that are brought out by your criminal defense specialist at a pre-trial motion.

6.5. Defenses Related to the Lawfulness of Your Arrest for OWI. The Fourth Amendment to the United States Constitution also protects you against any illegal or unlawful seizure (arrest) by the government.[101] A temporary non-custodial traffic stop turns into an "arrest" when a reasonable person in your position would think that the traffic stop was no longer temporary.[102] Just because you are in handcuffs by itself does not mean you are under arrest.[103] Nor does the officer drawing his or her weapon automatically mean you are under arrest.[104] Whether or not you are under arrest depends not on the opinion of the officer, but upon facts that reveal your subjective sense of lack of freedom.[105] To determine whether [***13] a defendant was in custody at the time of the interrogation, we look at the totality of the circumstances, with the key question being whether the accused reasonably could have believed that he was not free to leave.[106] However, in Michigan, the courts generally allow the police relative latitude to collect evidence during their investigation.

Whether or not there was sufficient probable cause or reasonable grounds for your arrest for OWI will depend on Michigan's case law, statutes and constitution, plus the circumstances surrounding your arrest.¹⁰⁷ Having the smell of alcohol on you alone can be enough "probable cause" for an officer to ask you to perform a field sobriety test or take a PBT.¹⁰⁸ This is why your OWI specialist attorney will need to know all of the smallest details of your arrest.

6.6. Defenses Related to an Unlawful Search and Seizure and Exclusion of Illegally Seized Evidence. Unless your blood was drawn pursuant to a search warrant, and there is little, if any, other evidence of intoxication, it is very rare for an OWI case to revolve exclusively around physical evidence that has been taken from you by the government in an unlawful manner. This is because most OWI cases focus around the officer's testimony as to what he or she observed, video tapes or audio recordings made by the officer in the line of duty, and lawfully obtained chemical testing (blood, breath or urine) performed on you to establish the presence and quantity of alcohol in your system at the time of your arrest.

Until you are arrested, you have the Fourth Amendment protection against an unlawful search of you and/or your vehicle.¹⁰⁹ The police cannot delay you too long before they either have to arrest you, or let you go, but you may be detained on reasonable suspicion in an investigatory stop as long as the police are diligently pursuing a means of investigation that is likely to confirm or dispel their suspicions quickly.¹¹⁰ Also, having a dog sniff your vehicle while it is stopped, as long as it does not delay the process of you being ticketed, is not an illegal search.¹¹¹

Certainly, anything that is considered in plain sight within your vehicle or on your vehicle can be cited by the police and used against you in your case.¹¹² The smell of intoxicants such as marijuana can be probably cause for an arrest and admitted into evidence.¹¹³ The police can also get around the warrant requirement by simply asking you at the time of your stop to allow them to search your vehicle or its contents. Voluntary consent is always an exception to the search warrant requirement. Even if you do not give your consent, at the time of your arrest, the police have certain rights to search not only you, but also the passenger compartment and any containers found in the passenger compartment of your vehicle.[114] A search done prior to your vehicle being towed away (called an "inventory search") is supposed to be done to assure that if valuables inside the vehicle disappear while the vehicle is impounded, the police department will not be held accountable.[115]

Because almost every custodial arrest leads to a vehicle tow and the "inventory search," you should never keep any contraband items in your vehicle. Most common are illegal drugs, but sometimes the police will seize prescription painkillers that are not in a proper container. Other types of "contraband" items might include pornography, an unlicensed weapon or obviously stolen merchandise. One of the more common successful challenges has been when police open locked or closed containers to look for illegal items.

However, while in custody the police do not have the right to search and inspect every item of your vehicle if your arrested for a violation such as suspended driving where there is no reasonable explanation to search a vehicle for contraband items.[116]

6.7. Defenses Related to the Violation by the Police of your Fifth Amendment Privilege Against Self-incrimination. The Fifth Amendment to the Constitution of the United States provides: "nor shall be compelled in any criminal case to be a witness against himself ..." and the Michigan Constitution reflects this requirement.[117] Once you have been placed under arrest, if you are to be questioned further, you have to receive from the law enforcement officer(s) a notification of this right.[118] However, once you are aware of this right you much explicitly invoke it.[119] This is true once the police stop has extended beyond a routine traffic stop and beyond doing any field sobriety evaluations.[120] Not only should you be notified of this right, but if you say something self-incriminating after being taken into custody or placed under arrest but before you receive this warning, these statements may not be used against you.[121] However, spontaneous utterances to police (especially those captured on videotapes) can be devastating to the case against you if they are ruled to be unprotected by the Fifth Amendment.[122]

6.8. Defenses Related to the Violation by the Police of Your Constitutional or Statutory Right to Counsel once Arrested. Under the Fifth Amendment you have the right against self-incrimination and your Sixth Amendment right to have an attorney available for your defense,[123] you after your arrest you have a right for your attorney to be present any time the police are questioning you **after** your arrest.[124] It is best, however, for you to invoke this right to have counsel present and to remain totally silent until your attorney arrives. Once you have unambiguously requested that your counsel be present, the police can no longer interrogate you without your permission. Nor can the police get someone else to ask their questions for them once you have requested the presence of your counsel.[125]

A "conversation" with you started by the police may be deemed to have been a contrivance to deprive you of your legal rights. If you were refused an attorney after you asked for one and the police continued to question you in spite of your request, proof of such a violation can be used by your attorney in your defense, or possibly used to get the entire charges against you dismissed.

6.9. Challenges to use of Improperly Administered Standardized and Non-standardized Field Sobriety Evaluations. It is highly likely that the police officer who stopped you, or found you behind the wheel in your stationary car, administered field sobriety tests to you before he or she arrested you. These evaluations are being done for one purpose; to gather further alleged incriminatory evidence against you and later use it at your trial.

Michigan does not require that the standardized field sobriety tests be given prior to every intoxicated driving arrest. Nevertheless, if these evaluations were given, but were done incorrectly,[126] or if the officer's decision to arrest you for OWI was based on non-standardized procedures,[127] your lawyer may be able to argue that the arrest for OWI was invalid.

6.10. Challenges Relating to the Officer's Competence to Administer Field Sobriety Evaluations. Simply put, if the officer who administered the field sobriety tests is not able to prove that he or she was well trained and competent to give you those tests, your attorney may be able to get the results of those tests thrown out of your case.[128] If the results cannot be thrown out because the officer is qualified to give the tests, then demonstrating his or her lack of experience or competence in properly administering, demonstrating or "grading" these evaluations may be used to challenge the weight and credibility of the evidence.[129] If your field sobriety evaluations are suppressed, it is likely the officer did not have enough probable cause to arrest you for OWI.

Except for the horizontal gaze nystagmus test which is considered a scientific test by the Michigan courts, the rest of the field sobriety evaluations are considered within common knowledge and the officers do not have to be considered "experts" in them to be able to testify against you.[130] If it is found the officer who conducted the field sobriety test includes false information and/or material information is omitted from their search warrant affidavit for a BAC test, the results of that test may be suppressed.[131] The standard is if after striking the false information and considering the omitted information the affidavit does or does not establish probable cause.[132] For more information about how to challenge these tests see: *"Do Standardized Field Sobriety Tests Reliably Predict Intoxication."*[133]

6.11. Challenges to the Officer's Ability and Experience in Determining an Impaired Driver from an Unimpaired Driver. Certainly, a law enforcement officer with years of OWI arrests and with advanced extensive training in OWI evaluations and arrests is much more likely to be able to distinguish an impaired driver from a driver who is unimpaired and safe to drive. An officer's lengthy police career is not a guarantee of the officer's competence level. Many newer officers receive modern intensive training that is far better than training from the 1980's. In Michigan, it is also becoming increasingly common for road patrol officers to be qualified participants in the National Highway Safety Administration's Standardized Field Sobriety Test Program. Most departments have at least one officer that has this advanced training, and nearly all Michigan State troopers on road patrol have attended this training and therefore participate in the standardized testing program. The training manuals for these programs suggest that the field sobriety tests, and even the roadside breath tests, are intended to assist the officer in making the arrest/no arrest decision. Nevertheless, some experienced officers will arrest **ANY** motorist with the smell of alcohol on his or her breath when the person declines to participate in voluntary field sobriety evaluations. If this happened in your case, then your attorney may be able to obtain a dismissal of the charges against you by arguing that your arrest was not supported by probable cause.

6.12. Defenses Relating to Discovery Abuse. In your OWI case, discovery is the formal process by which your side and the prosecution exchange information in accordance with state guidelines regarding possible evidence and testimony regarding your case. The prosecution must release some information. In Michigan, some prosecutors argue that the court rules provide that discovery does not apply to misdemeanor cases (like most OWIs). However, the more logical and thoughtful position is that the State is held to the same discovery rules in misdemeanors as in felonies.[134]

This may entail releasing as little as the results from any scientific (blood, breath or urine) tests that the state proposes to admit at your trial,[135] a copy of the police report,[136] the names of any witnesses they plan on using at trial,[137] any statements you made to the police,[138] and any exculpatory evidence.[139] (Evidence which shows or tends to show that you did not commit the crime). In Michigan, any state chemical tests need not be produced until 2 days prior to your trial.[140] Recent changes to the court rules provide that discovery is "reciprocal," meaning that your attorney has an obligation to turn over to the prosecutor evidence which he or she has obtained in your defense.[141]

6.13. Defenses Relating to Exculpatory Lost Video Evidence. In some OWI arrests, the arresting officer will have a video recording of all or part of the roadside conversation, field evaluations and chronology of the arrest process. If any law enforcement officer had a working camera at the arrest location, his or her department likely had in place a departmental policy that the entire arrest be recorded to be used later at trial. In the event a video was made at the scene, yet none can be located later, your attorney may be able to use the loss of this potentially exculpatory evidence as a defense in your case. If the prosecution fails to comply with rules of discovery, the court may order them to "provide the discovery or permit the inspection of materials not previously disclosed, grant a continuance, prohibit the party from introducing in evidence the material not disclosed, or enter such other order as it deems just under the circumstances."[142] This is particularly true in Michigan where the definition of reasonable doubt provides that doubt can grow out of the "lack of evidence". In fact, in certain circumstances, your attorney may even be able to require the judge to tell the jury at your trial that they must presume that the lost evidence was favorable to your case.

Combine this with your constitutionally guaranteed presumption of innocence until and unless proven guilty beyond a reasonable doubt, and the power of a jury trial becomes evident. The best OWI specialists can attempt to get the charges against you reduced or completely dropped on such facts. Your attorney must still demonstrate that the tape was favorable to you or that it may have shown your innocence and that the video was destroyed after your attorney had attempted to obtain a copy during discovery.[143] It is paramount to hire your attorney as soon as possible so they are afforded the opportunity to file for discovery before evidence is destroyed. A competent attorney will know what to specifically request so the prosecutor is made aware of such evidence. Without this knowledge, the prosecution is under no requirement to provide your defense with anything outside the range of mandatory disclosure.[144]

6.14. Defenses Related to the Failure of the Police to Comply with the Requirements of the State Implied Consent Statute. In Michigan, once you have been arrested for OWI, the police officer making the arrest must inform you of specific rights under state law relating to your obligation to take a state-administered test of your blood, breath or urine, as well as other rights to refuse this testing and your right to an independent test.[145] These rights include the right to be given the reasonable opportunity to obtain your own independent test of your breath, blood or urine. Once these rights are read, the arresting officer may give you no option but to submit to a test, even resorting to physical force to extract blood or gather urine through a catheter if the officer obtains a court order.[146]

If you were not read the correct implied consent warning at all, or if after reading them, the police interfered with your right to collect your own chemical test, then your attorney is likely to argue that your "implied consent" rights were violated by the police. In the past, if your attorney could prove that these rights were violated then such violation could result in the complete dismissal of the charges against you.[147] Today, however, the Michigan courts rule that procedural violations relative to chemical evidence "go to the weight rather than to admissibility." Consequently, it is now very difficult for your attorney to persuade a court to "suppress" any unfavorable test results and thereby exclude them from being introduced at trial.[148]

Making matters worse, a case from the Michigan Supreme Court further muddies these waters.[149] In this case the Court states that if it is determined that your implied consent rights were violated in any significant way then your case will not be dismissed and such wrongfully obtained evidence will not be excluded. Instead, it will be up to the jury to decide the significance of such police misconduct. So now, rather than having a judge with years of legal experience decide that illegally obtained evidence should not be used against you, all of the evidence comes in and the jury, not the judge, will decide what to do about the police wrongdoing. This is a radical change in Michigan law and places the jury in the position of having to understand the finest nuances of the law, then having them choose what parts of the evidence they should consider or ignore in deciding your guilt or innocence.

6.15. Defenses Related to the Failure of the Police to Comply with the Requirements of the State's Independent Test Statute. One of the requirements of the implied consent law is that you have the right to obtain an independent test of blood, breath or urine taken after the State test.[150] This sample can be tested independently by a laboratory of your choice (and at your expense) in order to permit you to challenge the State's test result that will be used against you at trial. Your independent test also protects against the possibility of a switched sample.

However, a more recent case from the Michigan Supreme Court challenges these rights. If you want to get your independent test at a hospital that the officer thinks is too far away and he or she suggests a closer one, and you refuse to go to this closer hospital, then such police misconduct will likely not result in the suppression of your state-administered breath test results. Instead, the test results may be introduced at your trial, and the judge will give the jury deciding your fate an instruction or instructions on what to do with this evidence. Of course such instruction will come only after they have already heard the damaging breath test evidence.[151]

Before deciding to request an independent test, however, know that the results of your independent test will be admissible at your trial.[152] Thus, if the result of your independent test confirms the police test, then your case becomes more difficult for your attorney to defend because it will include two chemical test results showing an unlawfully elevated alcohol level.

6.16. Defenses Related to Prosecution's Ability to Prove the Elements of the Offense, Other than Impairment. To be convicted of an OWI charge, the State has to prove each of the "elements" of each offense against you beyond a reasonable doubt. An "element" is an essential part of the offense charged. This means, even if the State can prove that you were intoxicated, they still typically have to prove that you were either "operating" or in "actual physical control" of your vehicle at the time of your intoxication. This type of defense is extremely fact-specific, and the case law in Michigan is not particularly clear on the issue. What is clear is that "circumstantial" evidence can be used by the State to prove this element. So, Michigan courts have found sufficient circumstantial evidence where a motorist was found outside of his car, but the hood of the car and the rear wheels of the car were warm, and also tree branches were stuck under the tires in an apparent effort to get the car out of the ditch. So, even if the police do not see you drive, and you are not found inside your car when the police arrive, you can sometimes still be convicted of OWI.

Nevertheless, if your lawyer can show to the court that the State cannot prove any one element of an OWI charge against you, then the entire charge typically can be defeated. Often, prosecutors are hesitant to reduce or dismiss these cases. This is why the best OWI attorneys challenge any inconsistencies in the police reports and investigate these cases thoroughly. Because these defenses are so detail specific, your attorney will need every fact that you can remember about the entire day leading up to your arrest.

6.17. Defenses Related to the Prosecution's Ability to Prove the Required Degree of Intoxication other than by Chemical Testing. If the State lacks any scientific test results of your blood, breath or urine (either because you refused, the police did not perform such a test, or possibly due to a machine or lab malfunction), the State may still attempt to prove the OUIL part of the OWI charge, that is, by showing that your ability to operate your motor vehicle was "substantially lessened".[153] These means include what might broadly be called "observational evidence", and includes your performance on any voluntary field sobriety tests, any physical evidence observed, detected or seized by the police at the time of your arrest (examples; smell of alcohol, open container of alcohol, seeing red, blood-shot eyes, hearing slurred speech), and "opinion" testimony from either the police or other witnesses that assert that you looked or acted somewhat "drunk." When the State does not have a scientific test "number" or illegal substance (such as marijuana in the blood), the only type of OWI charge that can be prosecuted is a common law OWI alcohol or OWI drug offense. The prosecutor can also attempt to prove the OWI by showing that your ability to operate was substantially lessened by a combination of alcohol and drugs.

Your attorney will likely need to anticipate the State's evidence and subpoena your own witnesses to help prepare your defense if he or she has found issues with the State's non-scientific testing, such as field sobriety testing. Remember, it is still the State's burden to prove beyond a reasonable doubt each and every element of any charge against you, including the element that it was alcohol that impaired your driving. The best OWI attorneys know the names and expert training of an array of expert witnesses, and the location of manuals or regulations that can provide evidence to challenge the State's observation evidence. Such witnesses or evidence will cost money to bring to court, but could be essential to your case.

6.18. Defenses Related to the Admissibility of the Prosecution's Breath Testing Evidence. If you did submit to a State administered breath test, in light of your presumption of innocence, the prosecution must prove the test to be "both relevant and reliable."[154] The DataMaster must be checked on a weekly basis and every 120 days by a Class IV operator of the machine. Logs must be maintained to ensure proper functioning of the machine.[155] If the prosecution fails to provide all of this proof, the test results may be excluded (not allowed) as part of the trial evidence against you. Such an exclusion is becoming increasingly rare in Michigan and the trend is to allow such "tainted" evidence to be submitted to the jury at trial. It then becomes your attorney's job to persuade the jury that they should give little "weight" to such tainted evidence.[156]

If a DataMaster DMT was used to test your breath, then there are additional issues related to dry gas simulation the use of the dry gas standard. The DMT however is fitted with a dry gas simulation canister that remains attached to the machine. Internal programming then directs the device to draw an appropriate dry gas sample for simulation every Monday at 10:00 a.m. The only thing left for "human hands" is the entering of the result of such simulation results onto the OD-33 (simulator logs).

The DMT therefore presents many new potential defense challenges. For example, the manufacture of the dry gas canisters and the closely related propriety and fulfillment of the "correction factors" necessary to account for changes in atmospheric pressure relevant to dry gas is likely to be extensively litigated. Unlike the wet bath process, a dry gas calibration or certification must take into account the barometric pressure when the machine measures the concentration of ethanol.

A rule effecting test admissibility and your confrontation rights coming into effect January 1, 2013 is referred to as "notice and demand." Within 14 days of receipt of a report *notice* must be given to opposing counsel. If opposing counsel does not *demand* the right to in-person testimony of the lab technician within 14 days of receipt of a lab report, they lose their right to cross-examination and the lab report is deemed admissible.[157]

6.19. Defenses Related to the Failure of the Police to Comply with Standard Operating Procedure During the Arrest or Forensic Testing. There is a "shortcut" method by which the State can introduce the breath test into evidence. This method usually involves the admission into evidence of the simulator logs based on the business record exception to the hearsay rule. After this, provided the prosecutor can show that the rules were followed in administering the test (a very light burden), then your breath test will be allowed into evidence. This saves costs, since the person who checked the machine's calibration is not necessarily required to appear to prove that the simulator tests were run properly, or to "prove" the underlying scientific theory and reliability of the breath analysis machine used in your case. In any event, showing the evidence necessary to get the test into evidence is called "laying the foundation."

The best OWI attorneys know the procedures that are utilized by the various police departments in their area. These experienced legal advisors also know the reasons behind the steps in the procedures. These procedures are more properly called quality assurance and quality control procedures. Failure to follow the proper procedures for either your OWI arrest or for handling the scientific or documentary evidence collected from your arrest (blood, urine or breath samples, the police video, any photos taken by the police of the scene or of you, etc.) can result in your attorney successfully arguing pre-trial motions that can either cause the case to be dismissed or be the basis for exclusion of key State evidence.

Missing videotapes or other critical evidence may be fatal to the State's case. While protections are put in place to protect the police officers during the arrest, a breach of the rules for storage and retention of evidence may be held against the police, due to the defense lawyer's argument that the destroyed or lost evidence would be favorable to you. Such destruction of evidence or mishandling of evidence is called "spoliation" of evidence, and operates to the State's detriment in most situations. Keep in mind that most law enforcement departments in Michigan have a policy to "recycle" tapes after 30 days, and sometimes in as few as 14 days. Thus, if you fail to properly find and retain an excellent lawyer, or if it turns out that you are not charged until after this 14-30 days, this important evidence can be destroyed without any adverse consequence to the State.

6.20. Defenses Related to the Credibility of the Prosecution's Breath Testing Evidence. To be allowed to tell the jury your breath tests' results, the prosecution must first "lay a foundation" to support the introduction of the "numbers" that are to be considered by the jury. The prosecutor must establish that the machine was in good working order and that it had been used in the manner approved by the State.[158]

In Michigan, only one breath exhalation is mandated.[159] If a second test is attempted and the results vary from the first, this goes only to the weight of the evidence, not its admissibility.[160] Still, from a scientific "weight" perspective, having only one test can be very important to your defense. This is because the rules in Michigan provide that the results of the second test are intended to confirm those of the first test. If a second test comes up as invalid, the person administering the test should, but is not required, to give you a third test.

The State's failure to "lay a proper foundation" will result in the test results not being admitted into evidence, such a failure of proof of a key part of the OWI case can either end the case or render the remaining "proof" inadequate to support your conviction.

6.21. Defenses Related to the Admissibility of the Prosecution's Blood Testing Evidence. As a general rule, it can be said that whole blood testing is more accurate and reliable than breath testing. The science behind blood testing is also considerably more complicated and requires a particularly high level of scientific and legal knowledge to properly defend. As with breath testing, it is essential that your attorney have a good science background to be effective in the courtroom when defending blood test results.

On the other hand, it is more difficult for the prosecutor to use blood test results, because admission of these results requires a more detailed "foundation," including more witness testimony. For example, in order for a blood test to be admissible as evidence, the prosecutor has to demonstrate the admissibility of the test by putting forth the officer who witnessed the blood being drawn from you, the nurse or practitioner that drew the blood, the "chain of evidence" witnesses who handled the blood before it was ever tested, and the forensic scientist who tested the blood at the State lab. Additionally, for the results of the State's test to be admissible, the State must show that the test results bear a minimum level of reliability. This will require the testimony of the forensic scientist who performed the actual testing, who must show that he or she did the testing according to the applicable rules and in such a way that the results obtained should be considered accurate. The State must also show, through the chain of evidence, that the biologic substance tested came from you and no one else.[161]

The first area of proof focuses upon whether or not the test machine itself was properly set up and calibrated, whether or not the test was run correctly, according to the lab's procedures, and run by someone capable, trained and authorized to operate the machine. If the blood test results being used against you were drawn as a part of a medical evaluation (in a hospital), rather than those drawn at the express direction of the police for evaluation in a crime lab, the testing must still have been done in compliance with the statutory standards.

The second area of inquiry focuses on the State's ability to establish the chain of custody for your sample. Your attorney focuses upon whether the sample was collected properly, whether the collection tubes were of the correct types, whether your arm was swabbed with a non-alcoholic pad, whether the nurse properly inverted the vial of blood before sealing the package for shipment to the crime lab, and issues that involve the "integrity" of the sample.

Even when grossly improper handling of your blood sample is shown by your attorney, the lab results may not be automatically excluded from evidence at trial. As with any blood tests, any discrepancies in the chain of custody may go to the *weight* of the evidence or cause the lab results to be excluded.[162]

6.22. Seven Defenses Related to the Credibility of the Prosecution's Blood Testing Evidence. Before a blood test result may be admitted into evidence against you by a trial judge, the prosecutor must be able to cross several "hurdles" that your defense lawyer may raise.

With blood testing defenses or problems may arise in any of the following areas:

1. **Collection** – Did the police properly aid in the collection of the blood, handle the blood tubes properly, and use the proper equipment? Did the person drawing the blood probably swab the arm, insert the needle, use the correct needle, withdraw the correct amount of blood, handle the blood tubes properly and was he/she properly qualified?

2. **Transportation** – How was the blood handled after it was collect? Where did the blood kit go, and ultimately how did the blood get to the lab for testing?

3. **Storage** – Under what conditions was the blood stored both before and after it go to the state lab?

4. **Preparation of Sample** – Was the blood properly prepared for testing? Did the analyst use the appropriate equipment and was this equipment properly calibrated?

5. **Testing** – How was the blood tested? Was the chromatograph used to test the blood properly maintained and in good

working order? Where any errors made during the testing? What is the uncertainty budget assigned to the equipment?

6. **Reporting** – How was the result reported, and was there any manipulation of the results to fit a prescribed method range?

7. **Cognitive Bias** - According to *"Cognitive Bias and The Evaluation of forensic Evidence"*[163] the debate about the influence of cognitive bias, which is the unconscious influence of bias on the reported results in criminal cases, has intensified recently. Cognitive bias is a universal, human phenomenon, and as it relates to intoxicated driving cases, cognitive bias can cause innocent drinking drivers to be convicted of a intoxicated driving crime they did not commit.

It is possible for defenses to a blood test result to arise from any of the seven categories above. For example, if the blood was not inverted correctly so as to mix with the preservative and anticoagulant,[164] or if it was drawn in the wrong type of blood tube (possibly a container with no preservatives), then any results can be challenged by your defense attorney. Your attorney will use cross-examination of the prosecutor's witnesses to start creating "reasonable doubt." Then, expert witnesses may be called to testify on your behalf to show how the flawed handling of the blood likely could result in a false elevated reading. If the tests are not scientifically credible, or reliable, then the alleged alcohol reading should not be used against you at trial.

It should be obvious that in order of there to be any real hope of meaningful challenge of blood testing the attorney handling your case must have a comprehensive understanding of both the administrate rules and applicable law and just as importantly, of the scientific principles that underlie the tests used.

6.23. Defenses Related to Police Misconduct or Perjury. For a variety of reasons, police and crime lab workers sometimes cheat. Instances of misconduct dealing with chemical evidence in intoxicated driving cases have been shown and often these errors are a result of efforts to save time or money. Other times, neglect or sloppiness is the problem. This misconduct overshadows and taints the State's "forensic" test results sought to be used against you.

Perjury is the crime of intentionally lying after being duly sworn (to tell the truth) by a notary public, judge, court clerk or other official. One of the most serious misconducts a law enforcement officer can do is to commit perjury. Jurors and judges tend to discredit all testimony of any witness who can be proven to have departed from telling the truth.

Showing perjury or a prior inconsistent statement is an important first step in convincing a jury (or a judge) that the officer or lab technician, is not worthy of belief on any issue. Your defense attorney will ask the judge for a jury instruction that tells the jurors that if they find a lack of credibility of any witness, they can disregard the witness' entire testimony.

It can often be very difficult to prove that a witness lied. However, experienced lawyers often have banks of prior transcripts of police witnesses or laboratory personnel. These prior transcripts can be used to show that the witness has testified differently in the past on an important issue. The goal of all this is to show your jury that reasonable doubt exists.

6.23.1 Why Police Lie When Making OWI Arrests. In the fascinating book *"Mistakes Were Made (but not by me)"*[165] the authors explain how people, even police officers, often justify behavior such as perjury and lying as somehow acceptable, if not actually moral. According to the book:

"The engine that drives self-justification (for lying), the energy that produces the need to justify our actions and decisions – especially the wrong ones – is an unpleasant feeling called "cognitive dissonance." This is a state of tension that occurs whenever a person holds two cognitions (ideas, attitudes, beliefs, opinions) that are psychologically inconsistent, such as "Smoking is a dumb thing because it could kill me" and "I smoke two packs a day."

Dissonance produces mental discomfort ranging from minor pangs to deep anguish; people don't rest easily until they find a way to reduce it. In this example, the most direct way for a smoker to reduce dissonance is by quitting. But if she has tried to quit and failed, now she must reduce dissonance by convincing herself that smoking isn't really so harmful, or that smoking is worth the risk because it helps her relax or prevents her gaining weight (after all obesity is a health risk too), and so on. Most smokers manage to reduce dissonance in many such ingenious, if self-deluding ways."[166]

It is precisely this kind of cognitive dissonance that allows police officers to lie in their OWI reports or when testifying. All that needs to happen is for the police officer to find some way to reduce the dissonance. Add to all this the increased focus on drunk and drugged driving throughout law enforcement, and a really dangerous recipe has been created; one that can lead to all sorts of abuses, including wrongful arrest and conviction for intoxicated driving.

6.24. The Defense of an Unconstitutional or Invalidly-adopted Drinking and Driving Statute or Related Ordinance or Invalidly Adopted Testing Equipment. In order for you to be guilty of a crime, you have to have violated a law that is constitutionally valid. As an example, if the government attempted to adopt a law which made it unlawful for you to speak openly in your own homes on Sundays, this law would certainly be found unconstitutional (against the First Amendment right of Free Speech among other protections) and thus invalid. If a statute is ruled to be unconstitutional, it cannot be used as the basis of charging you with a crime.

There is also the issue of whether or not the equipment used to test your breath or blood was properly approved for use. Even if approved for use, there is still the question of whether or not the equipment was changed or modified in any way after it was approved.

If it can be shown that it was, then it may follow that the equipment is no longer "approved" equipment. This should result in the test result being thrown out.

As discussed elsewhere, in 2013 Michigan began replacing existing breath testing machines with the new DataMaster DMT. This new equipment is subject to an approval process that may or may not have been followed in your case. The administrative rules were also changed to accommodate the new equipment. Plus, the DataMaster DMT is now owned by Intoximeters, Inc. All of these changes presents new defense opportunities. The most skilled intoxicated driving defense lawyers keep abreast of these changes, and will know whether or not the changes were made appropriately and according to the applicable law.

6.25. Defenses Related to Double Jeopardy. It is a violation of the Fifth Amendment of the United States Constitution for anyone to be held criminally accountable twice for the same issue by the same sovereign (legal entity).[167] What this means is that you cannot be made to stand trial a second time for any of your actions in a state court if the first trial in a state court has already had a final ruling in your favor. Believe it or not, in some countries, the government can start over and keep trying until they get a conviction.

Several important exceptions to "double jeopardy" exist. Michigan is a separate and distinct sovereign (independent government) from our federal government. With certain types of crimes, both Michigan and the federal government may try you for the same set of circumstances if your actions are possibly against different laws of each "sovereign."

Next, be aware that double jeopardy applies only at a certain point in the proceedings. If your proceedings get stopped before that time, you have no constitutional protection against a second trial. This point in time is after the jury has been empanelled and sworn in.[168] During a non-jury (bench) trial, the time is once the court first begins to hear evidence.[169] In Michigan, even if after the jury is sworn a mistrial is declared because of prosecutorial error, your case can be tried again. Such instances do not create double jeopardy protections.

Nevertheless, a mistake made by raising an issue too early may allow the prosecutor to stop the proceedings, correct the error, and begin your trial again — with the error resolved. This is yet another reason to have the best OWI attorney you can afford, because he or she will know exactly when and how to raise the double jeopardy issue that may win your case on this highly specialized legal issue.

It is not a double jeopardy situation for your license to be taken from you in an administrative hearing, and for you then to have to stand trial for OWI in a criminal court and possibly lose your license again.[170] Although the implied consent hearing at which your drivers' license is suspended immediately following an OWI arrest may seem like a criminal trial, the only question is whether or not you should lose a property interest (that is your driver's license).[171] You have no constitutional or statutory right to drive. You merely have a privilege from the state that granted your license to you. The administrative hearing is to determine if you violated the implied consent statute and therefore, if your license should be suspended for one or two years. In Michigan, this administrative suspension is considered to be "civil" in nature, and involves different issues than the legal issues involved in your criminal case, when your liberty interests are at stake (you could be put in jail or penalized with fines, lose your driving privileges or required to perform community service.) Because there are different interests at stake, the issue being litigated in the two related (but different proceedings) is not the same and double jeopardy does not apply.

6.26. Defenses Related to *Collateral Estoppel* or *Res Judicata*. "Collateral estoppel" is a legal doctrine related to issue preclusion. This means that the issue being raised by a party has been tried and settled in another court and there is no reason to try it again in your court.[172] In fact, one of the precepts of our legal system is that parties are bound to that earlier decision.

A common example in an OWI trial is what type of documents or testimony the State is required to bring into court in order to lay a proper "foundation" regarding its breath test results, and to create a presumption that the breath test "number" is admissible as evidence that the jury can hear. Based on extensive prior case law, it is usually fairly clear to your OWI attorney whether or not the State has produced enough evidence to carry its "burden" of persuasion.

"*Res judicata*" is Latin for "the thing has been judged," and is *claim preclusion*. That is, between the State and you, a specific issue has already been decided in a court of law and there is no reason to debate this issue again during your OWI trial.[173] *Collateral estoppel* is rarely an issue in an intoxicated driving case, but can be a powerful defense if it exists.

6.27. Defenses Related to the Denial of Your Right to a Speedy Trial. Speedy trial is a protection derived from the United States Constitution relating to the State unreasonably delaying your trial. This right is especially important for people who are incarcerated. Unreasonable delay is a violation of the "due process" provision of the Fifth Amendment.

Michigan has its own statute and constitutional provision limiting the time an accused person may be held in custody before trial (e.g. 180 days)[174] and guaranteeing a speedy trial.[175] Charges must be totally dismissed and the defendant released from any further legal obligation if the stated period expires without the State bringing you to trial. This type of dismissal would be "without prejudice," meaning that the charges against you can be reissued, you can be rearrested, and the entire criminal process against you starts over from the beginning.

Additionally, the 180 day rule applies only to people who are in jail for the entire period, and defendants often waive the right to a speedy trial in order to have additional time to prepare a stronger defense. Of course, there is also increasing pressure on the District

Courts in Michigan to resolve intoxicated driving cases as quickly as possible. The chief judge of every court is required to file a quarterly report listing the status of cases with the state court administrator regarding the time status of cases within their jurisdiction. If a judge is taking too long to resolve their case load, "corrective" action via direction of the Supreme Court of Michigan may be enacted. Clearly, no judge wishes to be admonished by and in front of their peers for being inefficient. This increases the pressure for cases to be resolved quickly.[176]

When an excessive amount of time has passed before the State charges you with a crime, or (after being indicted or accused) the process of getting to trial has been too slow, your attorney might be able to get the charges dropped because of this excessive delay. Three critical facts need to be shown by your attorney; (a) that the delay was not caused by your side, but by the State; (b) that you asked for a prompt trial (in some written filing with the court); and (c) that your ability to defend the case has been harmed or compromised in some way. There is sometimes a fourth factor considered, the length of the delay.[177]

However, your right to a speedy trial can be lost through lack of attention to details by your legal counsel. This is yet another reason to have a seasoned OWI attorney represent you.

6.28. The Defense of Necessity. Necessity in an OWI case is where you admittedly drove while impaired, but that you had a good (emergency) reason for doing it. Necessity is defined as:

> An act which would otherwise constitute a crime may also be excused on the ground that it was done under compulsion or duress. The compulsion which will excuse a criminal act, however, must be present, imminent and impending, and of such a nature as to induce a well-grounded apprehension of death or serious bodily harm if the act is not done. A threat of future injury is not enough.[178]

An example is if you are at home drinking, with no intention to drive, when your spouse suffers a deep knife wound. Rather than let your spouse die, you hurry to get to the hospital, despite knowing that you have had too much to drink before driving. You act upon this serious emergency and drive while intoxicated since you have "no other choice" if you want to save her.

To raise this "affirmative defense," Michigan requires that you notify the State that this will be part of your case. That way, the burden of proof shifts to the State to DISPROVE your assertion that "necessity" excuses you from being legally responsible for OWI.[179] Raising such a defense may put the State to a nearly impossible task of disproving the "affirmative defense." You may get a reduction in charges offered, to avoid trial on the more serious charge of OWI. Furthermore, even if you lose this trial, the judge's punishment will typically be less severe than in a normal case, due to your honest perception that you acted to protect the life of a loved one.

6.29. The Defense of Duress. Duress in a legal sense is breaking a law because something or someone else is making you break the law. It is the use of force, false imprisonment or threats (and possibly psychological torture or "brainwashing") to compel someone to act contrary to his/her wishes or interests.[180] An example would be if someone put a gun to your head and made you drive to another location even though you protested that you could not because you were intoxicated. This is a very rare "affirmative defense" in an OWI.

6.30. The Defense of Entrapment. In criminal law, entrapment is the act of law enforcement officers or government agents inducing or encouraging a person to commit a crime when the accused party indicates no prior intent or action to commit the crime on his or her own accord. The key to entrapment is whether the idea for the commission or encouragement of the criminal act originated with the police or government agents instead of with the supposed "criminal." Like duress, entrapment is an unlikely defense in an

OWI case. Entrapment, if proved, can be an affirmative defense to a criminal. Again, pre-trial notice of this affirmative defense is required in Michigan.

6.31. The Defense of Measurement Uncertainty. The "uncertainty defense" applies to both breath and blood testing, but has been most successfully applied to blood testing. The defense applies because all chemical tests claim to tell us something about a person's bodily alcohol content. Since they are measuring breath or blood alcohol, the test involves the science of measurement. This means that there is always some amount of uncertainty. Measurement uncertainty accounts for the fact that no measurement can ever tell us exactly what the "true" value of a thing being measured is. No matter how good a measurement is, there is always some doubt as to the "true" value of the thing being measured.

What a measurement actually represents is a range of values all of which can actually and reasonably be attributed to the "true" value with a given probability. If we want to properly interpret what a measurement means, then we must know this range of values and its accompanying probability. Taken together, the range and probability represent a measurement's uncertainty. Absent this information, a measurement is meaningless.

Uncertainty is typically expressed as a coverage interval consisting of a range of possible "true" values and the probability, otherwise referred to as the interval's level of confidence, that the values within the interval do indeed represent the "true" value. Like any other measurement, when dealing with a chemical test it is essential to know both. A proper expression of a person's breath or blood test results would be .08 +/- .02 at a 95% confidence level.[181]

In either the police station's breath testing room, or the laboratory of the state forensic scientist, there are a variety of things that can undermine a measurement that may be known or unknown, visible or invisible. Your attorney may explore how some of these things may have influenced the uncertainty of the breath or blood test in your case, and may challenge the police as to whether or not they are properly reporting the amount of uncertainty in your test results. A failure to do so might result in the breath or blood test being thrown out.

Alternatively, if the breath or blood test results are borderline, then your attorney may be able to present the defense that the State cannot prove beyond a reasonable doubt that your bodily alcohol level was actually above the requisite level. Usually, an expert witness is needed to assert this defense, as well as thorough discovery about the reliability of the State's measurement uncertainty calculation, and such things as calibration and simulator checks on the particular machine used to test your breath or blood.

6.32. The Defense of Different Partition Ratio than the Breath Machine is Programmed to Expect. The term "partition ratio" refers to the difference and comparison of your breath alcohol level and your blood alcohol level. In other words, at any moment, there is a specific relationship or ration between the measured level of alcohol in your breath compared to the level of alcohol in your blood. Partition ratios are an example of the divide between the law and the science that should underlie it. The science is that partition ratios differ between individuals, and for any individual, on a day to day, even an hour to hour basis. Nevertheless, the DataMaster in Michigan is programmed to calculate your breath test results by assuming that for every one molecule of alcohol in your breath, there are 2100 molecules of alcohol in your blood at that moment, even if this may or may not be true for you. If your partition ration was lower than the DataMaster expected, then your breath test result will be too high by a corresponding ration.

While the statement that partition rations vary from person to person cannot reasonably be disputed scientifically, state law usually makes it difficult or impossible to assert this challenge. It has been argued as a defense to an OWI charge that the basic breath machine is set up to evaluate a blood alcohol level based on a standard ratio of blood to breath of 2100 to 1. This defense is a legitimate, scientific attack if your ratio is always lower (e.g., 1400 to 1) and this can be documented. Again, the "partition ratio" defense requires the use of one or more expert witnesses to establish.[182] Most experienced OWI trial attorneys will only assert this attack if no better explanation of an errant breath test is available to your defense lawyer.

Many prosecutors will not agree to reduce or plea bargain any case where there is a high breath or blood test result, although this "number" varies from county to county in Michigan (even city to city), and depends largely on who is actually prosecuting your case.

Additionally, if you are facing a felony charge and you are convicted, the amount of time you will serve will depend in part on the level of your chemical test result. This is because you will be given more points for high test results, and the sentencing guidelines that apply will therefore be higher. In other words, a higher test result equals more points, and more points equals more jail time.

6.33. The Heartburn or GERD Breath Test Defense. GERD is an acronym meaning "Gastro-esophageal Reflux Disease." The common name for this is condition heart burn. If a person suffering from GERD is arrested for drunk driving and then given a breath test then it is possible for stomach gases containing alcohol to enter into the mouth thereby causing a false DataMaster result. In this instance the breath test machine is measuring stomach gas alcohol rather than deep lung air. If mouth alcohol rather than breath alcohol is being measured and reported, then your breath test result can often be way too high. So much too high in fact that the reported result is essentially meaningless. Your attorney can therefore argue therefore that the result should be thrown out.

This defense is not without its detractors, and you should expect the government lawyer to argue that the slope detector will cure this breath testing problem. Nevertheless, the GERD defense has been judicially recognized as a valid breath test defense in drunk driving cases and the defense has been upheld leading to the suppression of breath test results of a defendant who was suffering from GERD at the time of test.[183]

If you have been arrested for DUI, have been diagnosed with GERD and you think that your GERD may have impacted the DataMaster result, then it is important to substantiate this diagnosis. In other words, you must undergo confirmatory testing. Armed with these confirmatory tests your attorney might be able to work out a very favorable plea bargain.

6.24. Rising Bodily Alcohol Defense. When we look at the crime of intoxicated driving in Michigan we see that it is called OWI which of course means "Operating/While/Intoxicated." When thinking of the increasing blood alcohol defense we are addressing the "while" part of "while intoxicated."

Very simply, it takes for the alcohol to get from your stomach to your blood and eventually to your brain. If the alcohol is in your stomach when you are stopped but in your breath or blood when you are tested, then you may have a rising blood alcohol defense. Since evidentiary chemical test samples (breath or blood) are never taken at the roadside, based on the facts and circumstances of the case is it possible that you not drunk at the time you were actually driving?

In order to understand this issue/defense it is critical for your lawyer to understand the science of alcohol metabolism, which is governed by the absorption, distribution and elimination of alcohol. It is also important to provide your lawyer with a precise drinking history so that the time-course calculation of the alcohol consumed can be made.

The viability of this defense will depend on several factors, including the time of your last drink in relation to the time of the chemical test. Thus, it will also be important to have an accurate time line including (at a minimum) when the alcohol consumption started and ended, when the driving started and ended, and when the first chemical test sample was collected.

A proper analysis of this defense requires also an understanding of retrograde extrapolation, which is beyond the scope of this writing. If you are in raising this defense are encouraged to obtain one of the many resources on retrograde extrapolation so that this science can be well-understood. A failure to do so may lead to a failure of this defense.

Chapter 7:

Specific Challenges and Issues that Can Force Complete Dismissal of Your Case

7.0. Purpose of this Chapter. Based on the Fourth[184] and Fourteenth[185] Amendments to the United States Constitution, the police must have an adequate reason before they stop your vehicle. Michigan has state constitutional protections that offer equal or better protections to those found in the Federal Constitution.[186]

Once stopped by the police, any indication of impairment from alcohol or drugs will lead to an OWI investigation. Even a very minor tag or vehicle equipment problem will authorize an officer to pull the car over, even if the officer's real purpose is to look for other possible criminal activity.[187] If the "reason" for the stop is not proper or legally sufficient, then from the start, all further evidence gathered by the police is not admissible in court and all alcohol or drug related charges arising from this unlawful stop may be dismissed if a proper motion is filed. This is often referred to as "fruit of the poisonous tree."[188]

This chapter discusses some of the most common legal challenges your attorney might raise on your behalf at a pre-trial motion hearing. Your chances of success will often be based on all of the details you provide during your interview process when you tell your attorney your version of what happened at the time of your stop and arrest. In addition to your account of the incident details, the officer's traffic citations, other documents of your arrest, detention, vehicle towing and bonding out of jail will be of great value to your attorney. Any breath test results will also be important.

7.1. Stop Based Upon Traffic Offense or Vehicle Deficiency that is not Actually an Offense or Deficiency. The police officer must have a valid and proper reason to stop your vehicle.[189] If the officer who pulled you over made a MISTAKE OF LAW[190] (i.e., thought that an offense had been committed or that some equipment deficiency was "required" equipment), then the entire stop and all evidence recovered or collected by the police will be suppressed (excluded from evidence) at the time of the pre-trial motions hearing.

A specific example of a "mistake of law" case from another jurisdiction will help illustrate this point. During the very early morning, the police decided to run a license tag number through their system to check it. The officer entered the wrong number and the tag came up invalid. The officer then stopped the driver, who was later accused of OWI. The Kentucky Court of Appeals determined that because of the mistake of law, that the driver really did not have an invalid plate, and that the mistake was the officer's, there was no valid justification for the stop.

7.2. Stop Based Upon an Observed Equipment Defect that is not a Legally Required Item of Equipment. One valid and common reason a law enforcement officer may stop your vehicle is if he or she observes a missing piece of equipment on your vehicle or sees that a part of your vehicle is defective. A common example is if your brake lights are burned out, your tires are bald, or one of your headlamps is not working.[191]

However, if a law enforcement officer stops you because your rear view mirror is too small, and there is no law specifying the size of your rear view mirror, then the officer's pretext for the stop is invalid.[192] If that pretext is based on anything other than a published, existing law, then the stop itself will be declared invalid.

7.3. Stop for a Violation of Law and the Statute is Unconstitutional. In order for you to be guilty of a crime, you have to violate a law that is not unconstitutionally vague. Sometimes, state legislators pass laws that are too vague or ambiguous to be legally enforceable. In such situations, if the law is struck down by Michigan's appellate courts, this frees you of all charges, since the law under which you were arrested was not constitutional.

As an example, although roadblocks have been found to be a constitutionally based exception to search and seizure requirements in many other states, they have been found to be unconstitutional under the Michigan Constitution.[193] If you have been charged for OWI following your stop at a roadblock, or under another OWI statute or ordinance that is later declared unconstitutional or otherwise invalid or has already been declared so at the time of your arrest, your attorney can raise the defense that you had not in fact violated the law.

7.4. Stopped for a Paper License Plate Being on the Vehicle, and the Temporary Plate is in Good Order. It is certainly a lawful reason for a law enforcement officer to stop you if your paper license plate is no longer valid, or if it is not displayed in a valid manner. However, if the officer made a mistake and your temporary license plate is valid, or if the paper plate was in fact displayed in a valid manner, then in Michigan, the pretext for the stop was then invalid.[194] If the pretext for the stop was invalid, so was the stop. If proven at a pre-trial motion hearing, the motion to suppress will be granted by the judge and all charges would then be dismissed.

7.5. Stopped Because Vehicle is Coming from an Area where no Residences Currently are Occupied. Police officers certainly have a duty to protect the public as a whole. Part of this duty would be to protect areas under construction from thievery. However, just because you are driving on a public road out of one of these areas may not be by itself sufficient reasonable suspicion for a law enforcement officer to stop your vehicle, if this were to be the only detail to establish articulable suspicion. If an unlawful stop, then any other evidence arising from the stop (evidence of being under the influence of alcohol) cannot be held against you.

7.6. Stopped Based Solely Upon a "Be On the Look Out" (BOLO) Call from a Concerned Citizen, and the Information Given is Legally Insufficient. The police get a lot of calls from concerned citizens regarding what these citizens believe is an ongoing criminal offense. However, for the police to act on this information, it must be sufficiently detailed so as to allow the police to do something more than stop everyone.[195] The police likely could not legally stop your vehicle based only on a call from an unknown citizen who said that you were getting into your blue Ford and that you were drunk, although such a call can be one of many pieces which could lead to adequate sufficiency. On this flimsy information, any blue Ford could be pulled over, since no tag number was given. If you were stopped solely on the basis of this call, it is likely the court would consider such a stop legally lacking in detail. If declared to have been illegal, then other evidence developed following the traffic stop would also be excluded by the trial court (such as OWI evidence).

Finally, you also have a Constitutional right to "confront" the citizen who calls in the information used to make the stop.[196] Thus, if the caller does not provide information that would allow them to be later called as a witness, then your case should be dismissed on this basis.

7.7. Confronted by an Officer in a Legally Parked Car with no Reason to Suspect that a Crime had been Committed. In most circumstances, it is not illegal for you to be sitting in your parked car, as long as you are legally parked in a place that is open to the public. The cases that have ruled in favor of the police have generally involved a car parked in a high crime area or a place where burglaries had been occurring recently. Courts have also ruled in favor of the police where it is claimed that they approached your vehicle to make sure you were not in need of medical attention. This is called the "common caretaker" function of the police. Unless the police can verbalize a legitimate reason for confronting you in your parked car, any evidence gathered regarding OWI will be suppressed.

For the police to begin their investigation of a possible crime by confronting you as you sit otherwise legally in a parked car, they must have some other evidence that a crime is occurring.[197] This goes back to you having a constitutionally guaranteed right to be free from illegal searches and seizures found in the Fourth Amendment[198] and applied to actions of the officers who work for State agencies through the Due Process Clause of the Fourteenth Amendment.[199] If all the officer had prior to this investigation of you was your *legal* action, the officer's actions (and investigation that led to an impaired driving arrest) were unconstitutional, and any results that flowed from this unconstitutional act should not be used against you.[200]

7.8. Stopped Because the Officer Saw an Unusual but Insignificant Driving Error that did not Rise to the Level of Being Reasonable Suspicion of Impaired Driving. For the police to begin their investigation of a suspected crime (like OWI), by confronting you as you are driving, they must have some other evidence that a crime is occurring.[201] To stop you without justification violates your constitutionally guaranteed right to be free from illegal searches and seizures protected by the Fourth Amendment.[202]

For you to have a good challenge to an unconstitutional pullover, your driving behavior has to be unusual, but not illegal. Each of these cases is fact-specific and will be determined by how well your OWI attorney can use cross-examination to uncover the officer's baseless decision to pull you over.

7.9. Stopped After the Officer's Driving Actions Causes or "Creates" Weaving Due to the Driver's Preoccupation with the "Threatening" Actions of the Police Car in the Rear View Mirror. Brief lapses of staying in your lane alone may not necessarily be a violation of the law.[203] In Michigan, however, the courts have found that weaving within one's lane may be sufficient justification for the police to stop your vehicle. Nevertheless, if being followed by the police triggered your errant driving in your OWI stop by the police, and this weaving was the officer's only reason for stopping you, it is possible that (with the proper proof) the court will declare the stop to have been unjustified and not allow any evidence against you that arose out of the stop. This situation, like those in several other subsections of this chapter, depends on excellent representation by a high quality OWI attorney and fair consideration by a judge who truly honors and follows our Constitution.

Chapter 8:

The "Discovery" Process: How Your Attorney Learns What Evidence the Prosecutor Has and Decides How to Challenge or Explain It

8.0. Purpose of this Chapter. In fighting your OWI case, your side has the right to know some, if not all, information about your arrest and testing the prosecutor is preparing to use against you at your trial. The disclosure of some facts is mandatory. The process by which this information is released to your attorney by the prosecution, and possibly from your side to the prosecution is called "discovery."

The best OWI trial specialists know what to expect from the prosecutor in a typical case. They also know what they should be provided, and more importantly, when something important appears to be missing. They will also know when it is appropriate to ask the court to dismiss your case when discovery is not provided to you by the prosecution. This chapter explains part of the discovery process that applies to your case.

8.1. The United States Supreme Court Rulings Set the "Floor" to Discovery Below which Michigan Cannot Go. Certain minimum aspects of discovery must be complied with (if properly requested by your attorney). These are the items that must be handed over to a defendant that have been established by the United States Supreme Court. Under a case known as *Brady v. Maryland,* if the prosecution has any exculpatory evidence (evidence that tends to be favorable to you), he or she must eventually provide this evidence.[204]

When a prosecutor fails to divulge such important data, this is called a "discovery violation." There are three components of a true *Brady* violation: the evidence at issue must be favorable to the accused, either because it is exculpatory, or because it tends to impeach the police officer; the evidence must have been suppressed or withheld by the State, either willfully or inadvertently; and prejudice to your case must have occurred.[205]

Other limits to the "floor" of discovery exist. The Sixth Amendment compulsory process clause may be violated by imposition (through a court order sought by a prosecutor) of a discovery sanction that entirely excludes testimony of a material defense witness.[206]

If your OWI case is a misdemeanor (a first or second OWI offense within 7 years), then there may be some question as to whether or not you are entitled to any discovery. This is because the Michigan Supreme Court issued an "administrative order" that suggests that discovery is not available to misdemeanor offenders.[207] While the prosecutor may try to frustrate your attorney by citing this administrative order as an excuse to not providing discovery, most courts do not follow this rule. Also, the best OWI lawyers usually know how to get around this order and still obtain the necessary discovery. Regardless of the circumstances, rely upon your OWI trial specialist to understand Michigan laws.

8.2. Different Tools can be used to Uncover Information Relevant to Your Case. In Michigan, many different tools may be utilized by your attorney in a criminal prosecution in order to "discover" information regarding the evidence the prosecutor will use to prove your guilt. The prosecutor and your attorney can both require people to come to court to testify (through issuance of a subpoena), or require them to come to court and bring documents or other items with them to be used as possible evidence in your trial. This is called a "*subpoena duces tecum*." A motion to produce may also be used in Michigan. These and other possible tools are discussed below. Keep in mind that if the court issues an order to produce evidence, and the prosecutor ignores it, then your attorney can ask for your case to be dismissed.[208]

The primary purpose of forcing the state to reveal or turn over 100% of any available items that could be used at trial is that your skilled OWI defense attorney knows that the "smoking gun" that wins your case may be found in these materials. Pre-trial motions or evidentiary hearings may require the investigating police officers to give sworn testimony that "locks in" their statements. Then, if the same officers testify differently later, this prior testimony can be used for impeachment, that is, to show that he or she may not be testifying in an entirely truthful way. This approach can lead to helpful contradictions by the officer in two sworn statements, damaging his or her credibility, or their total collapse on the witness stand.

8.2.1. Subpoenas. A subpoena is an order of the court handling your case for a witness to appear at a particular time and place, for the purpose of giving sworn testimony. A subpoena may also be used to obtain pre-trial testimony from a witness at scheduled depositions (testimony under oath taken outside of court), pre-trial motions, evidentiary hearings, administrative license hearings and at trial. Subpoenas are issued by the hearing officer (e.g., administrative license suspension hearings), by your attorney, or by the court clerk of the tribunal you are in, but must be served personally on the party being summoned. Failure to appear as required by the subpoena can be punished as contempt of court if it appears the absence was intentional or occurred without justifiable cause.[209] The rules of criminal procedure in Michigan do not typically allow for depositions, but in some circumstances, depositions can be taken. A skilled OWI defense attorney knows when this might be an option.

8.2.2. Subpoena Duces Tecum. A subpoena duces tecum[210] (SDT) is a court order requiring a witness to bring documents in his or her possession or under the control of the witness to a certain place at a certain time. This subpoena must be served personally on the person whose appearance at court is commanded, and the list must be clear in stating what items are being requested. If the SDT is overly broad or oppressive, the prosecutor may seek a protective order from the judge restricting or limiting the SDT's scope.

Issuance of a subpoena duces tecum is the common way to obtain potentially useful evidence, such as police reports or videotapes that are in the possession of a third party.[211] A subpoena duces tecum must specify the documents or types of documents (e.g. "All DataMaster DMT maintenance records covering the time period between August 1, 2013 to January 1, 2014, for instrument number 930054 located at the Oakland County Jail) or it will be subject to an objection that the request is "too broad and burdensome."

Failure to respond to a subpoena duces tecum may expose the non-complying party to punishment for contempt of court for disobeying a court order. Fines or even jail sentences, or both, can be imposed by the judge. In some instances, the judge may order reimbursement of costs and attorney's fees to you for the State's non-compliance.

8.2.3. Freedom Of Information Act (F.O.I.A.). The Freedom of Information Act, as codified in 5 U.S.C.A. § 552, is a federal law which requires any federal agency to make available and provide to the party requesting disclosure certain information those agencies have in their possession. This may include documents such as copies of records and administrative staff training manuals.

Certain records may be protected from disclosure, such as records in an ongoing investigation by the police. On the other hand, prosecutors who cite Michigan Supreme Court administrative order 1999-3 (discussed above) may suggest using Michigan's F.O.I.A.[212] to obtain the necessary discovery. Also, some police departments (the Michigan State Police) often will not release records unless your attorney has complied with Michigan's F.O.I.A. Michigan has adopted statutes that are similar to the federal Freedom of Information Act. These laws allow for the public inspection of documents, papers, letters, maps, books, tapes and other materials in the possession of public agencies and officers.[213] However, like federal law, the police may refuse to provide discovery by claiming that certain materials are restricted from such disclosure - like information from ongoing investigations and the names of confidential informants.[214] This claim can be a source of great frustration where the prosecutor says he or she will not provide discovery and the police department claims they will not provide discovery either because the investigation of your case is "ongoing". Usually the court will need to become involved in these instances to sort it all out.

8.2.4. Motion to Compel. A motion to compel is a formal written request filed by your attorney, asking the court to order the prosecution to release a copy of some item of evidence or document to you that the prosecution possesses. A motion of this type can also come from the prosecution asking your side to produce some evidence, as long as it is not confidential or protected under the "attorney-client privilege". Whether or not the judge grants the motion depends on what is being asked for, and if the side asking has some clear legal right to obtain the evidence. Nevertheless, a motion to compel may be the only way to obtain certain documents or items necessary in your defense, especially if both the police and the prosecutor refuse to cooperate in providing discovery.

8.2.5. Depositions. A deposition is where both sides get a chance prior to trial or a hearing to question a witness, while the witness is under oath, and with the proceedings being recorded either as a transcript by a court reporter, by a videotape (or digital recording), or by a video recording. It allows either side's attorney to send written notice to require witnesses to appear at a specific time and place and provide sworn testimony. Michigan does not generally allow depositions in OWI or other criminal cases as a part of the discovery process.[215] In certain circumstances, such as where a court wishes to go to trial on a particular date and time and an expert witness is not otherwise available, a court may allow a deposition of this expert witness to be taken, but this happens very rarely. It is your choice (under the direction and guidance of your experienced trial attorney) whether you ever provide any testimony at trial or at pre-trial matters. Any sworn testimony you give at a pre-trial hearing for purposes of proving an issue relating to suppression of illegally obtained evidence cannot be introduced at your trial if you and your attorney decide to have you remain silent.

8.2.6. Private Investigator. Your attorney may feel that the use of a private investigator might be beneficial for your defense. This typically involves an additional cost, but these professionals can be worth their weight in gold. Such investigators often are retired law enforcement officers who have good contacts with police who are still on the job and they know how the other side thinks and operates. Most of the best OWI trial lawyers use private investigators in their cases, where the investigator's input or investigation could be vital.

Private investigators also know how to evaluate the scene of your stop for problems with the fairness of your field sobriety evaluations. The investigators might be able to uncover other discrepancies in the police report (or the video reports) and may help explain to the judge or jury some "problem" with your balance (that occurred during field testing on your roadside video) in order to help sway the ultimate "fact finder" of your innocence.

If your experienced OWI attorney recommends the hiring of a private investigator for your case, it is because your attorney is looking after your best interest, not just wanting to spend your money. Many times, the input of the private investigator can help uncover the

"Achilles heel" of the arresting officer. Other times, this investigator can provide the winning evidence in your OWI trial.

8.2.7. Officer's Disciplinary File. If any of the law enforcement officers involved in your OWI stop and arrest have had disciplinary problems in the past which could be relevant to your situation, this information can be obtained by your legal counsel as a part of the state discovery obligations.[216] If the last five of the officer's OWI stops and arrests were all thrown out due to sloppy or refuted police work, why should the jury believe the officer for your arrest? Or, if the officer was disciplined for not being truthful, this may be ammunition to challenge his or her credibility at trial. Once an officer has been officially sanctioned, disciplined, fired, suspended or otherwise "written up" as a liar, his or her ability to continue in work as a "street cop" is going to be short-lived. A private investigator can often learn this type of useful information as well.

8.2.9. Officer's Training Records for State Police Academy Central Records. All or part of the training records for the local law enforcement officers may be available to your attorney as a part of Michigan's F.O.I.A.[217] Two important details might come from these employment records.

First, it allows your attorney to prepare to more fully question law enforcement officers who will be testifying against you at either a pre-trial hearing or at your trial. The better prepared your attorney is, the more likely the questions asked of the police officers will provide answers for the possible legal issues in your case. Having ALL critical information derived from discovery is the best way to win an OWI case — either during a motions hearing or at your trial.

Second, if any police officer on the witness stand at either trial or at a pre-trial hearing states something on the record regarding his or her training or experience, especially if it is in regard to their OWI experience or training, and the records do not reflect similar information, the officer's candor with the judge or jury can be put in doubt. The more the officer is proved to be mistaken, or lack adequate training, the more the judge and jury have reason to believe you.

8.3. A Disclosure Motion Filed with the Court and Properly Served upon the Prosecutor will Cause List of Witnesses to be Produced. One of the most important things that comes from your discovery request of the State is that the prosecutor's office must release vital information about its witnesses against you at trial, such as name, phone number, address and similar information.[218] This information greatly increases the preparedness of your attorney, giving him or her valuable preparation time in order to best plan your defense. If the State produces a "surprise" witness at your trial, absent proof that the name or location of the witness was only discovered that day (or the day before trial), the State's use of that witness is likely prohibited.

Most experienced OWI specialists know the police officers, the usual state experts, as well as what kind of witnesses these people make when they are in front of a jury. Your defense is often designed around the strengths and weaknesses of the prosecutor's case, starting with their list of witnesses. A pre-trial investigation of the witnesses and their factual claims help your attorney comprehend how the State will attempt to prove the case against you.

8.4. Reciprocal Discovery Rules may Require Your Attorney to also Disclose to Prosecutor. Based on Michigan's discovery rules, certain information regarding documents and your expert or fact witnesses, potential evidence that they may provide at trial, must be released by your side to the prosecutor as well. This release is mandatory if it is sought by the prosecution to receive the information from your attorney.[219] It is important to understand this "reciprocal" requirement when deciding whether or not to have an independent test done of your breath or blood. Your experienced OWI lawyer will be able to help you understand the advantages and disadvantages of independent testing in light of the reciprocal discovery rules.

8.5. Video Tapes are Generally Discoverable. If the police officer who stopped you took video recordings on either analog or digital recording devices or tape, a copy of this video is generally available for your defense.[220] Unless allowed to be withheld by the court for good cause, failure of the prosecution or the police to release these tapes to your attorney prior to your trial usually means that the withheld information cannot be used against you in your trial.

Keep in mind, however, that most police departments "recycle" their videotapes after 14-30 days. Consequently, if you fail to retain a lawyer until 30 days after your arrest, you may not be able to obtain this videotape evidence, and under these circumstances, there would be no dismissal and no jury instruction. This would be unfortunate, because videotapes often contain a great deal of useful information, and may even show that you do not appear to be intoxicated. Also, at least one Michigan court held the videotapes may not be generally discoverable.[221] Nevertheless, in most instances, if a videotape exists and it is timely requested, your attorney will be able to obtain a copy of it.

8.6. Look for Private Security Video Footage from a Parking Lot or Business Camera Where Your Car was Stopped. One thing you can do, or a private investigator may do for you, is to investigate the vicinity of your stop and arrest. While the police may or may not have a video recording of your encounter with the police, other video cameras may have been positioned on buildings, in parking lots, or even set up on tall poles by private security services hired to maintain security for a mall or shopping center. In Michigan, there are also many areas where gambling has been legalized. This includes downtown Detroit and at various Indian gaming facilities. The parking lots for these establishments are nearly always videotaped.

An example where this might help is if the police officer testifies that the only reason your vehicle was stopped was because you were weaving illegally in and out of traffic or crossing the lane lines. Often, a police video is only activated at the time the officer decided to stop you, which is usually after these alleged traffic violations occurred. An independent video from an adjacent parking lot camera will be devastating to the state's case if it showed you didn't change lanes or weave.

8.7. Police Dispatch Tapes and Computer-aided Dispatch (CAD) Logs Available from Headquarters. Most police departments maintain tape copies of their dispatch radio communications and computer-aided dispatch (CAD) logs for several days to several months after any particular date. Even after recordings are disposed of, a printout or written account is usually maintained for a lengthy period of time. Under the F.O.I.A. in Michigan, this information may be available to you and your attorney.[222]

These tapes and logs may confirm or may refute what the police officer at the scene of your OWI arrest wrote down about the incident. In the alternative, these records might give your attorney a "smoking gun" as an independent source of highly credible data. The best OWI specialists will refuse to leave any stone unturned in their investigation of your arrest, and this information might help or hurt your case. This type of exhaustive search for **ANY** helpful information is part of what justifies higher fees for the best OWI attorneys.

One example of how these CAD logs can assist your OWI defense attorney is to help challenge or refute what a police officer claims a police informant said to the police. They can also be used to challenge the time of the stop. If these logs showed that there was a several hour delay between your stop and the time the police obtained your breath, blood or urine test, delays in procuring this test may cause this type of intoxicated driving prosecution to fail, based on a lack of proof that your "chemical test" accurately showed your blood alcohol level at the time you were stopped.[223] In Michigan however, this time limit may only go to the weight rather than the admissibility of the evidence.[224] There is no time limit to perform a blood test after an accident to test for alcohol.²²⁵ Another way to use the dispatch logs is to help show that it was physically impossible for the police to have completed their necessary "15 minute" observation time period prior to administering the breath test. This may help to establish a basis upon which to have the breath test "thrown out", and the UBAL (per se) charge dismissed. Beyond winning the "per se" count in your case, proof of false testimony by the officer may convince the jury (or your trial judge) to find you "not guilty" on all charges. On the other hand, there may be insufficient evidence of impairment without the chemical test evidence.

8.8. Any "BOLO" Cases Likely will have the Actual "911" Entirely Recorded. A "**B**e **O**n the **L**ook **O**ut" or BOLO call is where a concerned citizen has typically called the 911 operator or the police department directly to report a possible criminal violation. These emergencies conversations are likely to have been recorded.

Under the F.O.I.A. in Michigan, this information may be available to you.²²⁶ Finding errors or inconsistencies in the "reported" information can cause the entire police "stop" to be declared illegal. If the information given by the concerned citizen is not specific or detailed enough to have allowed the police to stop you, or if there were significant details regarding identification of you or your vehicle that were very different than described in the emergency call by the concerned citizen, your case can be won.

8.9. Accident Reports from Police Department that Investigated Accident. If you were involved in a motor vehicle accident as a part of your OWI arrest, it is likely that a police investigation of the accident occurred. This is particularly true if the accident involved a death or serious injury. If there was an injury reported, then either the officers at the scene, or a special team of police accident investigators, will have measured physical markings, ruts or skid distances, collected physical evidence at the scene, taken photographs and video footage, and may have done chemical or scientific analysis of certain items collected at the accident scene.

Whatever the police did, or if done by official representatives of the police or the crime lab, it is usually possible for your attorney to get copies of these investigative reports if it is not already part of the regular police report regarding your arrest for OWI.[227] Furthermore, your attorney may be able to get this information under an F.O.I.A. request.[228]

At times, your attorney may have to file a motion asking your court to require the prosecution to give up copies of these reports. If so requested and not produced by the prosecution before trial, the court may exclude this non-disclosed information from being used against you. Additionally, if it is later discovered (after your conviction) that the prosecutor hid "exculpatory" (favorable) information that would have aided your attorney in the defense of your case, a motion for a new trial or similar "post-conviction" filing may overturn your conviction.

8.10. Possible use of an Accident Reconstructionist. If your situation involved a motor vehicle accident, your attorney may recommend that you hire an accident reconstructionist. Such a witness will typically be most valuable to your case at the earliest possible date after the collision in order to document and measure any skid marks, obstructions of your view (such as hedges at an intersection) etc. An accident reconstructionist will almost always have either police or engineering training (or both) that allows him or her to look at the report of your accident and apply science to reconstruct or recreate what caused the accident.

These reconstruction experts may even be able to determine who was at fault and other critical details such as the speed of the vehicles at the time of the accident, the braking pattern of all vehicles, the relative positions of passengers inside the vehicles prior to the collision. Sometimes these details make the difference between a guilty verdict and an acquittal, or a reduction from a felony vehicular homicide or murder charge to a misdemeanor offense.

Your OWI attorney may suggest the use of a specific accident reconstructionist based on who is best for your particular type of accident, who might have the best courtroom presence at your trial, who has the best credentials or who best counters the proposed experts the state might be bringing to testify against you.

Chapter 9:
Understanding Michigan's Implied Consent Laws

9.0. Purpose of this Chapter. Simply by operating your vehicle on any public road in Michigan, you are assumed to have given consent to have your blood, breath or urine tested by law enforcement for the presence of either drugs or alcohol.[229] This "implied consent" however is not without limitations, and as with most other states, the State of Michigan is itself held to specific standards relative to the manner in which and under what circumstances such blood, breath or urine samples may be collected from you as a driver. This chapter describes these "implied consent" laws, and how you can use them if you have been arrested for OWI.

These laws, and the standards to which the State and law enforcement officers are held, can be very specific and technical. "Acts" or "omissions" by the officer can provide powerful defenses to your case and this is why your attorney will need to know as precisely as possible what happened between you and any law enforcement officer, what precisely was said and when, and also when exactly everything was done. Your recollection should begin at the time you were stopped, and should include everything up to and including your arrest and release.

9.1 Explanation of *Implied Consent* Laws in Michigan. Breath testing in OWI cases began in the United States in the late 1930s. Not surprisingly, "chemical" testing (referring to blood, breath or urine testing of any chemicals within these biological samples taken from a subject) quickly gained the favor of the law enforcement establishment. Michigan enacted its first OWI law in 1917,[230] and the first alcohol testing law in 1949.[231] Just as quickly, however, drinking drivers learned to refuse to submit to such tests.

To overcome these refusals, the concept of implied consent was adopted, wherein Michigan embraced the fiction that a person who drives a motor vehicle on their highways is **deemed to have consented** to the chemical testing of his or her body fluids upon being arrested for an OWI offense. All laws originally permitted the person's "implied" consent to be withdrawn (in other words, if asked to take a test by a police officer, the person could say "no"). However, when this happened, license loss penalties (or loss of the privilege to use the highways of the state where you refused) would be imposed. In 1970, Michigan passed its first implied consent law.[232]

The types of warnings or advisements that are required under the implied consent statute include: (i) If you take a chemical test of your blood, urine, or breath administered at the request of a peace officer, you have the right to demand that a person of your own choosing administer one of the chemical tests; (ii) The results of the test are admissible in a judicial proceeding as provided under this act and will be considered with other admissible evidence in determining your innocence or guilt; (iii) You are responsible for obtaining a chemical analysis of a test sample obtained at your own request; (iv) If you refuse the request of a peace officer to take a test described in subparagraph (i), a test shall not be given without a court order, but the peace officer may seek to obtain a court order; and (v) Refusing a peace officer's request to take a test described in subparagraph (i) will result in the suspension of your operator's or chauffeur's license and vehicle group designation or operating privilege and in the addition of 6 points to your driver record.[233]

In Michigan, police officers must substantially comply with the statutory warning or advisement requirements in order for implied consent penalties to be invoked.²³⁴ Warnings of the consequences of refusal typically must be clear and unequivocal. Inadequate or improper implied consent warnings may result in no driver license sanctions being imposed at the administrative hearing, and if you submitted to the State's chemical test, then the jury decides, after hearing all of the evidence at your trial and receiving an instruction or instructions from the judge, what the appropriate remedy for this violation of your rights should be.²³⁵

9.2. Can a Law Enforcement Officer Make the Request for an Implied Consent Blood, Breath or Urine Test Due to an Accident, with no Traditional Evidence of Impairment Due to Injuries? Symptoms such as red, bloodshot eyes, slurred speech, poor performance on your field sobriety evaluations, the smell of alcohol on your breath and your other physical manifestations at the time of your stop may provide a law enforcement officer circumstantial evidence of possible intoxication. These questions and field tests form "reasonable grounds" or "probable cause" for you to be arrested and then subjected to the scientific blood, urine or breath testing. Your submittal to such testing **MUST** be preceded by proper, timely and complete implied consent advisements.²³⁶

9.3. Does Michigan Require the Officer to Give a Formal, Pre-formatted Advisement? No constitutional or common law requirement compels the police to give such formal advisements.²³⁷ These advisements, and the requirements to give them, come from Michigan statutes. Instead of a strict, formatted advisement, the officer must adequately cover a list of items or steps.²³⁸

The importance of this advisement is at least two-fold to you as an OWI defendant. First, the words coming from the officer give you some idea of your rights and your testing obligations. However, this statement does not inform you of all of your rights, nor is this topic or subject matter commonly known to the common citizen.

Second, if the law enforcement officer failed to give the advisements to you, or gave it in an incomplete or inaccurate fashion, any test results which were obtained after this flawed advisement may be excluded from evidence at trial. However, this does not happen automatically, but first requires that the issue be raised by your OWI specialist in advance of your trial by way of a motion in limine.[239] (A motion made before trial that certain evidence be excluded from trial). The general rule is that if a warning of the consequences of refusal is required by statute and is not properly and timely given, you did not commit an implied consent violation.[240] Without these test results, most OWI cases fall apart and the charges against you may well be dismissed or reduced.

9.4. Does Michigan Law Require a Valid Arrest for OWI to Occur Prior to the Implied Consent Advisements Being Read? The order in which the steps of your arrest and the advisement was given to you can make a very significant difference in your case, which is yet another reason why your attorney will ask you to work very hard at remembering everything that happened to you in the hours surrounding your OWI arrest. In Michigan, you must be officially arrested before the implied consent is read to you.[241]

9.5. Does Michigan Mandate when the Officer is Required to Give the Implied Consent Notification? The law enforcement officer must give you some form of implied consent notification before the blood, breath or urine sample is taken from you.[242] The admonishment of your obligations and rights under implied consent does not have to be done word for word to match the precise words in the statutes. Nevertheless, the words are important, and if the advisement you were given does not match the words of the Michigan statute, your OWI specialist may want to bring this to the court's attention. Your case may be dismissed or the chemical test result suppressed.

9.6. Are there criminal penalties for refusing testing? Several states now consider a refusal to submit blood, urine or breath samples in an OWI a criminal act carrying criminal penalties.[243] This is not yet true in Michigan.

Whether or not criminal penalties are imposed for refusing to take a blood, urine or breath test, such refusals often badly damage your OWI case. The admission into evidence by the prosecution of your refusal to undergo chemical testing is often detrimental in the eyes of a jury. The admission of your refusal has been held to be constitutional by the United States Supreme Court and by nearly all states.[244] Unless satisfactorily explained, the jury will normally assume that you refused to be tested because you had consumed too much alcohol and were afraid of failing the test, an assumption that the prosecutor seldom fails to bring to the jury's attention. Offenders in Michigan do benefit from a jury instruction addressing this issue. Consequently, if you do refuse a chemical test, the jury will be told by the judge at the conclusion of the case that they may use this fact only for the purposes of determining if such a test was offered, and not for any evidence of your guilt.[245]

Still, as a practical matter when evidence of a refusal is admitted during the prosecution's case, it is often necessary for you to have to testify in order to effectively explain your reasons for refusing to submit. Most experienced trial lawyers handling OWI trials prefer to NOT put their clients on the witness stand. Obviously, then, the admission into evidence of a chemical test refusal should be avoided, if at all possible.

9.7. What are the Driving Restrictions or Loss of License Penalties for Refusal? Significant penalties typically exist for refusing to take the breath, blood or urine test when officially and properly requested to do so by the law enforcement officer. The specific automatic penalties depend on whether this is your first arrest for OWI. The automatic suspension upon your refusal is one year for a first refusal and 2 years for a second refusal within 7 years.[246] These are "hard" suspensions, meaning you cannot lawfully drive during the one or two year suspension period. However, a first implied consent suspension of your driver's license can be appealed on a "hardship" basis to the Circuit Court. If the appeal is successful, then partial or restricted driving privileges can sometimes be restored to you.

9.8. Can You Refuse Testing? In Michigan, unless the police officer gets a court order to obtain a sample, you typically have the right to refuse to allow the police to take a blood, breath or urine sample from you.[247] In other words, the drawing of your blood, or the taking of a urine or breath sample by the police must otherwise be voluntary.[248]

However, if the officer obtains the court order, Michigan courts have held that a person who refuses breath testing can be restrained or even physically harmed to forcibly draw blood or use a catheter in the person for a urine sample.[249]

9.9. Does the Procedure Used in Michigan Comply with *California v. Trombetta***?** In 1984, The United States Supreme Court decided that the constitutional protections against the destruction of breath test evidence by the prosecution or by law enforcement did not apply to the States by forcing them to preserve samples of your breath at the time they were also having your breath tested for your blood alcohol limit.[250] The theory was that the breath samples themselves were not being admitted as evidence against you in an OWI, but instead what was being admitted were the results of electronic reading from the breath testing device.

Under *Trombetta,* before you would have any Constitutional right to demand preservation of these samples, you would have to show these samples had a possible chance of showing you were not guilty, and if so, that you had no other means of showing this. Because Michigan gives you the right to obtain an independent sample, Michigan does not have to preserve any of your breath samples to be used as possible favorable evidence at your trial.

9.10. Is the Sample Being Requested for Implied Consent Usable for Possible Other Crimes? The fortunate answer in Michigan is no. Once the police have your blood, breath or urine sample, in some states it becomes evidence that can be used against you for other crimes. Michigan does not allow its use in prosecuting you in non-OWI situations.[251]

9.11. Do You Have the Right of Counsel Before Agreeing to Submit to the State's Test (or Refusing to Submit)? In Michigan, you do not have the right to have your lawyer present (or to even call an attorney on the telephone) while making your decision to either accept or to refuse the blood, breath or urine testing.[252] This means, the police do not have to give you access by phone or in person to an attorney when you are being pressed to make this critical decision.[253] However, relative to the implied consent law, there does appear to be a limited right to speak with an attorney before deciding whether or not to consent to the State's chemical test. Thus, if you refuse to voluntarily submit to the test requested by law enforcement, and are later charged with an implied consent refusal, you may be able to defend this case by showing that you made a request to speak with an attorney while making your decision, but your request was refused.[254] This fact can help show that your refusal was "reasonable," and thereby prevent your license from being suspended or points being added to your driving record.

9.12. Is the Preliminary Breath Testing Device Part of the Implied Consent Law, or is it a Non-evidential Test? No! The roadside breath test is not covered by Michigan's implied consent law. However, the law does require you to take this test.[255] If you refuse the roadside breath test you may be given a civil infraction ticket. This will result in a fine only. There are no points or driver license sanctions associated with a refusal of the preliminary (roadside) breath test.

The preliminary breath test is another field sobriety test the officer uses to determine if there is probable cause for your arrest.

This evidence might allow him or her to also request a blood or an "evidential" breath test at the jail or precinct (station) house. The numerical value that displays on these hand-held machines is not typically admissible at your trial. However, Michigan does allow the portable breath test result to be admissible prior to your trial if your attorney challenges the "probable cause" for your arrest. The result can also be admitted by the prosecutor if you make a "rising blood alcohol defense" at your trial. In this instance, the law allows the prosecutor to admit the portable breath test result at your trial to show that your alcohol level was actually higher, not lower as claimed, at the time you were driving.[256] Unfortunately, these hand-held devices can be fooled into giving a "positive" result for alcohol if you have recently used a commonly sold cough drop.[257]

9.13. Does the Officer Have to Advise You of Your Right to an Independent Test of Your Blood, Breath or Urine? One of your rights is to have an independent test of your own performed at a laboratory of your choice and at your own expense.[258] In Michigan, failure of the officer to inform you of this right or to comply with getting you this test may not absolutely preclude the State from using the evidence it gets from its testing.[259] Depending on the circumstances, an improper advisement may result in suppression of the result.

9.14. If You Request an Independent Test, does the Officer have to Reasonably Accommodate that Request? Michigan's independent test statute provides that a person who submits to chemical testing may, at the person's own expense, have additional chemical tests performed, and you are responsible for obtaining this test.[260] Generally speaking, however, if in the past the police unreasonably interfered with your reasonable request for independent testing, such interference could have resulted in the court dismissing your case.[261] However, the Michigan Supreme Court has ruled that it will now be the jury that decides the significance to place on an officer's failure to provide you with this right.[262] Your OWI specialist counsel will be able to evaluate the facts of your case to determine if your implied consent rights were violated and how best to handle this violation.

9.15. If You want to Request an Independent Test, do You have to First Submit to the State's Test? Michigan courts have generally upheld the proviso that only those who submit to chemical testing have the right to an independent test. Michigan courts have correspondingly denied the right to an independent test to those who refuse police testing.[263]

The denial of the right to an independent test cannot be used as a defense in implied consent proceedings. If you refuse, you refuse. However, it would seem that the denial by the police of your right to submit to a different form of testing that requested by the officer might be raised as a defense by you in an administrative "refusal" proceeding where the state seeks to administratively suspend your driving privileges for refusal of the officer's test. Consider the situation where an officer insists on blood testing and you (due to a fear of needles) say "I'll take any type of tests that does not involve needles."

9.16. For Breath Testing, what is Michigan's Observation Period (Deprivation Period) Prior to Taking the Test? When a breath test is requested, you must remain under observation of a law enforcement officer for fifteen minutes to ensure you have not vomited, smoked, put anything in your mouth, or not had anything more to drink. Such observation period must take place immediately before you take the evidential breath test, that is, the one offered to you at the jail or station house.[264] This rule is designed to ensure the accuracy of the test, so that undigested alcohol which is in your stomach (but not in your blood) does not affect the results of your breath test. A failure to follow this observation period requirement does not always result in the test result against you being thrown out. Often, Michigan courts indicate that such violations go to the evidential "weight" rather than to the admissibility of the result.[265]

9.17. How does Implied Consent Law Affect the Administrative License Suspension Hearing in your Case? The issues to be resolved at implied consent administrative hearings are limited by statute to the following: (1) Whether the peace officer had reasonable grounds to believe that you had committed a crime of operating a vehicle while intoxicated; (2) Whether you were placed under arrest for this crime; (3) If you refused to submit to the test upon the request of the officer, whether the refusal was reasonable; and (4) Whether you were advised of your implied consent rights.[266]

While the burden of proof at an implied consent hearing is always on the state to prove by a preponderance of the evidence that a violation of the implied consent rules occurred, this burden is typically met by introducing the report, statement, or testimony of the arresting officer. If your attorney can compel the attendance of the officer at your hearing, it is important that your attorney vigorously cross-examine the arresting and testing officers and get a transcript of the sworn testimony from the hearing officer, because it is often the only evidentiary hearing allowed prior to trial. Liberal discovery may be permitted in implied consent administrative cases, and the testimony or other evidence produced here might provide a winning defense strategy for your attorney.

9.18. Appeals from an Adverse Ruling from an Administrative Court. In Michigan, the hearing officer's decision may be appealed to the courts, but a "de novo"[267] hearing is not allowed. The court hearing the appeal must review the case based on the record established at the implied consent hearing. There are two types of appeals from these implied consent hearings, hardship appeals and legal appeals. For a "hardship" appeal, your attorney is simply arguing to the Circuit Court that not having a driver's license is a hardship for you, and he or she asks the Court to exercise its discretion in ordering the Department of State to return a partial or restricted driving privilege to you. On the other hand, a "legal" appeal is one where your attorney argues that the decision of the hearing officer was incorrect, as a matter of law when he or she found that you violated Michigan's implied consent law. If this appeal is successful, it may result in a restoration of your unrestricted driving privilege.

9.18.1. Winning or Losing the Administrative Hearing Will Not Affect the Criminal Case Afterward. Many of the issues determined at the implied consent hearing are identical to those faced in the criminal trial of the OWI offense. However, because the implied consent proceeding is deemed to be a civil proceeding and because of the differences in the burden of proof in the two proceedings, the doctrines of res judicata and collateral estoppel have consistently been held not to be applicable to the proceedings. Neither the prosecutor nor you are usually bound in one case by a finding in the other. Thus, if the hearing officer at the implied consent hearing finds that your stop or arrest was legally valid, this has no absolute effect on your underlying criminal case, which will nevertheless continue uninterrupted.

9.19. If You don't Understand English, and the Implied Consent was Read to You in English, how does this Affect the State's Tests? The results are mixed on this issue, depending very much on the state in which you were arrested for your OWI. In some states, you can avoid having the penalties of implied consent applied to your driving privileges if you can prove you did not comprehend English. If it can be shown that you did not understand English at the time of your arrest, and that you did not understand that you were being asked to perform a test, then some state appellate courts have decided that a refusal of testing did not occur. This has not been litigated in Michigan as of the time of the publishing of this book.

9.20. If the Officer Misstates Information or goes Beyond the Information Required to be Told to You, can this Additional Information Result in Your Test Result (or Refusal) being Excluded? If the additional comments by the officer are considered misleading enough, making it impossible for you to make an informed decision regarding the independent test, even if the rest of the implied consent advisory was read correctly, your test results may well have to be excluded. The burden is on your side to show that these improper warnings likely made a difference in your decision.

9.21. If You are Forced to Submit to Testing after You Verbally Refused to Cooperate, can the State Seek to Take away Your Driving Privileges even though they have Your Blood? While Michigan allows for the forcible drawing of your blood in some or all OWI cases if a court order is obtained,[268] it has not considered this issue as of the date this book went to print. In Michigan, your refusal to submit to the offered chemical test is reason itself to take away your driving privilege. Whether or not the State was successful in obtaining a warrant and forcibly taking your blood is of no consequence to this determination.

9.22. If You are Hearing-impaired, does it make a Difference that the Officer would not get an Interpreter? Persons who are legally deaf may have a defense to non-compliance with implied consent laws. Michigan's implied consent statute provides that deaf persons are entitled to an interpreter, and a failure to provide one should result in a successful challenge to any alleged implied consent refusal.[269] It may also result in a suppression of the test result.

9.23. If You Asked to be Taken to Acme Hospital for an Independent Test, and the Officer Declines because there are Closer Hospitals, does this Matter? It all depends on Michigan's definition of what would be a reasonable accommodation of your officer in obtaining your independent test. By statute, it is your responsibility to obtain the test.[270] However, in a very recent case from the Michigan Supreme Court, it was decided that dismissal is no longer appropriate. Because of this change in the law, if such police misconduct occurs and you don't get your fairly requested independent test, then it is up to the jury to decide the significance of this misconduct.[271]

9.24. If You Learn that the Hospital Requires Cash or a Check for an Independent Test, and you need to be taken by an ATM

Machine for Money, can the Officer Decline to do this for You? Unfortunately, this extra step of the officer having to take you to an ATM machine may or may not be considered to be beyond what was reasonably "accommodation." In the few cases on point from outside of Michigan, the officer was allowed to decline assistance and the state's test results were still admissible against the defendant in spite of the lack of the independent test,²⁷² while in another, when the suspect was short of the cash he needed, he requested that the officer stop by an ATM machine to allow him to get funds for the blood test at the hospital. The officer's refusal to accommodate this request caused the citizen's alleged refusal to be excluded from evidence.²⁷³

9.25. If You have been Injured in a Collision and (Due to Injuries) Submitting to the Breath Test would be Painful or Difficult, does this Constitute Refusal? The answer is maybe yes, maybe no. Your inability to provide a breath sample suitable for testing may constitute a refusal, unless it can be established that you were improperly instructed by the breath test operator, the instrument was improperly operated, or unless you can prove that your inability was caused by a valid physical or medical condition.²⁷⁴

It is generally held by appellate level courts that a refusal does not occur if you were unable to provide a sample or specimen for testing because of the presence of a medical or physical condition that made it impossible for you to provide the sample or specimen. However, unless the condition is obvious, the existence of the medical or physical condition and its effect on your ability to provide a sample must be established by credible medical evidence, and not simply on your word. Your attorney will need to fight this issue with admissible evidence of the medical problem. It should be noted that no court considers intoxication to be a valid reason for an inability to provide a sample for testing.²⁷⁵

9.26. If You just Never Answer by Saying "Yes" or "No" to the Request for a Forensic Test, does this Constitute Refusal? You do not have to expressly refuse chemical testing to be deemed to have refused. If you failed to respond "yes" or "no" to a request for testing, your silence might be considered a refusal. In other words, in the absence of an explicit refusal, your words or your conduct may be deemed to constitute a refusal to submit to chemical testing. It is generally held that a refusal occurs when you display conduct that would lead a reasonable person in the police officer's position to believe that you were unwilling to submit to testing.

Occasionally a citizen will initially refuse chemical testing and later decide to consent to testing. In situations, you may, under certain conditions, "cure" a refusal by subsequently consenting to testing. It is generally held that a refusal may be cured by a subsequent consent only if: (1) the consent was given within a reasonable time after the refusal and while the defendant was still in custody; (2) the delay caused by the initial refusal would not have affected the accuracy of the chemical test; and (3) honoring the request would not have caused an undue inconvenience or an additional expense to the police.

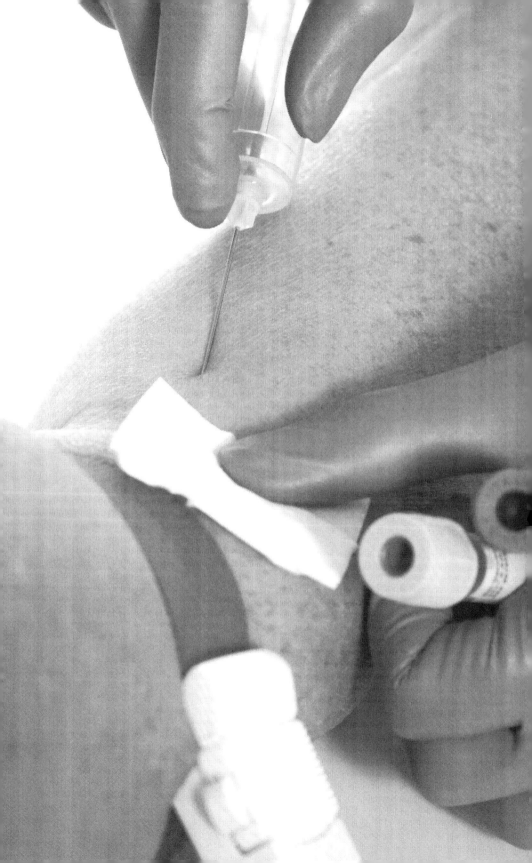

Chapter 10:
Understanding and Defending Breath and Blood Tests

10.0. Purpose of this Chapter. As a part of the investigation of your OWI case, it is almost certain that the police obtained a sample of your blood, breath or urine for a scientific evaluation, or that you refused to provide the same. If you refused, this chapter is otherwise irrelevant unless a warrant was obtained and a biologic sample was thereafter forced from you. Either way, if you have gone through one of these chemical tests, then this chapter will help you understand the scientific underpinnings of these tests, as well as their strengths and weaknesses.

10.1. Breath Test – Most Common Form of Testing. There are two general types of breath tests you may have taken in your OWI case, a roadside or portable field test and a more accurate and reliable test on a machine back at the jail or station house. The field test obtained from the handheld device is like any other field sobriety evaluation, that is, an officer can use it simply to determine the presence or absence of alcohol in your system and to a lesser extent, your possible level of alcohol impairment. Michigan has specifically authorized the use of these devices as a part of their OWI law.[276] Any numerical values obtained from the portable device at the time of your testing are typically legally irrelevant except when the court evaluates the propriety of your arrest. The portable test result is also admissible by the prosecutor when a "rising blood alcohol" defense is claimed by the defense. In this limited instance, the prosecutor can seek to have the portable breath test admitted into evidence to show that your blood alcohol level was higher at the time of your driving.[277]

The second breath test you may have typically taken is the more sophisticated and scientifically accurate machine used at the police station or at the jail. Michigan exclusively uses a device for this purpose that goes by the trade name "DataMaster." This is a table-top machine, and produced for you and the officer a print-out of the results after the testing.

The rest of this subsection addresses this table top machine, as these are the results that can be used in court as evidence by the prosecutor in order to attempt to gain a conviction for OWI based on the theory of UBAL, specifically that your actual blood alcohol level at the time of your driving was unlawful.

10.1.1. Michigan's New DataMaster DMT Breath Test Machine. For nearly the past 20 years Michigan has exclusively used the BAC DataMaster breath testing device in the investigation of alleged intoxicated drivers. This infrared breath alcohol analyzer was manufactured by National Patent Analytic Systems (NPAS), but in March 2013, the rights to the manufacture was sold to Intoximeter, Inc. The advanced age of the old breath testing device now being phased out has made it difficult to economically obtain replacement parts. Because of this and a variety of other reasons, Michigan made the decision in 2007 to "upgrade" the breath testing equipment and in 2008 spent at least 1.4 Million Dollars purchasing 228 updated DataMaster DMTs. The acronym DMT means "DataMaster Transportable."

The new DataMaster DMT began being placed into service in several Michigan counties in 2013, and over the next several years is likely to be rolled out throughout Michigan. Eventually, every old BAC DataMaster will be replaced with the new DMT.

Analytically, the DMT is the same breath test instrument as the older BAC DataMaster. Both measure breath alcohol by employing the principle of absorption of infrared energy. The same Grey-body infrared energy source is used, along with the same (albeit shorter) folded optical sample chamber, and the same thermo-electrically cooled lead selenide detector along with narrow bandwidth optical filters. Both Data Masters have the ability to electronically collect and store large volumes of test and simulator data. Despite this ability, the BAC DataMaster did not store any information, while in the customized DMT configuration for Michigan will store only the last simulator and last subject test in memory. No historical data is therefore saved or will otherwise be discoverable. This is unfortunate since the DMTs storage capacity has been increased. Such historical data regarding the operation of the DMT certainly might aid the defense in uncovering a problem that would otherwise remain concealed. Michigan's configuration only frustrates efforts to look for patterns that might reveal such latent problems impacting the accuracy or reliability of the device.

While the new DataMaster DMT uses the old infrared technology and has essentially the same optical bench, its software and computer functionality has been significantly updated.

The administration of the DMT change-over has required retraining of all police officers by the Breath Testing Unit of the Michigan State Police. Some of the administrative rules have also been changed. For example, to allow for the dry gas simulation as opposed to wet bath.

10.1.2. Does a Valid Breath Test Require Two Samples? In Michigan, the administrative rules applicable to breath tests require the police to request and obtain two samples of your breath. However, one sample is sufficient to satisfy the law, and the courts have interpreted this administrative rule such that only one sample is truly required.[278] If two breath samples are obtained and tested, then the results must be close enough to one another to demonstrate through consistency that the machine is working properly.[279]

10.1.3. If Two Samples, how Closely must the Results (Numbers) be to Each Other to Constitute a Valid Test? For the test results of either of the breath samples to be considered accurate enough to be used against you, Michigan requires that these results be within a given and allowable range of error or both results might be thrown out. This allowable range of error varies depending on the specific results of each test.[280] Generally speaking, the higher the test results the more the allowable variation between samples.

10.1.4. Regulations or Statutes Requiring Testing Officer to Follow Specified Protocol. Because scientific breath testing occurs so frequently and has been so competitively litigated, the State of Michigan has promulgated specific protocols or "administrative rules" with regard to performing this testing. If you did take a State administered breath test, in light of your presumption of innocence, the prosecution must typically prove that at the time of your test this particular equipment was in working order, was properly maintained and that the test was administered in a proper fashion, typically according to their protocol.[281] Ostensibly, these administrative rules were designed to assure and control the quality of the results obtained, but were also drafted in consultation the prosecutors as to what is required for such an arrest to be successfully followed by a conviction.

The best OWI specialists know these administrative rules for the breath testing, and more importantly, the reasons behind the steps in the rules. If the administrative rules for your breath test were not followed, this may imply to the court that there is a problem with either the arrest or with the evidence. While the administrative rules are used partly to protect the police officers during their investigation of your case, a failure to follow these rules may result in the dismissal of the UBAL charge or possibly an outright win at trial.

10.1.5. Manner of Blowing can Alter Final Results. The manner in which you blow into the DataMaster might affect your breath test result in one of several different ways. First, if you attempted to comply with the breath test, but there was a problem with the plastic mouthpiece, this might cause your machine to malfunction. The same might be true if you "overblow" (blow too hard or with too much air). A malfunction in the pressure switch may cause a false reading. If the officer does not realize what is causing the problem, he or she might believe that you have refused the test by non-compliance. On the other hand, if you attempt to blow five times within the two minute time-out period, the machine will determine that you have refused the test. This is called a "technical" refusal.

Next, you can hyperventilate by crying. As the air is circulating into and out of your lungs too quickly, the results of the amount of alcohol it reads in your breath does not accurately reflect what is in your blood stream. In addition, if you took the test while seated and leaning forward, this position may have caused a reflux of some of your stomach contents, including any alcohol in the stomach gases or free in your stomach. Because the machine automatically considers a ratio of alcohol in your breath verses your blood alcohol level, liquid alcohol or alcohol in this stomach gas can falsely and markedly increase the results.

10.1.6. Air Bag Residue may cause Elevated Readings. An automobile accident is often involved in many OWI cases. Since air bags were first tested in 1973, and first offered in automobiles for common sale in 1975, most automobiles are now fitted with them.[282] Air bags are packed either in baking soda or talc, or both. These powdery substances prevent "sticking" of the bag when it deploys. This fine powder can create the "Tyndall" effect, which is a false reading by the DataMaster machine if this powder is exhaled by you into the machine. This false reading is manifested in an erroneously high reading of alcohol on your breath. The propellants used to launch the air bags are gasses which may also affect the readings of the DataMaster, depending on which propellant was used in your car.

The important thing about all of this is to remember if your air bag deployed during any accident, you should report this to your attorney. Other details such as how much time between the accident and any breath test, the make and model of your car, may also be important.

10.1.7. Error Readings and the Importance of the Follow-up by the Testing Officer. If the breathing machine during your testing came up with an "error" reading on the monitor or the print-out, and you were subsequently considered to have refused to provide a sample, there are three possible reasons. First, you may not have been performing correctly because the instructions were not given correctly. Second, the instructions were given correctly but you did not understand them. Or, third, they were given correctly and you chose not to perform. If the problem was with either of the first two possibilities, then you may have a possible defense to the claim that you refused the test.

Additionally, if one of these problems did not cause the error reading to come up on the machine, then perhaps there was a problem with the machine itself? In this event your attorney will want to know: did the officer just stop trying after the first attempt, or did the officer try to fix the machine? Details that you remember about these few minutes during your breath test may lead to a defense to the claimed refusal. Specifically, a defense may lay in that you in reality wanted to perform, but that it was the fault of the machine in improperly determining that there was a refusal.

There are also a large number of other possible error codes from the DataMaster machine, such as an invalid sample, pump error and interferent detected. Most of these error codes will appear in addition to the breath test results on your OD-80 evidence ticket that you were given by the police. Some of these error codes require follow-up testing by the police. Your OWI specialist will know what these codes mean, and how they might assist in developing your defense.

Finally, if the machine produced an error reading, or several error readings, but a sample or samples were eventually found acceptable and tested, these added steps may place enough reasonable doubt in the mind of a judge or a jury to win your case. It likely depends on what the officer ultimately had to do to get an adequate sample, or what you did or did not do, that will make the difference in your defense.

10.1.8. Retention of All Evidence Tickets and Chemical Test Reports is Mandatory, because they are Part of Your Evidence. There are several possible evidence tickets or chemical test reports that could be very important to any defense in your OWI case. First, immediately after you were tested on the desk-top breath analysis machine at the jail or precinct/station, the machine printed a report of the results. You should have been given a copy of these results. While this test result is otherwise discoverable by the defense and must be disclosed by the prosecutor to your attorney not later than two days prior to your trial,[283] if you have your original, this assists in the process.

You may have received a second chemical test report if for any reason you had a blood alcohol test taken by a doctor, nurse or paramedic. These test results are typically not provided to you at the time of the test. If nothing else, you may have already received a bill, or a receipt, from the charges of the hospital for them to have performed a blood or urine test on you. If you do not have a copy of these results, your lawyer may ask you to obtain a copy. It is usually much easier for you to obtain this copy of these "medical records" than for lawyer to get them.

With either set of test results (police or medical), the defenses you may be able to raise can be based on these documents. Especially if there are significant discrepancies between these results, the sooner your attorney knows of all of these results, the sooner he or she can raise these defenses.

Last, there is always the chance that the prosecution will charge you using someone else's test results, in other words, where a human error or mistake has been made. Clerical errors do occur. If you have your copy of any evidence tickets or test results that you know are from you, and the tests the State attempts to admit in evidence does not match up, you may be able to get the entire case thrown out in your favor.

10.1.9. Computer Database Downloads and Vital Information from the DataMaster. The DataMaster has a built-in computer data base and this database information can be downloaded either by a modem or by an on-site computer. This allows for a complete and accurate history of all defects and aborted tests to be maintained. If this information were available, then this information could lead to a defense to your OWI case. This might happen if it could be shown, for example, that the machine upon which you were tested had a history of multiple failures or misreading's. However, in Michigan, the old DataMaster was specifically ordered by the State without this function turned on. State officials had the option of ordering the DataMaster with this capability, but chose not to include it for Michigan's testing equipment. It is not clear at the time of this writing whether or not the new DMT has been ordered with or without this functionality, and this topic is likely to be the subject of future litigation. However, the DMT has an enhanced data storage capability.

10.1.10. Person doing the Testing Must be Currently Certified to Run the Test. For any breath test on you to be considered valid, the person who ran the test on you must have been certified at that time to run the machine at the time you were tested.[284] Officers are being retrained for the DataMaster DMT so a lack of current training might also create a trial issue.

10.1.11. Periodic Calibration Checks and Service Records are Critical to Your Defense. The breath testing machines used by the police go through weeks or months of frequent use between "tune-ups." The rules in Michigan require that an appropriately qualified police officer run a simulator on the evidentiary breath testing device once per week to test the calibration of the device, and also that a manufacturer's representative test the device every 120 days.[285] In order for the breath test results to be used against you in court, the prosecution not only has to be able to show the results, but also that the machine was kept in good working order in compliance with these rules, and that it had been used appropriately.[286]

Part of this maintenance is calibration and periodic testing against known simulator samples to assure the accuracy of the machine. Calibration of each machine is done only as required, but is tested by the use of simulators every week and then every 120 days. If the results of your breath test are to be used against you in your OWI case, then it is considered a requirement for the prosecution to prove, by the admission of the test results of these weekly and quarterly simulator tests that the machine was in optimal working order. If produced, these records "prove" automatically that the machine was accurate.[287] Absent these documents, the UBAL charge against you may be dismissed. This is why your attorney may request these maintenance records from the prosecution as a part of the discovery process, or may want to closely inspect these records at the time of any hearing or at trial. And, with DMT the gas simulation is automatic, meaning there is no issue as to officer qualifications as under "old" rule.

However, with the advent of the new DataMaster DMT, some of the administrative rules have been changed. For example, to allow for the dry gas simulation as opposed to wet bath, the rules were changed to allow dry gas simulation that is within 5% of the compressed alcohol standard concentration after applying applicable altitude or topographic elevation correction factor supplied by the manufacturer.

This is a particularly significant change, because previously, simulation required an officer to prepare a water solution (wet bath) of alcohol and water and then run it through the machine. The DMT however is fitted with a dry gas simulation canister that remains attached to the machine. Records must still be kept, and improper records might still lead to the suppression of the result. The only difference is that a police officer is no longer personally preparing or running simulator solutions.

10.2. Blood Test – Most Reliable and Accurate Form of Testing. If drawn, handled and tested properly, a blood test is the most accurate and reliable direct measure of your blood alcohol level. The State considers your blood alcohol level in its determination of whether or not you are per se in violation of the OWI law by having an unlawful blood alcohol level (UBAL). Breath testing can be used the same way, but it is only a good approximation of your actual blood alcohol level and it involves numerous conversion factors to convert it.

10.2.1. Gas Chromatography for Blood Alcohol Tests. The process of gas chromatography involves the use of an instrument called a Gas Chromatograph (GC) to separate and analyze compounds that can be vaporized without decomposing the compound.

By use of a method called "head space," various foreign components of the blood such as drugs, drug metabolites, and alcohols in blood can be measured and identified. In a drunk driving case, we are primarily interested in the volatile ethyl (beverage) alcohol.

Like all chromatographic methods, with gas chromatography there is a "mobile phase," in this case a gas, which is used to carry the mixture over a "stationary phase." The gas is more fully called "headspace gas." With drunk driving cases, the stationary phase is typically a tube or capillary column. The components in the mixture containing a driver's blood leave this column in the order of their volatility, with the most volatile (first to vaporize) leaving the column first.[288] This "time of leaving the column" is used to qualitatively identify the component. The quantitative determination (amount) of the component, in this case alcohol, is determined by the amount of energy produced when burned as it leaves the column. This burning of the alcohol uses a "flame ionization detector."

10.2.2. GC-MS (Gas Chromatography Mass Spectrophotometry) for Blood Drug Analysis. GC-MS is the method of choice for drug analysis when determining the amount of any drug in your blood is required. In the forensic laboratory testing a sample of blood for an unknown drug or drugs, a gas chromatograph (GC) will be used at the front end to separate various volatiles in the blood. However, instead of a flame ionization detector (FID), the separated molecules then pass into the MS. The concept is the same as a GC chromatograph except that the detector FID is replaced with a mass spectrometer.[289] During the processing of the unknown, the drug molecules are broken apart and the resulting fragments then shoot down a tube called an "acceleration chamber" and are measured at the opposite end by a detector connected to a computer. Each fragment is charged and travels to the accelerator as an individual particle. As the charged molecular fragments reach the detector the instrument measures the charge and records the fragment mass. Fragment mass is proportional to the detected charge. These mass values are compared to a library of compounds from compounds that have been run in other labs. The computer looks for the best match. This matching substance is then reported as the identified unknown.[290]

10.2.3. Get the Entire Set of Records for the Batch that was Run, if Possible. Because GC-MS is a very sophisticated test to run, using a complex and expensive machine, the samples from all over the State are often brought to a central crime lab in Lansing, and tests are run each work day. One defense for you in your OWI case might be if there were problems with any part of the batch, or if the test results for the entire batch appeared skewed. Also, were there any similarities between your sample and any of the rest of the batch which might lead to a concern that your results are really yours?

10.2.4. Get Discovery on how the Standards were Created for Checking the Alcohol Accuracy for Gas Chromatography. Before any sample is run on the GC-MS device, standards, calibrators and controls (samples with known concentrations of drugs and alcohol) are run through the machine to help guarantee the machines accuracy. As of January 1, 2013, the State Forensic Toxicology Lab starting using an 8 point calibration curve with NIST traceable calibrators. If the results from running these standards, calibrators or controls does not match or are otherwise improper, then the machine is out of calibration and inherently inaccurate.

This accuracy is based upon the assumption that the standards are truly "standard." How these standards were created, how they are maintained and how they are used may all affect their reliability. If they were unreliable, or if there is any question of their reliability, this may throw enough doubt on the test results to get them thrown out of your OWI case, or to at least convince a jury that it is appropriate to disregard the results.

10.2.5. Get the Retention Manual for the GC-MS Device to Assure that the Peak was at the Expected Retention Time. Each GC-MS machine is a little different, with each one having slightly different results. Some defenses may arise from your side actually seeing the test result itself, the graph of the hard data, and comparing it to the manual. This should tell you what you should be seeing for any one drug result.

10.2.6. Get Service Records for Any Blood Test Device. The Michigan State Crime Lab owns at least six GCs that it uses to test blood for alcohol. As of January 1, 2013, the State Toxicology Lab in Lansing purchased new chromatography instruments and software and has written an entirely new written protocol for blood testing. No matter on what device your blood test was performed, you may have a defense if that machine was not correctly maintained, or if it has a history of frequent break-downs or false readings. For that reason, your attorney may attempt to get these records.

10.2.7. Look for Breaks in the "Chain of Custody" from Collection to Final Analysis. In order for the prosecutor to have any blood or urine sample entered into evidence against you in your OWI case, he or she must be able to show a "chain of custody" from you to the testing machine in the lab. In other words, the prosecution must be able to demonstrate to the court who had actual physical possession of this sample from the moment the sample left your body until it was actually analyzed in the machine.[291] This is what is called the "chain of custody." If there is a break in this chain of custody, your attorney may be able to use this fact in order to get the results of these tests suppressed. However, Michigan does not require a "perfect" chain of custody, and some breaks in the chain go to the weight of the evidence against you rather than to the admissibility of this evidence against you.[292]

10.2.8. Independent Tests to Confirm or Refute. If you are arrested for OWI and the police take any blood, breath or urine samples from you, then one of your rights is to have an independent blood or urine test of your own performed at a laboratory of your choice and at your own expense.[293] While there are many benefits to you undergoing this independent test, keep in mind that the result of your independent test is also admissible against you.[294] The primary benefit to this independent test is if the results of your test do not correlate with those drawn at the direction of the police. This is very significant evidence tending to show the invalidity of all of the test results.

10.2.9. DNA is Possible for Comparing the Blood Allegedly Collected by Police and the Defendant's. If there is a question about whether or not the sample the State is attempting to use against you is truly your sample, then if the State's sample has been properly preserved, the DNA in this sample can be compared to your DNA. The benefit to you is if the DNA does not match up, then no matter what any chain of custody paperwork may say, it is very unlikely that the sample the State has is from you. This additional information can then be used very strongly in your defense, and may result in the dismissal of your case.

10.2.10. Be Cautious to not Accept an Immunoassay Test for any "Quantitative" Drug Results, without a Confirmatory GC-MS. The GC-MS is a highly accurate way of determining not only the presence of drugs in your system, but also the amounts of those drugs as well. However, if you are charged with having marijuana or any other controlled substance in your body, then in Michigan you are charged with a "zero tolerance" crime, meaning the presence of the drug alone in your body is sufficient for you to be in violation of the law. This makes knowing the exact amount of these drugs in your body irrelevant. This will continue to be true even if you have a prescription for medical marijuana because the drug remains on schedule one. A recent court of appeals case concluded that any amount of THC metabolite in the system while driving constitutes an offense. Ostensibly, anybody who smokes medical marijuana with a card can be found guilty of driving under the influence even if over a week after ingesting any marijuana.[295]

10.3. Urine Test – Usually Reserved for Drugs and then Only to Determine Presence of a Class of Drugs. Urine testing does not reflect a measure of your blood alcohol because alcohol is one of the substances which is broken down by your liver instead of your kidneys. However, testing your urine is one of the most common methods of testing you for the presence of drugs, with simple dip-stick tests commonly available for screening tests for cocaine, amphetamines, methamphetamines, marijuana (THC), methadone and other opiates (narcotics), phencyclidine (PCP), barbiturates, benzodiazepines and tricyclic anti-depressants. These tests are as easy as you urinating in a cup and the officer waiting one to three minutes to determine if there is any color change.

10.3.1. If Quantitative Analysis of Either Drugs or Alcohol is Being used by the Prosecutor, get an Expert Witness to Assist to Refute the Results. Quantitative analysis means the prosecution is attempting to demonstrate the exact level of the prohibited substance in your blood rather than just the presence or absence. This type of analysis is not uncommon for alcohol, as if the level of alcohol in your system is above a certain level, (0.08 or 0.02 grams, depending on your circumstances); it is a crime in and of itself. This is the "per se" alcohol OWI charge.

If you are charged with OWI due to a prescribed drug that is not a controlled substance, then the prosecutor may need to show that the amount present in your body actually affected your driving ability. On the other hand, there can be times when a specific level of marijuana, or barbiturates, or any other drug may be irrelevant to the State in its prosecution. An example might be where you were charged with operating a vehicle with the presence of a "Schedule 'C'" drug in your blood.[296] In these instances, the crime is a "zero tolerance" criminal offense, and the exact amount of any drug or metabolite is of no consequence. Provided the exact amount of the drug or alcohol present is important in some way, then because these quantitative tests have inherent problems, an expert on your side may be able to attack the accuracy of these results. This expert may be the difference between you winning or losing.

10.3.2. Pooling is Always a Problem. Urine pooling means that your body is always making urine in your kidneys, then delivering that fluid to your bladder. Depending on how much you make, and how large your bladder, and how often you decide to do so socially, you empty your bladder anywhere from a couple times a day, to many times. Between these times, your urine is pooling in your bladder, waiting to be passed out of your body as urine. If you have not urinated for ten to twelve hours prior to being tested, and you had used some of those drugs in the recent past, the urine sample that is tested will have drug residue in it, even if those drugs were not affecting your mind or your reactions while you were driving. Of course, to use this defense against an OWI charge, you do have to admit to the drug use, and this would only be relevant if you are charged with OWI for a non-controlled, non-"Schedule 'C'" drug. Thus, depending on the drug and whether or not it was prescribed for you, simply having the drug in your urine could also be a crime.

10.3.3. Urine will Reveal Low Levels of Contraband Drugs Longer than a Blood Test. Your kidneys slowly and constantly remove the breakdown and waste products of most chemical substances from your body. Because your kidneys concentrate these waste products from your bloodstream, the residue of any drugs is detectable in your urine for much longer than in your blood. If all the police do is dip a test strip into your urine (the most common form of drug testing which can be done anywhere), illegal drugs such as marijuana, amphetamines, narcotics and barbiturates may all be detected in your urine sample for weeks after you were exposed to the drugs. If the police send the urine sample off for a more critical analysis to a crime lab, even more minute amounts of these drugs can be detected for months.

10.4. Saliva is not used for Forensic Alcohol Testing, due to Small Volume, but Good for Drug Screening or DNA. Yet another type of bodily fluid or tissue you might be asked to give to law enforcement may be some of your saliva. This can be done either by having you spit into a collection cup, or by swabbing the inside of your mouth. Either way, the amount of sample they get is too little to do any of the routine alcohol testing on it.

However, even this amount of saliva can be used to test for drugs in your system, or to check your DNA patterns. It is important for your defense to remember if you gave such a sample, as the prosecution may use any information so gathered to search for other crimes with which to charge you, or as a basis for the OWI charges against you.

Chapter 11:
Understanding Michigan's License Suspension and Revocation Laws

11.0. Purpose of this Chapter. Michigan does not currently provide for an automatic suspension of your driver's license if you are arrested for OWI. However, your license may be suspended for up to two years if you refuse the blood, urine or breath testing requested by your arresting officer.[297] If you want to avoid this "implied consent" suspension, then it will be necessary for you to face an administrative process that is separate from your criminal case.

These administrative hearings are considered to be "civil" in nature, and even though these administrative hearings and your criminal hearing or trial may appear to be superficially similar type procedures, they are not. This is true, even though the decisions reached usually pertain to some of the same facts surrounding your stop and arrest. The main difference is that your criminal case involves whether or not you broke the OWI "criminal" law, and whether the State can prove every element of this crime beyond a reasonable doubt. However, the administrative license suspension has little to do with whether or not you broke the OWI law. Instead, it is based on the allegation that you violated the implied consent law. This violation, if it can be proved, is considered a "civil" violation. This chapter discusses this administrative procedure, and how this interacts with your criminal case.

11.1. Administrative License Suspension ("Implied Consent") Proceedings are Almost Always Prior to Any Significant Criminal

Court Date. It is unlikely that any criminal hearing or your trial will be held before many weeks, if not many months have passed after your OWI arrest. It will typically take that long for your attorney to investigate your case, gather all the information he or she can, and then organize experts and your defenses. Even if you have a constitutional right to a speedy trial such speed typically benefits only the prosecution because they usually have all their information within hours of your arrest.

On the other hand, your administrative hearing is usually held within a few weeks after your arrest.[298] Because the police often appear without representation (the prosecutor does not usually attend), these hearings can often yield important testimony from your arresting officer that can be used later in your criminal case.

11.2. Implied Consent Proceedings are Civil in Nature. Implied consent proceedings are civil in nature, not having anything to do with any criminal penalties. Losing your license in one of these hearings may seem like a criminal penalty, but it is not.[299]

Because it is a civil and not a criminal proceeding, the burden of proof is much lower at these administrative hearings. To suspend your license, all the State needs to meet is proving your errors by a preponderance of the evidence.[300] Also, if your attorney requires the assistance of the hearing officer in obtaining witnesses, he or she can request that the department issue these witnesses subpoenas.[301]

11.3. Department of State Hearing Officers are Appointed, not Elected, so the Fairness and Due Process Compliance Varies. There is no requirement that the "judge" for these administrative hearings be an attorney.[302] That being the case, and considering the legal nature of the proceeding, the fairness and the "due process" compliance varies greatly from hearing to hearing. There may be times when your OWI specialist lawyer may almost have to coach these judges.

11.4. Your Arresting Officer is Required to Attend the Implied Consent Hearing and any Failure to do so will Result in the Driver

Prevailing Automatically. The rules provide that if the arresting officer is more than 20 minutes late for any scheduled implied consent hearing, then the driver automatically wins. The same is true, however, if you are late, with the State automatically winning, so it is essential for you to be on time for your implied consent hearing.

Even if you are not able to win your implied consent hearing (your driver's license is suspended or revoked), one benefit to you in these proceedings may be if your attorney will have the opportunity to ask your arresting officer questions while the officer is under oath and on the record. If there were other police officers involved in this process, they may also attend and testify. This information can then be used against your arresting officer, who is often a key witness for the prosecution, in your criminal case. Knowing what this person is going to say, what other officers may have to say, and locking them into their answers, gives your attorney an idea of which of your defenses have the best chance of success. And, if any officer changes their mind and testifies differently at your trial, this is very much in your favor as the officer's reliability is placed directly into question.

11.5. Your Failure to Make a Request for an Administrative Hearing Within 14 Days of your Arrest will Result in the Automatic Suspension of Your Driving Privilege. Unless you request an implied consent hearing, your license suspension is automatic. If you do request a hearing, be sure that you or your attorney indicates that all four issues are being contested. At the hearing, officers have the burden of proof, and unless you have waived one or more issues, the officer must testify to all four statutory requirements listed in 625f.[303]

Because the officer must testify and has the burden of proof, you may not be required to say or do anything at the hearing. Nevertheless, your presence is required and your lawyer may believe that it important for you to testify, perhaps to rebut something the officer has stated. If you do testify, this does not waive your Fifth Amendment right against self-incrimination during the underlying criminal case against you. Also, because the officer has the burden of proof, the Hearing Officer does not usually have any questions to ask you.

11.6. Often, it is Best not to Show Your "Hand" to the State During the Implied Consent Hearing, and use the Proceeding to Obtain More Information that may Assist in Winning the Criminal Case. Just as it may be very useful to your criminal case to put your arresting law enforcement officer on the stand in the implied consent hearing and "lock" him or her into their testimony so as to best plan your case and defenses, if you take the stand, or you have witnesses testify in your behalf, the prosecution will want to do the same to you.

If you have good defenses to your OWI charges, giving the prosecutor knowledge of these gives them more time to attempt to refute them. Unless getting your license back immediately is critical to your life, and you have rock-solid defenses in your criminal case, and because Michigan has a mandatory suspension of your license anyway if you are convicted, giving the prosecution any useful information at this hearing may win a battle but lose the war.

11.7. Implied Consent Proceedings may Offer the Chance to "Negotiate" with the Officer (or the State Attorney Handling the Hearing) to Withdraw the Proposed Suspension/Revocation. Any time you can get your attorney and the prosecutor in the same room, with the proposed facts of the case before both of them, there is always a chance for negotiation. Both sides have likely seen similar cases many times, and hopefully both know the courts, the judges and the local laws. The best OWI specialists have worked with these people for **YEARS**, with hundreds, if not thousands, of similar cases. He or she knows how to negotiate with either the presiding officer or the prosecution to get you your best chance at getting your license back, or of not pursuing this option if it would mean harming your criminal case. Of course, this negotiation may need to take place prior to the scheduled hearing date because there is often no prosecutor present at the implied consent hearing.

11.8. In some Situations, the Same Criminal Prosecutor Handles Both the Implied Consent and the Criminal Proceedings, but in Others this does not Apply. In some situations, the same prosecutor who will be trying your criminal case handles the administrative license suspension or revocation hearing. If it is the same prosecutor in both situations, then this may be all the more reason not to bring forth any of your "best" evidence because while you might get your license back sooner, you may lose your criminal OWI case.

11.9. Obtaining a Copy of the Transcript may be Advisable so that a Record of the Sworn Testimony can be used Later in the Criminal Case. The implied consent hearing will be tape recorded by the Hearing Officer, and a copy of the sworn testimony can be obtained by your attorney for later use. In the rare circumstances where the tape is destroyed or is otherwise not useable, a new hearing will be scheduled simply for the purpose of making a record for later use. The cost for such a transcript may run several hundred dollars, but because your attorney will have the opportunity to question the arresting officer, locking in their side of the story, a transcript of this testimony can be worth its weight in gold to your case. Having the testimony written in a transcript gives your attorney a better chance to prepare for trial and to be present and to prove your case to the judge or jury. This testimony may confirm defenses available to you, or may show your attorney which ones might not likely work.

11.10. Obtaining the Video Tape of the Arrest or Breath Testing can be Important to Facilitate the Balance of the Case. In spite of the limited issues which must be proven in an implied consent hearing, the best proof for your side in either this hearing or for your criminal trial may be the video tape of your arrest or your breath testing. A picture may be worth a thousand words, but a video recording may mean the difference between freedom and jail and a criminal record. Also, if your attorney can argue your side from only this video evidence and your experts, it means you have not had to take the stand in your defense. Taking the stand allows the prosecutor to also ask you questions, something which can be very harmful to your hearing or your criminal case. Thus, whether for the hearing or for your criminal case, obtaining any videotape of your arrest or your breath testing is very important. However, bear in mind that it is not appropriate to request an adjournment of the hearing simply because you do not have the videotape, or any other discovery for that matter.[304]

11.11. The Issues at the Implied Consent Hearing are Limited, so Your Attorney may only be able to Explore a Limited Number of Points Relating to the Criminal Case. The issues which can be discussed at your implied hearing are very limited. Typically, the only issues presented at these hearings revolve around: (1) Whether the peace officer had reasonable grounds to believe that you had committed a crime of operating a vehicle while intoxicated; (2) Whether you were placed under arrest for this crime; (3) If you refused to submit to the test upon the request of the officer, whether the refusal was reasonable; and (4) Whether you were advised of your implied consent rights.[305] The standard of evidence the state must prove is not nearly as high as at your criminal trial, being only by preponderance of the evidence rather than beyond a reasonable doubt.

Keep in mind that it will be fruitless for your attorney to argue at this hearing that a suspension of your driver's license will cause undue hardship to you, or that you were not in fact drunk, or that the chemical test was improperly obtained. None of this is relevant and such testimony or argument will not be allowed. Also, even if any blood obtained from you pursuant to a search warrant later tests below the legal limit, this is not a defense to the allegation of an implied consent suspension. Remember, the only issue is not in fact if you violated the OWI law, only if you violated the implied consent laws.

11.12. A Knowledgeable Attorney will know the Pluses and Minuses of Holding the Hearing Versus Possibly Seeking to Negotiate a Withdrawal of the "Hard" Suspension that could Occur. Because the burden of proof on the police officer is relatively low, and because the issues presented and discussed so limited, it is fair to say that it is often very difficult to win at the implied consent hearing. However, this does not necessarily mean that you should give up your right to such a hearing. Based on their years of experience with criminal law and the history of such hearings in your particular region, these OWI specialists know what might be gained, and more importantly, what you may lose by going through this administrative hearing.

Even if you do lose the hearing, simply going through the process may open avenues of defenses to your case through the questioning on the record of the police officers involved in your arrest. Consequently, it is almost always worthwhile to conduct the hearing, if only to obtain such sworn testimony for later use at your trial.

11.13. Your Right to Appeal in the Event You Lose the Implied Consent Hearing. There are two types of appeals that are available in the event that you lose the implied consent hearing. The first is a "hardship" appeals. This appeal is heard at the Circuit Court, and involves your attorney indicating to the court that there is a significant hardship to you in not having a driver's license. You will also need to show that there is no alternative form of public transportation and no one in your household who can provide transportation for you. Additionally, before granting you a hardship license, most Circuit Court judges will want to see a favorable substance abuse evaluation showing that you are at low risk for repeat behavior. Finally, hardship appeals are available to you only if you have no prior implied consent refusals within the prior seven years.[306] If you are given a hardship license, your privilege to drive will be very limited both with regard to the type of driving allowed as well as the days and time of day you may lawfully drive. A successful hardship appeal will not remove the six points that were added to your driving record as a result of originally losing the implied consent hearing.

You may also take a legal appeal from the implied consent administrative hearing. With this type of appeal, you are arguing to the court that the hearing officer committed a legal error in finding that you violated the implied consent law. Legal appeals are very difficult to win because your attorney must show that the hearing officer abused his or her discretion.[307] Legal appeals may always be taken, regardless of if you have prior implied consent refusals, and the biggest advantage to such an appeal is that winning means full restoration of your driving privilege. Also, the six points previously added to your record will be removed.

Any driving privileges that are restored to you through either the hardship or the legal appeal are subject to any further criminal action against your driving privilege for the underlying OWI charge. Thus, any restored driving privileges may be quite short lived.

Chapter 12:
Your Attorney's Pre-Trial Activities

12.0. The Purpose of this Chapter. It is likely that prior to your trial or your pretrial hearings you will meet with your OWI specialist attorney, communicate with him or her by phone or e-mail, and spend time with his or her experts and investigators. You will probably also be in contact with your attorney's office staff and paralegal(s) several times before you appear in court. Nevertheless, you may think that not much is happening on your case during these waiting periods, and therefore it may seem as if you are not getting your money's worth. The purpose of this chapter is to help you understand just how much work is required by your attorney during this "behind the scenes" preparation of your case.

12.1. Working Behind the Scenes. The vast majority of what goes on in your OWI case happens behind the scenes. You may spend hours with your attorney at different stages of the case. However, what you do not see are the long hours of training and preparation, legal research, telephone calls and face-to-face conversations your attorney may have with members of his or her staff, experts, investigators and witnesses for the prosecution. Your attorney may also be talking directly with the prosecutors, and perhaps under certain circumstances, with the judge. In addition to these forms of communication, your attorney may be preparing various discovery demands or other types of pleadings, and will be filing these in court. Motions and briefs may also be filed in court on your behalf. In most instances, you will know exactly what is happening with your case based on documents you receive from your attorney through either traditional or electronic mail. A strong defense to the OWI charge will require a large number of hours from all members of the attorney's staff, and these hours are dedicated directly to your file and your defense.

Also, the best OWI attorneys know everyone in your court system, from the judges, through the clerks, the court reporters, and the prosecutors and their staff, and these relationships can be of great benefit to you. However, your attorney should never promise you that they can work you a "deal" because of whom he or she knows. That is not the way the court system works. Prosecutors do not have to offer deals. Nevertheless, personal contacts are important, and through them your attorney can make things work as smoothly as possible.

12.2. Using an Investigator to get Answers that the Attorney Cannot. Private investigators can add a great amount of benefit and value to your defense. Typically, these investigators are retired law enforcement officers and many of them have decades of law enforcement experience. They may have even been a member of the police department that investigated your case, or otherwise know the police officers involved. Most often, an investigator will go to the scene of your arrest and take photographs and make measurements. He or she may also speak with witnesses and possibly even the officers involved in your case. Finally, the investigator may be able to obtain specific information regarding the chemical tests given in your case. Thus, if you truly want to leave no stone unturned in your defense, then find an OWI specialist that has an investigator on staff or contacts with one or more experienced investigators that can be used to increase the chances of winning your case.

12.3. Being "Connected" Without Being a Crook. One of the reasons you need an experienced OWI expert to represent you is their knowledge of the court system, the judges and the prosecutors. You should take it as a very good sign when the judge or the prosecutor warmly greets your attorney when he or she enters the courtroom. It is typically a sign of respect, even positive personal feelings between them. These relationships will assist the defense of your case in many ways, starting out with your pretrial and continuing on to your evidentiary hearing and/or trial. It will also carry over to any phone calls between your attorney and the prosecution. However, do not expect miracles, or for your lawyer to try to swing things in your favor just because of this respect and these relationships. Also, do not expect anything based on "backroom" or illegal negotiations. The best OWI attorneys have gained the reputations they enjoy because they are perceived as being ethical. You should never ask or expect your attorney to compromise his or her excellent reputation for some short term gain in your case.

12.4. Timely, Targeted Filing of Pleadings is Critical. The well-seasoned OWI attorney will develop your defense through an exhaustive investigation of your case. This will begin with obtaining from you all of the facts about your case that you can remember. The investigation will continue with a close examination of all the evidence he or she can uncover through his or her own investigator, as well as the information obtained from the police and the prosecutor. After the investigation is complete, your attorney might then make specific and timely pleadings or requests of the court and the prosecutor. The best OWI lawyers know exactly what they should expect to receive from the police, and know the best time in which to get it. They will not make the mistake of demanding this information so late in the game that it will have been lawfully destroyed or be otherwise useless, or so late as to allow the prosecutor to argue that the court should deny such requests. Your seasoned OWI attorney also will not demand this information too early, such as before all of the information may be available from the other side or before the prosecution is obligated to release anything.

By filing pleadings and discovery demands that are both specific and timely, the prosecution is less likely to be able to argue to the court that the sought information or evidence should not be released to your side. If your pleading is asking the court to order something, if the request is well thought out, specific, reasonable and backed by the law, it is hard for the court to refuse. As the information sought or requested of the court is often critical to your case (video recordings, asking the court to deny admission of certain evidence), making these requests in a timely and targeted fashion is critical as well. If not correctly done, your side can lose the access to this material, or lose the hearing. The unfortunate result of such poor timing may be that you ultimately lose a defense or perhaps even lose your case.[308]

12.5. Assisting You in Hiring an Expert to Consult or Testify. There can be no question that proper use of expert testimony can make or break an OWI case. Because your OWI specialist knows the Michigan courts, knows the likely juries in the county of your arrest and knows your best defenses, he or she also knows who will make the best expert for your case. Based on decades of OWI trial experience, your lawyer knows who is best for your situation among the thousands of possible experts available to either consult on your case or to testify at your trial or hearing. He or she will have many experts whom they have worked with in the past, and they can help you in hiring these experts.

12.6. Arraignment (where you Plead Guilty or Not Guilty) and a Point in the Case where Certain Motions and Challenges must be Filed. Usually within 14 days of your arrest, yet months before any hearing or trial, you will be brought before a judge and asked how you want to plead, guilty or not guilty.[309] Many courts will allow your attorney to "waive" this first court appearance by filing the appropriate paperwork before your scheduled hearing date. Courts are becoming increasingly reluctant to allow such waivers, particularly if yours is a second or subsequent OWI offense. Also, you will not want to waive your arraignment if you have to ask the court to appoint you an attorney for your defense because this is usually done at this proceeding.

Most motions or challenges to the proposed evidence or testimony must be made before your trial and many courts will schedule "cut-off" dates.[310] If your attorney does not file any appropriate motions or otherwise make these requests by this cut-off date, you usually lose the opportunity to do so. Should this occur, then defenses you might have had will be lost forever. Because of pressure being placed on the District Courts from the Michigan Supreme Court,[311] these timing issues are becoming increasingly important, with deadlines coming sooner and sooner. This is yet another reason to hire a well-seasoned OWI trial attorney so that you do not lose your case because of lost opportunities.

12.7. Pretrial Conferences with Prosecutor or Judge (with Prosecutor also Participating). A pretrial conference is essentially a scheduling conference, and your attendance will usually be required. The purpose of the pretrial is to allow the prosecutor and your defense attorney to discuss what needs to be done to prepare the case for trial, or to determine if the case can be resolved without a trial. It is not unusual for issues which can or must be decided before your trial, but for which neither you or the prosecution will need to present witnesses or admit evidence, to be handled at a pretrial conference. This is a situation where your attorney, the judge and the prosecutor get together, often in the chambers (office) of the judge. It is unusual for a court reporter to be present. Examples of issues which might be handled or discussed at a pretrial conference include logistic issues, in which order witnesses will be heard, discussion of how long the trial may take, negotiations for sentencing recommendations if there is a possible plea bargain on the table, atypical or unusual sentencing concerns which the judge would have to approve, and arguments by either lawyer that can be supported by prior decisional law.

In Michigan, if you are arrested for an OWI offense, state law mandates a pre-trial conference which typically must be scheduled within 35 days of your arrest.[312] However, the law also indicates that a failure to follow this scheduling guideline is NOT cause for dismissal of the charges against you. The options to consider would be to basically adjourn the pretrial to another date (as an example, if discovery is not yet complete), to schedule a hearing on a pretrial issue (called an "evidentiary hearing), to schedule jury selection and a trial date, or for you to plead guilty based on the plea/sentence bargain that your attorney would work out.

12.8. Pre-trial Motion and Evidentiary Hearings. Some pretrial motions may result in the entire dismissal of your case. This is particularly true if during these motion hearings specific questions of law or fact are answered in your favor. Thus, in certain circumstances, such dismissals can occur before a trial. Examples of such "dispositive" questions are whether or not the stop by the police or your subsequent arrest was lawful, whether or not your blood, breath or urine tests were properly obtained, or in the case of a refusal, whether or not the warrant obtained was legally valid. The court may also determine whether or not all of your constitutional rights were otherwise properly protected. These are all examples of issues that can be presented and argued without a jury being present. In other words, they are preliminary decisions for the judge to make.

A major difference between a pre-trial motion hearing and an evidentiary hearing is that with an evidentiary hearing, testimony is taken in open court and witnesses are often questioned by both sides. An evidentiary hearing is as if a small segment of your trial was cut out of the trial, isolated and worked out, outside of the presence of a jury. If you have a subsequent trial, then this segment often is replayed before the jury. Unless your case takes place in a "video" court room, a court reporter or court recorder will often be present at the hearing. This is because as the judge is making rulings on points of law, these decisions can form the basis of an appeal if your side loses. Appeals are based entirely on the trial court "record", so everything that happens in court must be recorded in some way.

The winning of a pre-trial hearing by your side gives your attorney great leverage in getting the charges against you either lessened or even dropped. Because they are so much shorter than a trial, your attorney may place a great deal of effort into winning such important points in your favor. Such hearings also lock in the testimony of the prosecution's witnesses, giving your attorney a better chance to prepare to question them at your trial. It may also be true that your best chance at winning will occur at such a hearing. Consequently, if you lose at the hearing, you may decide to forgo a trial and have your attorney attempt to negotiate a plea or sentence bargain in your behalf.

12.9. Being on a Trial Calendar. Criminal jury trials are only heard by the courts during certain days or weeks each month. The court's "docket" or jury trial calendar is the entire list of all of the cases which may be handled by a particular court during this jury trial term. There are typically countless more cases on the trial calendar than can ever be handled by the judge during the specific criminal jury term. Those that are not settled before trial are usually taken starting with the oldest case on the list and continuing with the next oldest until the end of the time period is reached. At that point, the cases that remain unsettled are shifted to the next trial calendar, moving up closer to the start of the new list as they become older in time.

Another method used by some district courts in Michigan is for all cases scheduled for a particular jury term to pick their juries on the same day from the same "jury pool" (group of prospective jurors), and then schedule the actual trials for these cases over the next one to two weeks. While this does not prevent there from being too many cases to try each term, it does assist the court in making efficient use of each trial term. It may not, however, be so beneficial to the criminally accused. An experienced OWI attorney knows how to "read" the trial calendar, giving you a reasonable estimate of your chances of having your trial and when.

12.10. Letting Your Attorney Decide who (if Anyone) Testifies.

If you are soon to be at trial, or you are already starting your OWI trial, it is important at this point to accept the fact that your attorney knows the best way to present the facts and circumstances of your case and your defenses to the court. It is quite likely that he or she already has in their head an image of the trial and plan of how best to present your defense. This plan should remain flexible until he or she sees what the prosecution puts forward as far as their testimony and evidence. The plan may then very well change so as to present to the judge and jury your best point of view. Part of this plan is deciding who, if anyone, should testify on your behalf. As a defendant, you have no duty to put on any defense, and you have an absolute right not to testify.

If your attorney does think it advisable for you to put forward any defense, he or she does so based on such factors as decades of experience with the court you are in, with the judge who is running the court and with the same type juries you now face. Many defendants in your position will want to testify for themselves. They want to tell their side of the story, will want to clear up any misstatements or exaggerations by the arresting officer, and basically they just want their day in court. However, there are many pitfalls associated with such a decision, and many things to consider before a decision to allow you to testify can be reached by your attorney. What do you have to say, and could it be said better by someone else?

Also, if you take the stand in your defense, while you get to tell your side of the story, the prosecution gets to cross-examine you. They get to ask you embarrassing and difficult questions, making you appear to be a liar or a fool. The prosecutor will also attempt to have you "fill in the blanks" for the police officer. In other words, if you never told the officer where you were drinking, when you started or stopped, or how much you actually had to drink, these questions are fair game at your trial. Typically, the prosecutor will also ask you what a drunk person looks like. The goal of this question is to have you testify about the same balance or speech problems the arresting officer claims to have observed in your case.

Thus, while you may make a few points by testifying on your own behalf, because your attorney knows your case, the prosecutor, the jury and the judge, your well-seasoned OWI trial attorney also knows just how much you stand to lose by taking the stand. If they recommend you do not take the stand in your defense, there are many good reasons for this decision.

12.11. Preparing Jury "Charges" (Instructions). Before jury selection, before the trial begins, and at the end of your trial, the judge reads to the jury a series of instructions, or charges, laying out the law they are to follow when deliberating and reaching your verdict. They will be told for example that they are the only "finders of fact" and that any decision they make as to the facts of the case is final, but that they must follow the law as it is provided to them by the judge.

The decision as to exactly which charges are given is made by the judge, outside of the presence of the jury, usually toward the end of your trial. Sometimes getting the judge to change a word or two, or accept one "turn of a phrase" rather than another, makes the difference between a not guilty verdict and you going to jail. OWI specialists know their case law, what instructions have worked for their clients before, and the best chance of getting your judge to accept them.

Even the denial of your attorney's suggested jury charges can be important. If your lawyer makes a written suggestion for a jury charge which is denied by the judge, this may form the basis of an appeal if you are found guilty by the jury. That makes preparing the jury charges for your case yet another critical step in your OWI case, and why you need a specialist in this field defending you.

12.12. Being Ready for the Worst Case Scenario. In spite of a good case, the best attorneys on your side, and rock solid defenses, in the end, you may be found guilty of OWI. There is always the chance you will be led from the courtroom in handcuffs, having been found guilty of one or more criminal offenses, but unless you are a multiple offender, or if your case involves the death or serious injury of another, you will probably remain on bond prior to your sentencing.

You should discuss with your attorney before trial the likelihood that if you are found guilty, you will go directly to jail. If this is a possibility in your case, then it is important for you to be prepared for this eventuality, even if you are told by your attorney the chance of it is slight. If you have a family, work to get your financial situation such that if you do end up in jail, your family's suffering is minimized. If you can save up your vacation time, and have an understanding boss, perhaps you will not lose your job while you are incarcerated.

Talk to your spouse, your children, your parents about what you face, and that you could end up in jail. Arrange to have support for your family if the worst scenario happens. Be mentally prepared for being carted off to jail. If the worst happens, get through it with dignity. Know that you will come out the other side.

12.13. Your Attorney's "Time and Expertise." Even though all lawyers in Michigan have graduated from law school, and all have to have passed the bar to be allowed to practice, all lawyers are not created equal. One of the reasons you have hired this particular lawyer is his or her "time and expertise."

Time. You will spend hours, perhaps even days, with your attorney and their staff in the preparation and investigation of your case, and in hearings and at trial. However, what you may not see, and may not be otherwise aware of is the long hours that might include late night and early morning preparation sessions that your attorney goes through as he or she prepares your case. These hours might be spent with the experts or investigators in your case, or with your attorney's staff, or in preparing legal research. What you typically do see is a polished end product, such as an expert putting decades of experience into action before a judge or jury when they testify in your behalf in court, or when your attorney makes a persuasive closing statement to the jury. It is as much these behind the scenes hours as the actual hours you spend with your attorney that you are paying for when you hired this attorney.

Unfortunately, you are also paying for the times when the two of you are waiting in court, while the judge handles legal matters besides your case. Both of you are almost always required to be there, sitting, patiently waiting for your turn. Because it could turn out you that rather than waiting, you end up going first (even if others may be ahead of you in the scheduled order), your attorney must show up fully prepared from the first moment in court. Most often, there will be several court appearances before your case is fully resolved, and each of them will likely require several hours of you and your attorney's time.

Expertise. For an OWI attorney to be at the top of his or her game, he or she must have not only a vivid understanding of the intricacies of OWI law, but an equally comprehensive understanding of the science involved in intoxicated driving. This includes subjects such as the metabolism of alcohol and the technical aspects of breath and blood testing. So, while you may not be able to fully see or appreciate the complete mastery of the subject matter possessed by your attorney, it is often easy to see the lack of this expertise among other lawyers who do not possess this OWI expertise. This is because OWI is a particularly complicated area of law. Watching an excellent lawyer perform in the courtroom is kind of like watching a professional athlete make something look too easy on the field. Either way, you don't see the years of training and experience that goes into making the actions of the seasoned professional seem effortless. It is this combination of training and experience that allows them to be one of the best. In court, if you see a polished attorney by your side, it is because of the many, many hours of preparation on their part with your case, and their years of experience in defending those accused of intoxicated driving.

What you seldom see is their connections, the relationships your attorney has spent time cultivating among the judges, prosecutors and court staff. Nevertheless, do not expect your lawyer to get favorable treatment for you just because of who they are and who they know. However, if a judge or the prosecutor knows and respects your attorney because of his or her reputation and expertise, then they may chose not to fight as hard on some issues. They may also be prepared to give your side the benefit of the doubt, and this may just translate to results in the courtroom.

12.14. Be Realistic and be Flexible. Even the best OWI specialists are not magicians, and even the most experienced OWI attorney can only put forth the optimal view of your case. When your attorney presents your case to the judge and jury he or she will lay out the facts and the opinions of experts in a way that will put you in the best possible light. While they have decades of criminal defenses experience, with cases like yours and in your court, there is still a need for you to be realistic and flexible.

This is because your attorney is not in charge of all aspects of your case. The prosecutor has much to do with deciding which charges to bring, the timing of hearings and any trial. They may also have some input into any punishment you may face. While the prosecutor has a great deal of leverage, ultimately it is the judge and his or her clerk who actually decides the specific timing of your hearings and your trial. Your attorney will, of course, also have some say into the manner in which dates are scheduled.

Also, the court system is set up for the convenience of the court, not for you or your attorney. It is not unusual for hundreds of cases to be scheduled for the same day as your arraignment, for thirty or more cases scheduled for the same week as your trial or hearing. This redundancy exists just in case some cases cancel, settle or are not ready to progress. It keeps the court busy, even if you are forced to sit around and wait your turn, or are asked to come back another week or month because they did not get to you this time.

You know the importance of the charges you face and how they will affect your life. You best understand your financial situation and what you can afford. After listening to your side of the story, investigating the facts and the evidence for and against you, your attorney can inform you as to what you realistically face as far as likely punishment. He or she may give you news or opinions you do not want to hear. Sometimes, there are no technicalities to exonerate you, and the facts and evidence against you are impressive. In light of all this, it is also important for you to be realistic. Yes, no matter how skillful your attorney may be, you may still face the bleak prospect of being convicted of intoxicated driving.

12.15. Compromise – it may be the Best Bet for You. Compromise is defined as a settlement of differences by arbitration or by consent reached by mutual concessions.[313] The prosecution and the police believe you have committed a crime. If they did not then, in theory at least, they should not be pursuing you and attempting to gain a conviction. There are times when the middle ground of accepting a guilty or nolo contendere plea against you for some lesser offense furthers the need of the prosecutor and police to feel as if they are making the world a little safer. This means you will have a criminal record, and you will face some penalty, but that the punishment will likely be somewhat less than what you faced for an OWI conviction.

There may also be times in your case when you have to compromise internally, with yourself and your family. You may have to make decisions that are not as positive for you specifically but that are better for your family. You may face a decision such that your desire for a sense of justice may ruin everyone else, and of course, you should try to avoid giving in to such desire.

A number of factors go into this decision making process. These include the facts of your case, the expense you face if you continue the fight, the ramifications of any criminal offenses on your record (even if for something more minor than OWI), the effect your case is having on others, and your attorney's experience with your court, your prosecutor and your arresting officer. As you begin to weigh and otherwise add up all of these factors, you should be able to come to an informed decision as to whether or not you should compromise or keep on fighting.

12.16. When "No Deals" are Available: Your Decision. In the end, there may be no "deal" on the table. This may be because you are a repeat offender, because the chemical evidence is above a certain arbitrary number, because you were involved in an accident and the prosecutor wants to appease the "victims" or simply because the evidence against you is strong. On the other hand, you may not want to deal because you believe that your defenses are so strong that you feel sure you will win, or possibly you have decided that you simply cannot accept the prospect of having a conviction on your record. These factors may lead you to the conclusion that accepting any "deal" is not in your best interest.

In the end, any decision in this regard is **YOURS**. Such a decision may include pleading to a deal, or when to continue to fight even a difficult and almost hopeless battle. It may also include deciding when to fight tooth and nail to the very end or to change your plea to guilty in order to accept the consequences of your actions. You may also decide that you simply want to fight because you believe that your cause is just.

The best OWI attorneys are experts at explaining to you the repercussions and benefits of any decision at any point in your case, but the ultimate decision is yours and yours alone. You may ask the opinion of your attorney, but whether or not you take this advice is **YOUR** decision. No matter how skilled or experienced your attorney, no one can ever put him or her in your position and fully understand what is in your best interest. You should look to your attorney only to provide you with sufficient information to reach a fully informed decision including all of the aspects of this decision mentioned above.

Chapter 13:

Should You Have a Trial or Negotiate a Plea Bargain?

13.0. Purpose of this Chapter. From the time you are arrested, through the time that your case is first scheduled for trial, you will have numerous opportunities to decide either to fight the charges against you, or to work out a plea bargain with the prosecution and/or a sentence bargain with the judge. If you decide to fight, and your attorney has not been successful in obtaining a pretrial dismissal, then you are likely to continue on to trial. The subject of trials will be handled in subsequent chapters.

On the other hand, you may be able to significantly shorten the prosecutorial process by electing to allow your attorney to reach the best possible deal with the prosecution or judge. In this instance, there might be a plea bargain where you might agree to plead guilty to some other lesser or non-alcohol related offense, or under certain circumstances, possibly even to plead guilty to your OWI offense. On the other hand, you may wish to have your attorney attempt to work out a sentence bargain with the judge, and if your case is a felony, then your attorney will probably try to work out a "Cobbs" agreement.[314] This is essentially a sentence agreement where the judge first performs a "preliminary" evaluation of your case and your prior criminal record, if any, and indicates to you before you plead guilty what your sentence will be. If at the time of your sentencing the judge reconsiders and decides not to follow the prior "Cobbs" agreement, then you have a chance to withdraw your plea and go to trial. In Michigan there is also a Killebrew Plea[315]. In this instance, a defendant enters a conditional guilty plea which can be withdrawn if the judge's eventual sentence falls outside terms negotiated by the defense and prosecutor.

Another kind of plea is a "blind" plea. This is where there is no agreement between your side and the judge relative to sentencing. Instead, you stand before the court, plead guilty (or nolo contendere[316]) and accept the punishment as determined by the judge after hearing anything pertinent you or your attorney want to say. If you do not like the punishment, you have no chance to take back your plea. Needless to say, this type of plea requires an experienced attorney who can discuss with you the particular judge's prior sentencing practices. This might make your plea a little less blind.

This chapter discusses this "plea" process, when you should strongly consider it, and when it might not be in your best interest. In the end, the decision of when to accept a plea, and when to chance a trial, is yours and only yours. An experienced OWI attorney can give you opinions and a recommendation based on their knowledge and decades of experience, but the ultimate decision on going to trial or accepting and type of plea is **YOURS**.

13.1. Getting a Handle on Your Case. Your attorney needs to figure out what happened to you during the entire time period surrounding your arrest, and you need to relate this information with as much detail as possible. Without this information, even the best and most experienced OWI attorney cannot give you a worthwhile opinion of how you should proceed with your case. This information comes from the very detailed questionnaire your attorney will have you complete, information your attorney's staff will get from the investigator, from the police, from the prosecutor, and from the results of any chemical tests you took.

Your attorney or his or her staff also investigates the court to which your case has been assigned. Who is the judge, and who is the prosecutor? Who works in those offices and how do they usually proceed with OWI cases? The answers to these questions will inevitably have an impact on the strategy your attorney employs to defend your case.

13.1.1 A Great Defense Begins with a Great Investigation.[317] When we think about an investigation in an intoxicated driving case, we typically think of serving the prosecutor with a discovery demand. In return we hope to obtain the police reports, the videotapes and the documents necessary to support a valid chemical test. We look them all over, and try to spot issues. We know, of course, that the investigation is one-sided, and that the police might mislead, embellish and, in some cases, outright lie about what happened. The most common lie is one of omission.

Too often lawyers base their case preparation on this discovery, yet we know that this has been manufactured by the police with one goal in mind—and that goal is a conviction. In order to counteract or contradict what we've been told by the police, we often hire our own experts or investigators to assist us with our case. Most states now require reciprocal discovery, which of course means that the information we obtain through our experts and investigators must be provided to the prosecutor.

Even in the age of reciprocal discovery, there is some information that must never be shared with the prosecutor and there is only one person with whom the prosecutor will never be able to speak, and this person often knows more about the case than anyone else: YOU. No reciprocal discovery rule will ever require that we share this discovery with the prosecutor. Your statements are protected by the Constitutional right to remain silent, and by the ethical rules of confidentiality. Thus, unlike your expert witnesses or investigators, a prosecutor will never be able to call you to find out what you will say at trial or what you have told your attorney about the case.

Consequently, this is the one greatest advantage we can obtain and the only element of surprise that we can never be compelled to share. It is important to make full use of this advantage. We may then use this information to tell your story at trial; a story the prosecutor will have little way of learning about prior to trial. The only way to really know, that is to "discover," your story, is to perform a thorough interview which must include your attorney spending considerable time with you. Some of this time may involve case reenactments, particularly if your lawyer is trained at the Trial Lawyer's College.

13.2. Evaluating the "Quality" of Your Case. A thorough investigation of this kind typically takes place over a period of several weeks. After all this information has been gathered and digested, your attorney can begin to give you some insight as to the "quality" of your defense, as well as the strengths of the prosecution's case. He or she should be able to give you a pretty authoritative idea as to how good or poor the police work was, and comment also on any potential witnesses. By this point, your attorney should also be able to comment on how good a witness any officer involved in your arrest might turn out to be. Some officers make excellent, essentially unflappable witnesses.

Your seasoned OWI attorney also knows how the court in which your charges will be prosecuted has handled cases like yours in the past, and the likely result of a plea, pre-trial hearing or trial. All of the above factors go into his or her evaluation of the "quality" of your case. Any recommendation they make to you is based on his or her decades of experience.

13.3. Evaluating the Fairness of the Assigned Judge. All judges in Michigan are elected officials. Most, but not all sitting judges started out by practicing law. Some were criminal defense attorneys, while more and more of them were former prosecutors. Those who have been sitting judges for any time have histories of how they rule on situations like yours.

Misdemeanors like first or second offense OWI are always tried at the lower level courts called the "district court." It is quite likely that your lawyer has appeared before your judge assigned to hear your case on numerous prior occasions and has already developed some sort of relationship with the judge. Some judges, it seems, just cannot be fair on OWI cases, while others seem to frequently side with the defense. Knowing this can help you and your attorney streamline your case, and not waste time pursuing defenses or issues that have no chance of success with your particular judge.

13.4. Evaluating the Prosecutor's Experience, "Relationships" and "Personal Charisma." It is highly likely that early in your case, it will be assigned to a specific prosecutor or particular prosecutorial team. As with judges and police officers, each prosecutor has their own strengths, weaknesses and personality.

Unless the prosecutor is new to the game, the well-seasoned OWI attorney will usually have tried cases like yours against this particular prosecutor, maybe even many times. It may not be unusual for each prosecutor to use the same experts, use the same trial techniques, even the same themes to their opening and closing statements. This is often the case for city or township attorneys who may have represented the same municipality for decades.

Your lawyer's knowledge and experience of your particular prosecutor adds to his or her ability to make better recommendations to you in your OWI case. A prospective trial against a very worthy opponent, who is well respected by the judge and well-liked by past juries, might lead to a different recommendation by your attorney than if your prosecutor has limited experience or has a harsher personality that does not play well to the jury.

13.5. In Your Jurisdiction, do You even get a Jury Trial? It is a fundamental right for anyone facing any criminal trial, including misdemeanors like OWI,[318] to have a jury if they want one.[319] All district courts in Michigan are equipped to handle jury trials, and if you want a jury to decide your case, you need only request it. However, you may also "waive" the jury and have the judge decide your innocence or guilt. To opt out of a jury trial, you must knowingly, voluntarily and intentionally waive your right to a jury trial.[320] The prosecutor also has a right to have his or her case heard by a jury. Thus, even if you waive your right to a jury, the judge might not accept your decision if the prosecutor objects. In any event, a well-seasoned OWI attorney will know the benefits and risks of a jury trial verses a bench trial in your region.

13.6. Where do You Find Good Jurors and Bad Jurors in Your State? If you decide to have a jury hear your OWI case, you certainly will want the best possible persons on your jury, that is, people like you, who are open and fair-minded. Knowing the chance of getting such "good" jurors, and hopefully being able to get rid of "bad" jurors, can be the difference between a good trial lawyer and an OWI expert.

An experienced OWI attorney understands the likely jury pool starting point in your case based on the numerous juries they have selected in cases just like yours over the years in the same court. Because they always pull from the same county, it is not unusual for subsequent jury pools to be similar. Their experience allows them to give you the best possible guidance as you make difficult and critical choices, like whether to accept a plea bargain or to go to trial.

13.7. If Convicted, who Sentences You? The judge who accepts your plea of guilty or who presides over your trial will be the one who sentences you.[321] This sentence may include time in jail, time on probation, fines and costs, and there may be other requirements such as community service and an ignition interlock device. If you are convicted of an alcohol related crime, then you will also be screened by the court's probation department to determine if you have an alcohol or drug abuse problem. There are specific sentencing guidelines - maximums and minimums - to help whoever decides your punishment.[322] A well-seasoned OWI specialist can offer guidance based on their decades of experience as to what penalty you likely face. This information may assist you in making your decisions to go to trial or to accept an offered deal.

13.8. Is a "Deferred Adjudication," Diversion, or a "Plea in Abeyance" Possible? In some situations, with crimes other than OWI, you might be allowed to defer your conviction while you complete a prolonged period of evaluation, community service and drug and alcohol evaluation and treatment. If you successfully complete your program, and commit no further violations of the law during this period, the charges against you might be dropped or reduced to a lower charge. This is called a deferred adjudication, diversion program or a plea in abeyance. Under certain circumstances, some Michigan judges may allow a similar arrangement; though they are not generally allowed by law to do so with an OWI case. Another similar incarnation of this approach to sentencing is the increasingly popular "drug court" where the alcohol offender undergoes various levels of addiction treatment in exchange for much lighter punitive sanctions .

These options are typically not offered for the more serious criminal charges, such as where a death has occurred, as they are usually reserved for typically less severe criminal acts. Additionally, and as a general rule, these types of pleas or sentencing arrangements are also only usually offered to people who have no other criminal record. However, many courts are using "diversion" programs for felony intoxicated driving cases, where the emphasis is again on treatment rather than punishment.

In Michigan, similar terms are available for adults for certain other crimes including simple possession of some drugs[323] and for some other crimes committed by youthful offenders between the ages of 17 and 21. These alternative sentences are not a statutorily mandated option for OWI offenses.[324]

13.8.1 Michigan's Sobriety Court. Though not addressing the conviction itself, the sobriety court law does allow a certain kind of reduced driver license sanction. After an initial forty-five day suspension, qualifying repeat offenders might be able to obtain restricted driving privileges with a breath-alcohol ignition interlock device, provided they have successfully participated in a sobriety court program.

The law has a broad definition of "prior offense." It requires the Secretary of State to issue a restricted license to an individual whose license was restricted, suspended, revoked, or denied because the individual either has (1) two or more convictions of driving while intoxicated or visibly impaired under Michigan Law; or (2) one under Michigan Law preceded by one or more convictions for violating a "substantially similar" local ordinance or law from another jurisdiction. An underage drinking and driving conviction from outside of Michigan may also count, provided they meet the "substantially similar" requirement.[325]

Provided the repeat offender is otherwise eligible, a restricted license will be issued after the individual's drivers license has been suspended or revoked for forty-five days. In order for this to occur, the assigned judge must certify to the Secretary of State that the individual has been enrolled in a DWI/sobriety program and that an approved ignition interlock device has been installed on each motor vehicle the individual operates or owns.[326] This restricted license only allows the individual to operate the vehicle while traveling to and from the individual's residence, workplace, school, and court ordered drug/alcohol education or treatment programs and only if the vehicle equipped with an approved ignition interlock device.[327] During the restricted driving period, the Secretary of State may also require the driver to submit to driving skills tests.[328]

The restricted license remains effective until a hearing officer orders an unrestricted license.[329] The individual who holds the restricted license only becomes eligible for an unrestricted license when the later of the following events occurs: court notification to the Secretary of State that the individual has successfully completed the DWI/sobriety court program, or upon the completion of the minimum license sanction that would have been imposed in absence of this section.[330] Because the law is written in the conjunctive, it appears that both of these events must occur. For example, if the minimum license sanction for a particular offender is one year, and they successfully completed the sobriety program in nine months, they still do not become eligible for the unrestricted license until the one-year sanction has lapsed. In contrast, if the one-year sanction lapses and the individual has yet to complete the sobriety program, the individual remains ineligible for the unrestricted license until they successfully completed the program.

13.9. Is a "First Offender" Plea an Option, to Keep Your Long-term Record Clean? In many states, if your OWI conviction is your first ever criminal conviction, and if you keep your subsequent criminal record clean for five years following this conviction, all record of this conviction can be expunged from your criminal record.[331] Because sentencing for subsequent OWI offenses is based on prior similar convictions, this is not an option for OWI convictions. Unfortunately, Michigan does not allow expungement of any OWI crimes under any circumstances.[332] Michigan has also made it difficult to attack the legal sufficiency of prior convictions. This is called a "collateral" attack, and is rarely an option in Michigan. However, if a collateral attack is possible, it can result in a great benefit to you, particularly if it causes a felony charge to become a misdemeanor.

13.10. Is a "Nolo" Plea or an "Alford" Plea Available, and will it Help You on your OWI Case in Avoiding License Loss or Protecting a Job? A plea of nolo contendere (or "no contest") means that while you do not admit to committing the crime, you do not contest the charge either. In accepting a no-contest plea, the judge will usually review the police report and chemical test reports and accept everything contained in them as true. In this way, the court is able to make out a "factual basis" for your plea. A "nolo" plea means you are willing to accept the punishment even though you do not admit to any guilt. Under certain circumstances a nolo plea may be allowed to an OWI charge in Michigan.[333] As it relates to the criminal matter however, keep in mind that while it may "sound" better, a nolo plea has exactly the same effect as a plea of guilty, and can be used for enhancement in the future. The effect on your driver's license is exactly the same as well. There may be a benefit if you face civil liability for the crime, such as where there has been a death or serious injury.

An "Alford plea" is a guilty plea where you do not admit that you did the act, yet you accept that the prosecution likely has enough evidence with which they could convict you. This plea originated in the United States Supreme Court case of *North Carolina v. Alford*, 400 U.S. 25 (1970). After the Alford decision, an "Alford" plea generally has the same effect as a plea of guilty with respect to sentencing. Later use of the conviction as an aggravating factor (if you are later convicted of another offense) is allowed in all courts. Your OWI specialist will know your situation, and counsel you as to the applicability as well as the benefits or lack thereof, of either of these pleas.

13.11. Is a Reduction to a Lesser Offense Always a Good Solution? Whether or not a reduction to a lesser offense from the OWI charges is in your best interest depends on your particular situation. An OWI specialist knows not only the law and the court in which your charges are pending, but also the likely results of your case. Just as importantly, your attorney has taken the time to know you and your situation.

There may be times when to have even a single OWI conviction on your criminal record can be devastating to your life, and the consequences can be even worse for additional OWI convictions. It may be that having such convictions on your record ruins your job or chances for promotion, or otherwise limits your ability to care for your family. On the other hand, to some in your position, getting the criminal case over with sooner rather than later, getting it behind you now rather than having it hanging around for a year or more is actually in your best interest.

There are also other times when accepting a reduction in your case may also not be in your best interest. Your attorney may feel you have an excellent chance of beating the charges against you. While this can never be promised with certainty, part of the reason you hired an OWI specialist is exactly for this expertise. The prosecution may be very willing to offer you a reduced charge precisely because they know the case against you is weak, or missing a critical element.

There may also be times when it is the punishment that matters to you and your life, not the crime of which you are convicted. It could be that you going to jail for whatever reason, having to pay a large fine or having to serve mandatory community service for any length of time, could be harmful to you or your family. When thinking about these issues, bear in mind that for a conviction of any misdemeanor, no matter what the misdemeanor, you are at least theoretically facing some jail time. You could face exactly the same punishment if you accept a guilty plea to a lesser charge rather than being found guilty on an OWI charge. In the end, it could be that a plea produces nothing of true value to you. Your OWI specialist will be best able to recommend which pathway is best for you, and help you sort out all of the various concerns.

13.12. How Long will a Conviction Stay on Your Record? In Michigan, any conviction stays on your record forever. So, if you ever plead anything but not guilty (guilty, nolo contendere, an "Alford" plea), or if you are subsequently convicted at trial of anything, you will always have this result on your criminal record. Some states do allow for its removal, and even Michigan allows for your record to be cleaned of any first misdemeanor offense (other than OWIs) after five years and assuming you commit no other criminal offenses.[334] When it comes to intoxicated driving, this is simply not an option.

13.13. The "Stipulated" Bench Trial or "Conditional Plea" to Set up Appeal. There may be times or circumstances when your attorney recommends that you go through a "stipulated" bench trial or a "conditional plea." This is done just so that a critical legal point in your case can be decided by a court superior to the one in which your trial is being held. These higher courts, "appellate courts," will not usually decide whether or not there has been an error in your case, until your case is "final". To get your case finalized, your attorney, the prosecutor and the judge may agree to proceed in this manner, even in spite of a significant disagreement of law. The thought is that if you are found not guilty under the debated view of the law, then there is no reason for you to appeal. If you are found guilty, then your case is final and the court of appeals will decide whether or not your trial court applied the right interpretation of the law.

A stipulated bench trial is where you go through an entire trial, but there are stipulations. A stipulation is an agreement between the prosecution and your defense attorney. Both attorneys and the judge may agree to proceed along one interpretation of the law, even while your attorney has noted on the record his or her objection.

A conditional plea is where you may plead guilty, nolo contendere or render an Alford plea (even though you feel you are innocent) in order to have some critical point of law in your favor presented to an appellate court because by making one of these pleas, your case is otherwise closed at the trial court level. Because Michigan law provides that you have no right to an appeal after a plea of guilty,[335] conditional pleas are not usually a viable option.

Either way, the decision to proceed, in spite of a disagreement in the law, is a difficult one to manage. It takes an experienced OWI attorney, who knows and understands the relevant law to be able to best make recommendations to you regarding these options. You are accepting a potentially difficult fate if you plead guilty or make a statement of accepting guilt, and betting on an appellate court to eventually find the law in your favor.

13.14. Is Punishment Going to be Worse After Trial? It is a common concern that if you go all the way through trial for your OWI charges and are convicted, you face a likely worse punishment than if you accept a negotiated plea bargain offered by the prosecutor. In other words, the concern is that the judge will impose a trial penalty. This may or may not be true. It may depend on the judge, the deal on the table, the factors that may come out at trial, and whether or not you take the stand and testify. Many judges believe that if you take the stand and say that you were not drunk driving, but you are later convicted, that you have committed perjury. On that basis alone, the judge may impose a more severe sentence.

Regardless of what happens, however, the sentence for an OWI conviction or guilty plea must stay within a mandated minimum and maximum. These are based on whether this is your first OWI offense, and if not your first OWI offense, the timing of your prior convictions.[336] If you face multiple charges, the maximum cumulative sentence if found guilty on all counts is likely to be longer than if you just accept a plea bargain to a single count. However, because multiple sentences can and often run concurrently, the actual amount of jail time you face is usually the same either way. On the other hand, if you are found not guilty of most of the charges against you, you face only penalties based on the remaining charges rather than all of the charges.

Chapter 14:

Using Motions Practice to Handicap the Prosecutor and Possibly Win in Court

14.1. Overview of this Chapter's Purpose. During the pendency of your case, and even during your trial, many questions of law may arise that the court is called upon to answer. Defenses or challenges may be asserted by your attorney before trial that cause the State to drop some or all of the charges. Your attorney makes some of these different requests of the court. The prosecutor can also assert motions in certain circumstances. When an attorney asks the court to do something or to decide something, this is called a "motion." The court either grants or denies the motion, based on both the law established by the legislature and the law that has been decided by appellate-level courts. On many issues that are "fact specific," decisions are often rendered based upon the personal and legal knowledge and opinion of the judge.

Because this is **your** defense for the **criminal charges** against **you**, you will be receiving a large number of forms (copies of the motions and the judge's decision on each motion) from your lawyer. It is best if you understand what each of these might mean. The purpose of this chapter is not to make you into a lawyer. It is instead to allow you to have a more intelligent conversation with your lawyer at any critical point during the legal proceedings so that you can help raise the best possible defense to your charges.

14.2. Challenging the Accusatory Document. To be held liable for a crime, the State, or the Federal government, has to inform you of the crime with which you are charged. The accusatory document can be as simple as the traffic citation itself, or it may be another particular form. The Michigan Constitution requires that this document be accurate so that the person being accused of the crime may raise an adequate defense.[337]

A demurrer (or motion to quash) is an attack by you against this accusatory document. A special demurrer is an attack on the FORM of the document - that the crime with which you are charged cannot be specified on this kind of document or that the document is lacking some essential "part." A general demurrer is a challenge to the SUBSTANCE of what is written in the document. In other words, does the accusatory document contain the correct information relating to stating all the elements of the offense rather than just some of the elements? If it is defective, you can ask the judge to throw out the criminal charges against you. The timing of when to bring this kind of challenge is very important, so that the prosecutor cannot just redo the paperwork correctly. Your OWI specialist will be familiar with Michigan's laws regarding how to assert the proper motion to quash (demurrer) at the appropriate time.

14.3. Statute of Limitations Challenges. A statute of limitations is the maximum time period determined by the Michigan legislature during which a criminal charge may be brought against you. The theory is that if what happened was too long ago, it will be too hard to defend against (witnesses have died, moved or forgotten details). For some crimes, no statute of limitations exists, such as murder.

Although it is very uncommon for a long period of time to elapse between your being stopped and your being charged with an OWI crime, if for some reason this has happened, your lawyer could bring a motion to dismiss the charges against you based on the statute of limitations being violated. In Michigan, all misdemeanors have a statute of limitations of six years, and this is true for misdemeanor OWI offenses as well.[338]

14.5. Speedy Trial. Unreasonable delay by the State to charge you with a crime can lead to a motion to dismiss or a motion to discharge you of the offense. This may occur because the process to bring your case to trial once you are charged has been too slow and your attorney might be able to get the charges dropped because of this unreasonably lengthy pace.[339] In Michigan, if you are arrested for a misdemeanor OWI and you remain in jail, your trial must occur within 28 days of your arraignment, unless you waive your right to a speedy trial or you are released.[340] However, these situations are very rare.

14.6. Pre-trial Motions. In an attempt to better define what issues and facts have to be decided at trial by either the jury or the judge, pre-trial motions may be filed by your attorney and heard by your judge before your trial begins. These concerns and questions are framed by the motions, and because they are made before the trial starts, they are called pre-trial motions. The answers the judge gives to these questions, called "rulings" or "orders" often determine whether or not the case even goes to trial and how much negotiating room your attorney has with the prosecution to obtain a reduction of the charges. Pre-trial motions may also assist the parties and the judge to determine an appropriate punishment, in the event of your conviction.

14.7. Motion in Limine - Latin for "threshold," a motion in limine is a request made at the start of a trial requesting the judge rule that certain evidence may not be introduced in trial.[341] An easy way to remember what "in limine" means is to think of this motion as being one to LIMIT the other side in some fashion.

These motions are very common in criminal trials where the admissibility of evidence is subject to constitutional or statutory limitations, such as suppression of your statements made without the Miranda warnings (reading your rights to you).[342] In a litigation-oriented OWI practice, these may be the most common and most successful motions brought before the court. They can be made either in writing or orally, if your state law does not mandate that the particular type of motion be put in writing. Prosecutors often object to these motions for lack of notice. Ultimately, it may be up to the judge to allow or disallow motions in limine.

The purpose of a motion in limine is to prevent certain evidence (usually proposed testimony) from ever being mentioned once the case is in front of the jury. If this motion is granted, neither the prosecution nor your attorney may mention the prohibited subject.[343] Both sides must caution their witnesses against mentioning the subject of the prohibited evidence. It must not be brought to the attention of the jury. If a witness violates the judge's order, a mistrial can be granted by the judge, thereby stopping the trial, and requiring that the entire trial proceeding be started over with a new jury.

A hearing is when the judge meets with both side's attorneys, usually in open court with a court reporter present. Either side can ask the judge to rule on motions (ask the judge to answer legal questions or to otherwise make a decision) based on witnesses and other evidence, including oral argument (oral presentations) from the attorneys. Because a motion in limine pertains to prohibiting testimony regarding a specific subject, those subject limits often can be determined with or without a hearing based on the lawyers submitting briefs (written documents that argue their side based on the statutes or prior case law). It is at the judge's discretion whether or not the lawyers get a chance for a hearing or for oral argument.

14.8. Motion to Suppress. This is a motion (filed on behalf of a criminal defendant) to disallow certain evidence (usually some form of tangible property or "thing") in an upcoming trial from ever being considered by the jury. Example: a written confession which you allege was signed while you were drunk or without the reading of your Miranda rights. Probably the most common such motion in an OWI case, however, is a motion to suppress the chemical evidence.

Motions to suppress have to do with the question of whether evidence (property) that has been seized is admissible at trial or not.[344] These motions determine critical evidentiary issues and "frame" the issues the jury will hear. Different than a motion in limine, a motion to suppress generally must be made in writing and the motion also must raise a constitutional issue.[345] You will know if your attorney has made this kind of motion when you get a copy of it.

The Fourth Amendment of the Constitution of the United States prohibits the taking of anyone's property (a seizure) by the police unless there is a legal basis and specific reason for allowing the taking.[346] Some constitutional right is usually at question in a motion to suppress because it usually involves a seizure by the police or other law enforcement. Testimony is typically required by the ones who either ordered the seizure or carried out the seizure. The hearing is held to determine whether or not the seizure was legally valid. That being the case, a pre-trial hearing is required so that each side may question and counter-question those giving sworn testimony before the judge.

14.9. Jackson Denno Hearings and Related Challenges. In your case, your lawyer may want to argue that any confession or admission that you made at the time of your OWI arrest was not voluntary, and if it was not voluntary, then the jury should not be allowed to hear anything about it.[347] This is a very uncommon situation in an OWI arrest because so much of the evidence is based on either the field sobriety tests done by the law enforcement officer at the scene or on medical/scientific tests. Yet, some officers are very good at tricking people into uttering incriminating statements after custody is already clear.

14.10. Double Jeopardy. It is against the Fifth Amendment of the United States Constitution for anyone to be held criminally accountable twice for the same issue by the same sovereign.[348] What this means is that you cannot be made to stand trial a second time for any of your actions if the first trial regarding these actions was complete enough to be lawful.

However, several important exceptions to this rule exist. Because Michigan is a separate sovereign (independent government) from the federal government, each may try you for the same set of circumstances if your actions are possibly against their law and they had jurisdiction (legal control) over you or the events at the time they occurred. Second, your legal situation only reaches a level where double jeopardy applies at a certain point in the proceedings. If the trial get stopped before that (usually due to a "mistrial"), you have no constitutional protection against a second trial in most instances. If a prosecutor or judge makes an error at your trial, certain facts may block a new trial after a mistrial is granted. These are rare, but provide a total victory for you if it occurs.[349] This is yet another reason to have the best lawyer you can find, so that if something happens, they know when to pull the plug on your proceedings, and when not to, to protect your best interests.

Although the implied consent hearing at which your drivers' license is suspended immediately following an OWI arrest may seem like a criminal trial, the only question is whether or not you should lose a property interest (that is your driver's license).[350] Your driver's license is not a right that you have, but instead a privilege from the state that granted it to you. This administrative hearing is a determination if this privilege should be revoked. This is a different issue than your criminal process, by which your liberty interests are at stake (that is they can put you in jail, put you on probation, or penalize you with fines and community service[351]). Because there are different interests at stake, the issue at hand is not the same, and having to go through both proceedings is not double jeopardy.

14.10.1. "Same Conduct"—Procedural Double Jeopardy. Until recently, if the conduct causing your arrest was such that you are or could be charged with several different crimes, that are all known to the prosecutor, and can be all tried in the same court, then a trial on one issue precludes a subsequent trial on any of the other possible offenses.[352] In other words, if you were speeding at the time of your stop by the police, then found to be possibly OWI, if you are tried only for the speeding by a court that could have also heard the OWI, by a prosecutor who knew about the OWI question, you cannot later be tried on the OWI.[353] However, this rule was overturned three years later[354] which instead incorporates the "same element test."[355] If you have any questions, your OWI specialist will be able to help you.

14.10.2. Prosecution of one Offense Bars Prosecution of Others. If you are charged with more than one crime (different counts), and one or more of these counts are dismissed, the State has the option of appealing the dismissal immediately or proceeding with the prosecution of the other counts. If the prosecution elects to proceed on the remaining counts, you cannot later be tried on the counts that were dismissed (and NOT appealed by the prosecutor) because of double jeopardy.

14.10.3. Municipal Versus State Prosecutions. Only certain types of cases can be heard in the different levels or types of court. If you are tried in a court that has a very limited ability to hear only specific crimes, a court with a broader or more general ability to consider these cases can still try you on the other counts without a claim of double jeopardy. An example would be if you were charged with following too closely and OWI, the first charge may be properly brought in a municipal traffic court or a local magistrate judge. Michigan law might provide that this court cannot hear intoxicated driving cases. In such a case, it is possible that the OWI could be tried later in a State, Circuit or Superior court.

14.10.4. Plea Constitutes Jeopardy. Once you plead guilty before a trial judge and this plea is properly recorded and accepted by the judge, this constitutes jeopardy, for which your sentence cannot be changed.[356] Once a guilty plea is entered, you cannot be retried on the charge due to double jeopardy protections.

14.10.5. Instances where Prosecution Barred. Your attorney may assert a legal argument in your case that seeks to obtain a ruling from your judge that subsequent prosecution is barred. As noted above, if the subsequent charges against you arose out of the same transaction for which you have already been tried, double jeopardy applies, banning the second trial. Other situations might arise, such as your paperwork being drawn up incorrectly by the state, where the prosecutor tries to add charges at an improper time. This can bar a subsequent prosecution if a jury has already been empanelled. As these situations can be legally challenging to the court, this is yet another reason to have the best OWI lawyer possible.

14.10.6. Instances where Prosecution not Barred. In certain situations, a subsequent prosecution is not barred after your trial has been "terminated" by mistrial. Prosecutors can file what is called a nolle prosequi on charges. This is a dismissal of these charges against you. It is usually based upon a decision that to prosecute you at this time is not in the best interest of the government. So long as the statute of limitations has not expired, the prosecutor can change his or her mind and prosecute you later. If a prior termination of your legal proceedings was proper, or if you are being subsequently charged for a transaction that was not the same as your prior trial, you may be able to be prosecuted.

14.10.7. Direct Appeal—when is it Available? If your lawyer argues to the court that double jeopardy protections should be applied to your subsequent prosecution before trial, and he or she loses the argument, your lawyer may be able to directly appeal this decision to a higher court without waiting for the results of the second trial.[357] The reason for this is that if the legal issue is decided in your favor, you will walk away from the charges "Scot free."

14.11. Motion to Sever – or Severance. In a criminal trial practice, this is a separating of some part of the overall proceedings by court order, such as separate trials for criminal defendants who were charged with the same crime. Such division of issues in a trial is sometimes also called "bifurcation."

Severance is granted in criminal proceedings when a joint trial might be unfair. In a criminal trial, there may be times when there are two defendants charged with the same crime, and it might be fairer to try them separately rather than together. Believe it or not, when a police officer does not see which person drove the vehicle, he or she may charge both of the people in the vehicle with OWI. The defense attorneys representing each defendant could then file a motion to sever the trials with the court to accomplish this.

14.12. Plea of Autrefois Acquittal. "Autrefois" is a French word, now part of English criminal law terminology which means "in the past." It refers to an accused who cannot be tried for a crime because the record shows he has already been subjected to trial for the same conduct and was acquitted. If the accused maintains that the previous trial resulted in conviction, he or she pleads "autrefois convict." "Autrefois attaint" is another similar term; "attainted" for a felony, a person cannot be tried again for the same offense. These types of motion rarely arise in an OWI practice. Your OWI specialist will be familiar with how to use these "tools" if the occasion arises in your case.

14.13. Similar Transactions. In general, evidence that you have committed a "prior act" that is similar to the one presently charged, is inadmissible.[358] You are supposed to be tried for the present charges only, and not have your character impugned by raising prior conduct. In other words, someone with a long criminal record should not automatically be assumed to have committed another crime.

However, if you or your legal counsel raises some issue of character, what you present can be rebutted by the prosecutor. Example - Just because you have 15 speeding tickets cannot normally be presented in a speeding case. However, if you take the stand and testify as to just how careful a driver you are, in an attempt to convince the jury you are not prone to drink and drive, the prosecution may introduce evidence of your prior speeding tickets to challenge these claims which were made under oath.

Michigan allows a prosecutor to introduce "prior act" evidence if some purpose can be asserted and proven by the prosecutor.[359] For example, if you were alleged to have been the driver of a vehicle involved in a "hit and run" case, and (when the police found your car) you were not around, the State may seek to introduce the fact that you had a prior intoxicated driving conviction to try to prove "identity" of you as the driver of the hit and run.

Like all evidence, the judge performs a balancing act.[360] In the foregoing example about a hit and run case, the judge may not allow the prosecutor to use "similar act" evidence. If evidence is important to the case, it has a prejudicial effect on one of the parties involved, hurting either the State's or the defendant's case. The judge balances this harm against how important the information is to prove some "missing" element of the charges you are facing.

14.14. Motion to recuse. This is a request by either the prosecutor or your attorney to have your original judge removed and to be replaced by another judge. Sometimes the grounds for recusal arise due to a conflict of interest or some other good reason (acquaintanceship with one of the parties, for example).

Recusal also applies to a judge being removed or voluntarily removing himself/herself from a criminal case in which he/she has a conflict of interest, such as friendship or known enmity to you.[361] This is why your attorney may ask you if you personally know any judges, any other lawyers, or have had a bad experience with anyone in the local judiciary before.

14.15. OWI-related Affirmative Defenses. An affirmative defense is a claim by the defendant that there was either a good reason why he or she committed the otherwise criminal act or that for some reason they were justified in doing the act. If assessed properly, and if accepted by the jury, an affirmative defense constitutes a complete exoneration of the offense that you have been accused of committing. Once you claim an affirmative defense, the burden starts with your attorney to put forth a preponderance of the evidence to establish the affirmative defense and then the burden shifts back to the prosecutor to disprove it.[362]

14.15.1. Entrapment. In criminal law, entrapment is the act of law enforcement officers or government agents inducing or encouraging you to commit a crime when you have expressed no desire to commit it. The key to entrapment is whether the idea for the commission or encouragement of the criminal act originated with the police or government agents instead of with the supposed "criminal." Entrapment, if proved, is a complete defense to a criminal prosecution. The factual question the court (the judge or jury) has to answer is: Would you have drunk the alcohol and driven his vehicle if not pressed by the police officer?

14.15.2. Involuntary Intoxication. Intoxication is the condition of being drunk as the result of consuming an excessive quantity of alcoholic beverages or narcotics. As it applies to drunk driving (OWI) intoxication can come from alcohol alone, or from a combination of alcohol and narcotics or prescription medications which would produce the same effect even though the amount of alcohol may be below the per se limit. Involuntary intoxication is an affirmative defense to specific intent crimes, for which you have the burden of proof by a preponderance of the evidence, that you voluntarily consumed a legally obtained and properly used medication or other substance and did not know and reasonably should not have known that he or she would become intoxicated or impaired.[363] However, as OWI's are general intent crimes, this defense is generally invalid in Michigan. On the other hand, if you were to claim an unexpected reaction (involuntary intoxication) of prescription medication with moderate alcohol use, you would be raising an insanity claim and statutory notice and procedures must be followed, including obtaining a forensic evaluation establishing your temporary insanity by involuntary intoxication.[364]

14.15.3. Automatism Defense. Automatism refers to behavior performed in a state of unconsciousness or semi-consciousness such that the behavior cannot be deemed volitional. This unconscious or semi-conscious state may be brought about by any one of a variety of circumstances including epilepsy, stroke, concussion, or involuntary intoxication. In those cases that have discussed automatism, evidence supporting that defense is generally in the form of testimony by law enforcement officers or medical experts.[365] Under the appropriate circumstances, automatism can be used as a defense to an intoxicated driving charge, and in this context the defense serves as a way to avoid culpability because the act of the driving itself was not volitional.

In Missoula, the defendant driver ran one stop sign then slammed her brakes on at another. She had slurred speech and her breath smelled of alcohol. The officer unsuccessfully attempted to administer field sobriety tests, and the driver refused to give a breath sample. Before trial the driver claimed that she'd been given a date rape drug. She raised an automatism defense arguing not that there was involuntary intoxication but rather that the drug precluded her ability to form the intent to drive voluntarily or be in actual physical control of the vehicle.

In analyzing the defense, the court agreed that drinking a non-intoxicating quantity of alcohol is not illegal, and posed the question this way: "what if prior to driving on the night she was arrested, the defendant drank a non-alcoholic beverage such as a glass of water or a soft drink that unbeknownst to her contained a "date rape" drug? Under the State's theory, she would still be guilty of DUI. The court was apprehensive of this position because, as stated in the opinion, it is a basic premise of Anglo–American criminal law that the physical conduct and the state of mind must concur, and when a crime requires certain attendant circumstances, those circumstances must concur with the conduct and the fault as well.

In this case the defendant argued that she could demonstrate by several independent witnesses and medical professionals that she was drugged against her will, that she did not exercise "independent judgment" in taking a "date rape" drug that resulted in her impairment, and that her act of driving was result of an "independent event"—the drugging.

Provided the appropriate notice was given to the prosecutor, the court concluded that the defendant would be entitled to raise automatism as an affirmative defense in this case, but that she would bear the burden of proving the affirmative defense at trial. Therefore, in the instant case, in order to prove her automatism defense by reason of someone allegedly putting a "date rape" drug in her drink, she would have to prove by admissible evidence that she did not act voluntarily when she drove her vehicle. This evidence may include expert medical or pharmacological evidence, non-expert evidence, or a combination of both. It remains always the State's obligation to prove every element of the offense charged beyond a reasonable doubt. Thus, to the extent that the defendant offers admissible evidence supporting her automatism defense that she did not act voluntarily, it will remain the State's burden to prove that she did act voluntarily beyond a reasonable doubt.

14.15.4. Justification or "Necessity" Defense. Circumstances may arise such that you may be justified in driving drunk. For example, while intoxicated, if you are trying to save another person's life, society might consider it justified for you to drive. An example would be if you were legally intoxicated, and your wife who was 8½ months pregnant went into labor and no one else was available to drive her to the hospital. However, true necessity is nearly impossible to establish. In nearly every circumstance, the court will require you to call 911 rather than try to solve the emergency yourself by driving while intoxicated.

14.15.5. Ignorance Defense. In some crimes, not knowing what you are doing, or ignorance, is a defense to being punished for the crime. This is not true for OWI offenses.

Chapter 15:
Bench Verses Jury Trials

15.0. Purpose of this Chapter - The purpose of this chapter is to help you understand the two types of trial available to you, bench trials and jury trials, and how the two differ. Also, this chapter will help you understand why your attorney may recommend one type of trial over another.

Simply stated, a bench trial is a trial before only the judge, without a jury being present. Instead of the jury deciding the issues of fact (like whether or not you are guilty of driving while intoxicated), it is the judge who makes this decision. In a jury trial, the judge decides issues of law (i.e., which evidence is admissible and which is not) while the jury decides issues of fact. So, do you want the judge or a jury deciding the issues of fact in your case?

15.1. Who gets to Opt for a "Bench" Trial or a Jury Trial? It is a fundamental right for anyone facing any criminal trial, including misdemeanors like OWI,[366] to have a jury if they want one.[367] To opt out of a jury trial and have only the judge decide your innocence or guilt, you must knowingly, voluntarily and intentionally (also written as "expressly, intelligently and personally") waive your right to a jury trial,[368] and in Michigan, you must get the consent of the prosecutor and the court.[369] The reason you need the consent of the prosecutor is because in Michigan, the "State" also has the right to have the case heard by a jury as well. Both sides must agree to allow the judge to be the fact-finder rather than the jury to have a bench trial.

15.2. Why would Your Attorney Prefer a Bench Trial or a Jury Trial? A number of factors go into a decision to have a bench trial rather a jury trial, or the other way around. The first factor goes directly to your attorney's knowledge of the judge's prior rulings on OWI issues, as well as the judge's basic sense of fairness. Your experienced OWI lawyer may personally know of the judge's record, may know the prosecutor, may have tried both bench and jury trials in the specific court where your trial will be held. Based on this experience, your lawyer may recommend a bench trial. The true test comes down to this: Can you expect a jury of randomly selected citizens to be any better at deciding this case than this judge?

Other reasons for a bench or a jury trial go to the facts of the case. If strong emotions are involved (someone died in the accident related to your alleged OWI offense or if people in the other vehicle suffered significant injuries), if you have prior OWI convictions that the jury will learn about at trial, a fair minded judge might be a much better choice than leaving the decision of your guilt or innocence to a jury who may be more easily swayed by your prior driving history rather than the facts and the law. In other situations, an experienced OWI lawyer may know that the judge scheduled to try your case has a poor "barometer" of guilt or innocence.

Jury trials involve numerous steps, processes and procedures not present in a bench trial. These "steps" include the judge providing the jury with some orientation, instructions and oaths,[370] and the selecting or empanelling of the jury (something that can sometimes take half a day or more in an OWI trial). In presenting the case to the jury, the lawyers will almost always take longer to elucidate their side than if before the judge. The opening statements and closing arguments are longer and more detailed. In addition, the time it takes a jury to deliberate (decide guilt or innocence) can often run from hours to several days.

If you are paying your attorney by the hour, this extra time will add to the cost of your legal bill. Also, in order to explain things to a jury, your lawyer may need to use different or additional expert witnesses. These expert witnesses might be necessary to help bring the jurors "up to speed" about your legal defense. These different or extra experts cost money out of your pocket. Also, if the jury trial requires more days in court than a bench trial, this will also add to your defense expenses because while you are in court, you are not at work making money. Despite these differences, some lawyers charge the same for bench of jury trials. You should consult your fee agreement if you are not sure.

On the other hand, based on your attorney's knowledge of your case, his or her knowledge of the different courts, prosecutors and judges, and his or her experience with the juries in the jurisdiction in which your OWI trial will be held, good reasons may exist why a jury trial is your only realistic chance to win your case. Certain types of cases are usually not good candidates for a bench trial. For example, if your case involves a breath test result of 0.10% and your defense is that your high protein diet may have caused a false, elevated reading; few judges would accept this defense as a reason to disregard the test result and find you not guilty.

15.3. Who is Present at Either Type of Trial? Unless otherwise determined by order of the judge, both types of trial are open to the public. Therefore, there may be an audience. However, most trials have no observers other than the lawyers, the witnesses, court personnel, bailiff and court reporter.

Otherwise, in either type of trial, you and your lawyer will be present. Your lawyer may have a paralegal or associate, an assistant or a secretary with him or her, and these people usually sit with you or just behind your table. You will sit at one of the two tables in the middle of the room, in front of the audience section for the public. The prosecutor will be present and will sit at the other table for legal counsel. Typically, the only person sitting with the prosecutor is the "officer in charge," which is almost always the arresting officer in your case.

The judge will be present, as will a court reporter, both usually sitting at the front of the courtroom. The judge's desk (bench) is often elevated, and in the name of security, may be behind a complex platform. Other people from the judge's office, the clerk or a secretary may or may not be present, and they often sit near the judge's bench. The court bailiff (the person who calls witnesses into court from a waiting room or the outer hallway) and a member of the sheriff's department (especially if you are coming to trial from the jail) may also be present in court for security purposes.

Those who are to be witnesses either for the prosecution or for you may be present in the courtroom until just before the trial starts. Either the prosecutor or your lawyer may invoke the "Rule of Sequestration."[371] If invoked, all witnesses who are going to testify (with the notable exception of the officer in charge) must physically leave the courtroom and wait outside. This is done so that their own testimony is not patterned after or "improved" by hearing any other witness' testimony. As each witness is called, the bailiff goes to the waiting area and retrieves that witness.

15.4. How Long will Your Trial Take? A bench trial is almost always shorter in duration than a jury trial. The same witnesses testify, and often the same evidence is admitted to the court. However, because a bench trial is usually two lawyers (the prosecutor and your defense attorney) presenting evidence and testimony to another lawyer (the judge), the flow of information is often quicker and more efficient when compared to having to present information and evidence to a jury of lay citizens, as is the questioning of witnesses and the presentation of physical evidence. Also, when presenting a case to a jury, it is often necessary to spend a great deal of time "laying foundations" for the admission of evidence or testimony. These foundations are typically unnecessary with a bench trial. Finally, when a judge is deciding the case, the opening and closing arguments are either much shorter or possibly even waived altogether by either or both sides. This is because the judge already knows the fine legal points relating to OWI law, so no lengthy explanations are needed by the attorneys.

In addition, because there is no jury, the jury selection process is eliminated, cutting out several hours in a typical OWI trial. Jury trials also involve numerous steps, processes and procedures not present in a bench trial. These "steps" include the judge providing the jury with some orientation, instructions and oaths,[372] and the selecting or empanelling of the jury (something that can sometimes take half a day or more in an OWI trial). In presenting the case to the jury, the lawyers will almost always take longer to explain things than they would to the judge. The opening statements and closing arguments are longer and more detailed. In addition, the time it takes a jury to deliberate (decide guilt or innocence) can often run from hours to several days. In a bench trial, no jurors are questioned or sworn in, nor does the judge need to read the jury instructions at the end of the trial, and then wait for a jury to make a decision.

Thus, a jury trial for an OWI which might take several days is often compressed into a two to eight hour time frame in a bench trial for the same legal issue.

15.5. What is Lost by Opting for a Bench Trial Instead of a Jury Trial? Certain types of cases such as breath or blood test per se alcohol cases usually are best heard by a jury. This is true in part because many judges are invested in the belief that breath and blood testing is always reliable and accurate. Judges are simply not likely, in most circumstances, to disregard a breath or blood test and find you not guilty of UBAL. This is yet another reason to use a skilled OWI lawyer who can help assess the judge.

In other types of cases, such as a case with a sympathetic defendant, a skilled lawyer may be able to sway a jury better than they might be able to sway a judge. At other times, the opposite may be true. In making its decision, a jury can vote "guilty" or "not guilty" on the charges based on a multitude of issues regardless of how the judge words the "instructions" on the law that they must apply to the case. A criminal defense lawyer with strong persuasive skills can often sway a jury to vote "not guilty."

15.6. What may be Gained by Choosing a Bench Trial Rather than a Jury Trial? Because bench trials are often shorter in duration than are jury trials, they are cheaper if you are paying your lawyer by the hour. Some "flat fee" attorneys charge less for bench trials in their fee agreements. As noted above, it is often quicker to get a bench trial than to set up a jury trial. A bench trial may be a better option if the key to winning your trial rests upon a "legal" issue being decided in your favor. For example, if all pre-trial issues are heard as part of a bench trial, then a favorable ruling on a motion to suppress for an illegal stop will win the entire case, and the prosecutor cannot appeal the judge's decision. However, some judges will require that these issues be raised before the bench trial, effectively precluding this rational.

15.7. Who Testifies at Your Trial? In many cases, the testimony, and who gives it, will be the same at a jury trial and at a bench trial. At times, your attorney may add or delete a witness when a judge hears the case without a jury. This is the exception rather than the rule.

In their case-in-chief, the prosecution will put up the officer who first decided that your vehicle needed to be stopped, or the witness who first thought your driving was suspicious and that you were driving under the influence. If another officer administered your field sobriety tests, this officer will testify. If a different officer or technician did your breath, urine or blood tests, this person will often also be requested to testify.

In a breath test case, the prosecution may need to have a witness testify concerning the machine's periodic simulator reports as this testimony is usually necessary to show that the machine was in good working order. If you underwent a blood or urine test, the person who drew your blood or watched you urinate as well as the person who actually did the laboratory test may testify. The prosecution may also have other fact witnesses testify if this information may help prove their case against you.

Once the prosecution has rested (finished putting up the evidence and testimony they think is required to convict you of OWI), you and your attorney will decide whether or not to present any evidence. In some cases, you may testify. It is highly likely the two of you will have discussed this alternative extensively before trial, but the final decision is often made in the midst of your trial. Unlike the rules for civil cases, in a criminal trial you cannot be forced to testify.[373] As will be discussed below, the prosecution has the burden of proving you guilty. Therefore, you have no burden of proof and you can remain silent.[374]

Your attorney may also have one or more experts prepared to testify. Expert testimony is often helpful and sometimes necessary to refute or dispute the prosecution's witnesses. Also, your attorney may have other "fact witnesses" testify as to other issues that might be legally relevant to your arrest. For example, a person who was with you all evening may testify that you drank only two beers over a three hour period, and that you acted totally sober. The order in which each of these defense witnesses is presented, including your testimony, will depend on an assessment of how best to present your side of the story.

After your side (the defense) rests, the prosecution has the option of putting on rebuttal witnesses to testify. These can be some of the same witnesses as they put before the court during their case-in-chief, or they can be new witnesses. This testimony is supposed to refute or dispute anything your witnesses said or other documentary evidence your side introduced.

After any rebuttal evidence by the State, you and your lawyer get a chance to rebut anything the prosecution's rebuttal witnesses said, or any new evidence they put before the court. This stage of the case is called "surrebuttal." This may be some of the same witnesses you used during your defense, or they can be new witnesses. The use of rebuttal and surrebuttal witnesses is often a matter of strategy and requires a thorough understanding of the intricacies of trial and the art of persuasion.

15.8. Who will not be Allowed to be a Juror? If you elect to have a jury trial, the first part of the trial is the empanelling of your jury. The United States Constitution does not forbid Michigan from establishing relevant qualifications for jurors.[375] In Michigan, to be on a jury, you must be 18 years old or older, be able to speak English, be mentally and physically able to serve as a juror and have not committed a felony.[376] Michigan pulls juror's names from those who have a Michigan driver's license. Also, you must live within the jurisdiction of the court to serve as a juror in that court. Thus, courts that reside in communities that are traditionally thought of as conservative tend to have a more conservative jury pool. A common requirement or qualification in most regions is that a juror be a qualified elector or voter of the county or district in which the trial will be held or hold a valid Michigan driver's license.

However, anyone called may also ask to be excused. Typical excuses include professional or personal duties which would make serving on a jury difficult as well as being age 70 or older.[377]

15.8.1. "Striking" a Jury: Eliminating the Bad Jurors. At the start of your jury trial, both the prosecutor and your attorney get a chance to eliminate potential jurors from a larger pool based on several factors, to form the actual 6 or 12 person jury that will serve for your trial. In Michigan, every jury for a felony case has 12 members (unless you agree otherwise),³⁷⁸ and must come to a unanimous verdict. The jury for a misdemeanor OWI will have six members, and must also reach a unanimous decision.

Based on "voir dire", prospective jurors can be eliminated from the jury pool by the judge or the attorneys either "for cause" or based on a "peremptory challenge." This concept of "elimination" rather than "picking" jurors may surprise you, since some people think that each lawyer gets to ADD selective jurors to the ultimate panel.

15.8.2. Is Jury Questioning ("*Voir Dire*") Available? Voir dire (vwahr [with a near-silent "r"] deer), loosely translated from French, means "to speak the truth." It is the questioning of prospective jurors by a judge and the attorneys in court to assist in the final selection of the actual jury. It is available any time a jury is involved in a jury trial.³⁷⁹ Voir dire is used to determine if a juror is biased and/or cannot deal with the issues involved in a particular kind of case fairly. As mentioned before, each attorney's job is to not allow a juror to serve if he or she has knowledge of the facts; acquaintanceship with parties, witnesses or attorneys; engages in an occupation which might lead to bias; prejudice against drinking and driving; or has had previous experiences that have left him or her with an indelible "impression" that would cause that juror to favor or disfavor one side.

Actually, one of the unspoken purposes of the voir dire is for the attorneys to get a feel for the personalities and likely views of the people on the jury panel. When the attorneys are permitted to actively participate and question the jurors, your chances of acquittal are usually improved. In some courts the judge asks most and perhaps even all of the questions. In others, the lawyers are given substantial latitude and ample time to ask questions.³⁸⁰ The trend is to limit the time allowed during voir dire, and it is becoming increasingly common for judges in Michigan to disallow the attorneys to conduct any voir dire. The court rules and case law in Michigan are solidly behind taking voir dire away from the parties. Acquittals are more difficult to obtain if the judge does all of the voir dire.

Following the voir dire, the judge and the attorneys will have a brief conference. Then, after all eliminations for "cause" are established, the remaining panel is "struck." The final jury is the "remainder" after the lawyers use their limited number of "strikes" for peremptory challenges.

15.8.3. For Cause – Unlimited. A Challenge for Cause is a request by a party to the judge that a prospective juror be dismissed due to a specific and important reason that the juror has prejudged the case or has somehow indicated that he or she cannot be fair, unbiased or is otherwise not capable of serving impartially as a juror.[381] Such challenges are based upon answers given to questions during voir dire (see above). A challenge for cause includes for example where a juror discloses that they have a close acquaintanceship with you, one of the attorneys or a witness.[382] The general categories out of which challenges for cause might arise are more broadly set forth in Michigan court rules.[383] A potential juror's answers showing obvious prejudice or an inability to serve due to a mental condition, inability to hear well or a language barrier can also lead to exclusion.

In making a challenge for cause, your attorney must articulate the specific reason he or she believes the juror is disqualified. If the judge agrees, then the judge will "grant" the challenge, and the potential juror will be excused. A new juror will then be selected from the jury pool, and will be seated in the spot vacated by the excused juror. If the judge disagrees with your attorney's arguments, then the challenge will be denied. In this way, the judge determines if the potential juror shall be dismissed.[384] The judge's discretion is not without guidelines however, and a judge can create reversible error if he or she refuses to remove a juror for cause when grounds exist that the juror should have been removed. An unlimited number of challenges for cause can be raised.

15.8.4. Peremptory Challenges. The other type of challenge is called a "peremptory" challenge. With a peremptory challenge, both the prosecutor and the defendant can ask for a particular juror to be excused without stating a reason.[385] The court must grant these challenges, but they are limited in number. Experienced trial attorneys develop a sort of "sixth sense" for knowing when a juror is "against" his or her client's case. The decision to remove a juror may come down to a lack of eye contact or negative body language. A peremptory challenge will also commonly be used after a challenge for cause has been made unsuccessfully, or where the juror has given answers that suggest bias, but do not rise to the level of a challenge for cause.

The number of peremptory challenges for each side is controlled by the number of parties on trial in a case (usually there is only one party in an OWI).[386] For most misdemeanor OWI cases, each party will have 3 peremptory challenges. Further, if a case has substantial publicity or other good cause more peremptory challenges may be requested.[387] The selection process may be by the use of "silent" strikes, where the list of qualified jurors is passed back and forth between the attorneys, with the prosecutor striking first, and then alternating "strikes." Another method is for the attorneys to either "accept" or "excuse" each juror, starting with number 1 and progressing until a jury of either 6 or 12 is selected.

There are some limits to the use of peremptory challenges. For example, peremptory challenges must be based on some other reason than race,[388] gender[389] or religious affiliation. Either side can challenge any pattern of eliminating jurors based on race, gender or religious affiliation alone, without having a legitimate, identifiable "dislike" about the juror's background or answers during jury selection questioning.

15.8.5. Background Information on Jurors: can Your Attorney get it? Unlike what you may see in the movies or on television, in a jury trial for misdemeanors like OWI, neither the prosecutor nor the defense attorney typically gets an advanced list of potential jurors or more than a few details about the prospective juror's background information. Usually, the list of jurors arrives minutes before the selection begins.

As jurors report for jury duty, before they are ever assigned to any trial, they are typically asked to fill out a brief questionnaire, giving such information as their name, age, occupation, marital status, employment history, any prior personal litigation experience with the courts (criminal or civil) and possibly if they have prior experience of serving on a jury. They are also asked to indicate if they have any prior law enforcement experience or if they have ever been an elected official, if they have a criminal history, and whether or not they have ever been involved in an alcohol related traffic accident. The attorneys get a copy of this questionnaire and a list of the juror's names just before the pool of prospective jurors comes into the courtroom. Some courts will allow attorneys to review this information prior to trial, but this depends on court policy and whether or not the questionnaires are actually available when the request is made.

15.8.6. What if jurors Don't tell the Truth at *Voir Dire*? If a prospective juror makes a misstatement during voir dire with no deliberate attempt to mislead, this will not usually authorize a new trial if you are convicted in the first trial.[390] If such an issue is discovered, your attorney may file a motion for a new trial alleging that a juror was not truthful during the voir dire. The motion will cause an inquiry into the "good faith" (or lack of good faith) in the misstatement, and the judge will decide the significance of the situation.

15.9. What is the Procedure for Conducting Your Trial? Both bench and jury trials follow a similar pattern. However, a jury trial has more stages or steps that must be completed in a specific order and fashion. Hence, jury trials usually take longer to complete.

The procedure for either type of trial starts with everyone (but the jury if a jury trial) gathering in a courtroom. You and your defense team gather around one table, while the prosecution and their team gathers around another. Only after everyone else is present does the judge enter. The bailiff usually announces the judge coming in. When the judge enters the courtroom, it is expected for you to stand until you are told to take your seat.

Next, the judge and the lawyers involved with your case may have some preliminary discussions on whether everyone is ready to proceed, or the judge may ask if any unresolved issues need to be discussed (before the jury enters the courtroom). Often, some off the cuff or lighthearted comment may be made between the attorneys and the judge, so do not be alarmed by this. You need not be annoyed or feel that your attorney is fraternizing with the opponent. The fact that this "familiarity" between the judge and your attorney exists is usually an excellent sign for your case. The more open and related all the attorneys are with each other, the better it will be for your case. (Yes, the judge is one of the attorneys!)

The judge will then more formally ask each side if they are ready to proceed. The prosecutor is typically required to answer first, followed by your attorney. If either says no, your trial is halted so that the judge can look into the cause or the reason for any delay. If it is due to the defense, this may not be good, unless the State caused a problem with your lawyer being ready to proceed. If some violation of the discovery rules by the prosecutor has occurred, your charges may be dropped. This may also occur if key witnesses for the prosecution are not present. The judge may grant either side an "adjournment" or a reset of the trial date if good cause can be shown that justifies the present delay.

If both announce "ready", if it is a bench trial, the prosecutor starts with his or her opening remarks. In a jury trial, the jury must first be empaneled. At this point in a jury trial, the judge will instruct the bailiff to bring the prospective jurors into the courtroom. It is usually a good idea to stand any time the jury enters or leaves the courtroom. This is done out of respect for their position as your "decision-makers."

The bailiff will provide for both the prosecutor and your attorney a brief summary of some personal details of each potential juror. The details deal with job data, marital status, age, etc. The idea behind giving the attorneys some background information is to shorten the process and give both sides some basic information that both lawyers will likely need to know.

Once everyone is again seated, the judge will have some preliminary remarks or "qualifying" questions for the jury. The judge may administer an oath to the jury pool, or may have the clerk do this. Next, the judge may describe for the jury the charges you are facing and the expected duration of the trial. The judge may ask the jurors some questions, either as a group or individually. Then, assuming that your judge allows the attorney(s) from each side to ask questions, both sides are permitted to ask additional questions.

The judge will ask the prosecutor to conduct his or her questions of the jury panel. The prosecutor will likely stand up, often at a podium between the two counsel tables, though in some courtrooms, the attorneys are able to walk about freely, and may stand directly before the jury. He or she will first introduce themselves, and then ask some general questions that have to do with whether or not any member of the jury pool would have trouble being a disinterested and fair juror. These questions are typically of the type that can be answered "yes" or "no," with each member of the pool raising his or her number if they are saying yes.

Once these general questions are finished and the prosecutor has again taken his or her seat, your attorney will stand up, greet the jurors, and introduce himself or herself and introduce you. Your attorney may ask you to stand briefly for your introduction. He or she will then ask general questions of the jury pool.

During the questioning by either attorney, the other attorney may object to the form or the content of a question. The judge will make a ruling each time that either allows the question or rejects the question as being a proper area for inquiry. The judge may need to confer with the attorneys at the bench (the judge's elevated desk), or ask the jurors to take a short break outside of the courtroom for purposes of letting both attorneys put all of the details of the challenge or objection "on the record" before making a ruling.

During voir dire, each attorney may also be allowed to ask each juror individually some very pointed questions, using the information that was divulged during the general questions or taken from the information sheet that each juror completed before coming into court. The prosecution asks his or her individual questions, followed by your attorney, for each potential juror in turn. It is important for you to take notes as to how you think each potential juror is responding, how forthcoming you think each is being, or how favorable you think each might be toward you, based on demeanor or body language. Your attorney will usually take a few minutes to discuss possible jury "strikes" with you and both explain his or her "rationale" for the proposed strikes, and listen to your thoughts.

At any point in the jury selection process, both your attorney and the prosecutor may be called to the front of the courtroom, to stand just in front of the judge's bench. It is likely that this is being done to discuss removing a potential juror from the jury pool "for cause." They may also be speaking about details of the trial which are matters that the jury need not hear. These conversations are conducted in hushed tones so that the jurors do not hear the discussions. The judge may then excuse these selected jurors, without necessarily telling anyone why they are being excused. At some point, the judge may make a point to state "on the record" which jurors were "struck" for cause and possible share the reasons for each strike.

After each of the jurors has been asked the more personal questions by both of the lawyers, the judge may then ask a few more questions of his or her own curiosity. Then, the challenges begin. The judge will first ask each party if they have any challenges for cause. If challenges for cause are made and granted, a new juror will take the seat of the juror excused. When the new juror is seated, the attorneys and the judge will be able to ask this new juror questions.

After each lawyer has either "moved" or "passed" for cause, each lawyer then gets to utilize a certain number of peremptory "strikes." This means that each attorney is allowed to eliminate a fixed number of the remaining potential jurors for ANY reason he or she believes would justify excusing a particular juror from the panel. The usual pattern of eliminating jurors starts with the prosecutor going first, followed by the defense, then a second elimination by the prosecution and a second elimination by the defense, and so on. Once all peremptory challenges have been made, or once both sides pass on the opportunity to make such challenges, the jury selection process is complete. Those who are excused leave.

The judge then administers yet another oath to the jury. This oath generally has the jurors all confirm that they will fairly and honestly listen to all the evidence, follow the judge's instructions and render a verdict that "speaks the truth" in your case. The bailiff may distribute pads of paper and pens for the jurors to take notes, if the judge authorizes this to be done.

At this point, the process of a bench trial and a jury trial again merges. The prosecutor has the option of making an opening statement. This is done nearly 100% of the time. The opening statement is supposed to be an outlining of what the State intends to prove in their case. This is an overview of the case "story," and it is not a time for the prosecutor to "argue" the facts of the case.[391] After a brief opening statement, the prosecutor will sit down.

When the prosecution is done speaking, the judge will ask if your attorney wishes to make an opening statement. Your attorney can answer "yes" and outline the evidence he or she expects to be proven in the trial. Instead of giving an opening statement, your attorney may "reserve" opening until AFTER the State rests its case. Unless some strategic reason to do so exists, it is usually best to go ahead with the defense opening immediately after the prosecutor so that the contested issues are "framed" for the jurors at or near the same time.

Like the prosecution, your lawyer is not supposed to do any arguing. Your opening statement is like a movie preview. Either side may use visual aids such as a chalkboard or a PowerPoint presentation, as long as they are presenting only what they plan on proving during trial. Such graphic presentations are more common in jury trials than in bench trials.

Both sides then have the opportunity to present evidence and witnesses, examine and cross-examine the witnesses, rebut and surrebut. The exact witnesses and what evidence is admitted may differ between a jury and a bench trial, depending on what your experienced OWI attorney feels is required to educate and convince the jury when compared to convincing only the judge. The jury members have likely never seen or heard evidence or testimony in an OWI trial, the judge has heard similar in perhaps hundreds.

It should be noted that because of the greater length of a jury OWI trial when compared to a bench trial, the judge may take several "comfort" breaks during the proceedings. You may expect a short break every few hours, and for lunch. If your trial appears to be likely to extend several hours beyond 5 PM or so, the judge may decide to adjourn court for the day. The choice on any of these breaks, when they occur and how long they last, is always at the discretion of the judge. The decision of when to adjourn is also left to the judge's discretion.

Both sides get a final chance to talk to the jury (or to the judge in a bench trial) in closing arguments.[392] However, before closing arguments begin, in a jury trial, the judge will usually need to meet with the attorneys to review what "jury instructions" he or she will be giving to the jury after the closing arguments. These jury instructions (or jury "charges") are the rule of law and procedure that apply to this case and these facts as presented.

Since the prosecution has the burden of proof in criminal cases, the prosecutor will have the option of addressing the jury (or the judge in a bench trial) first and last, as a general rule. Sometimes, the prosecutor will "waive" the initial remarks and save his or her time to conclude the closing argument. This is an advantage, since the prosecutor's words will then be the last thing the jury (or the judge) hears prior to the judge giving them his or her jury instructions.

It is your constitutional right to have your attorney make a closing argument. The purpose of this closing argument is for your attorney to take the facts that have been presented by either side, refer to any controlling legal precedent, and put forward to the judge the best possible reasons why you are **NOT GUILTY** of the charges.[393] This is one of the few chances your lawyer will have to utilize his or her persuasive skills. Often, your OWI defense specialist will play an emotion or highlight some issue of how you were treated unfairly during the arrest process.

When both sides have finished in a jury trial, the judge then reads the extensive rules of law that the jury is to apply to the facts that they have heard during your trial. The judge will read the charges against you, word for word. The judge will also read as many as 100 jury instructions, outlining the jury's duties and the rules of law they are required to follow. This reading of all of the applicable legal rules can run from 20 to 35 minutes in a garden-variety misdemeanor OWI case, or easily exceed an hour in a felony prosecution. Based on a recent case from the Michigan Supreme Court, based on these instructions, the jury may also be asked to determine any appropriate remedies for violations of your implied consent rights.[394]

The jury is then excused and the bailiff leads them to a jury deliberation room. Once there, following the judge's instructions, they elect a foreperson who becomes their speaker. The jury then decides your guilt or innocence, taking as much time as they need. With most OWIs, these deliberations typically take at least an hour.

No correlation exists between the length of the deliberations and the likelihood of an acquittal. Do not ask your attorney to guess what the jurors are "doing back there" or how the case will be decided. The jury makes its decision when they make their decision.

After several hours or even several days, the jurors may decide they are making no progress and send written notice of this to the judge. In some situations, the judge may even ask the jurors if they want to keep trying or go home for the night and resume the next day. The judge may also instruct them to keep trying to reach a verdict. As a last resort, the judge may decide to declare a mistrial.

If the jury comes to a verdict, both sides are notified, and everyone again gathers in the courtroom. Because your lawyer must keep themselves free for this eventuality, he or she cannot do anything else. Whether you are being billed by the hour or were charged a flat fee, this "unknown" time committed to your case is part of that fee.

The judge enters and takes the bench any time issues relating to the jury are being discussed or handled. Once the judge and attorneys have spoken, the bailiff then brings the jury into the courtroom. The judge asks the foreperson if the jury has reached a verdict. If they have, the bailiff takes the written verdict from the foreperson and hands it to the judge. The judge will then make certain that the verdict is in the proper form. Then, the verdict is given back to the bailiff so that the foreperson or the bailiff can "publish" it (read it into the record).

Once the verdict is read, either lawyer has the option of requesting the judge to "poll" the jury. This involves the judge asking each juror one at a time, if this is his or her verdict in the jury room, and whether it is still his or her verdict. This process gives a juror to speak up if he or she was pressured into voting in a manner he or she did not believe was the correct verdict.

A "not guilty" verdict is final, once entered, absent a one-in-a-million request for a "polling" of the jury and a recanting by one or more jurors. The State cannot appeal a "not guilty" verdict rendered by your jury. After the "not guilty" verdict is made the order of the court, you are "discharged" of any responsibility for that charge.

A guilty verdict usually leads to a defense request for the jury to be polled. Absent a juror "recanting" his or her vote, the guilty verdict will typically be made the order of the court. Certain rarely used motions may be asserted by your legal team, but these usually only arise when an unusual mid-trial motion was made by the defense attorney and the judge reserved ruling or initially ruled against your attorney's motion, only to later change his or her mind after hearing the guilty verdict. Barring this, some form of post-trial motion or appeal can be pursued. See **Chapter 16** for more details.

If the jury never can agree on a verdict and their vote must be unanimous unless you agree otherwise,[395] a mistrial can and eventually will be granted by the judge. This means that the State can start over to try your case before a new jury. Often, these cases get resolved at this point by negotiations between the attorneys for a reduced charge.

In a bench trial, the judge makes a decision as to your guilt or innocence. Unlike with a jury, often this is done right away, or after a very short break. With intoxicated driving cases, Michigan law requires that you be screened by the court's probation department prior to your sentencing.[396] The purpose of this probation interview is for the court to determine if you have an alcohol or drug abuse problem. Consequently, it is usually not possible to have the judge sentence you to your punishment at the same proceeding. Instead, your sentencing is usually scheduled for several days or weeks after your trial. This is further discussed in Chapter 16. If you are found not guilty, your trial is over, your bond is released and you are "discharged" from responsibility for this crime.

15.10. Would You be More Likely to Testify at a Bench Trial Verses a Jury Trial? No rule of thumb applies here. In some cases, you may need to testify to explain some factual issue. Your attorney may have decided on a bench trial because some inflammatory issue may be exposed by the evidence. For example, if you made a racial comment to the officer in a moment of anger or rage over your arrest. It may be helpful to have you testify at trial just so the judge can get a better idea of who you are. The strategy here may not be to help you win at trial, but instead to help you obtain a better sentence in the event you do not prevail.

15.11. Burden of Proof. Burden of proof basically refers to who has the requirement to prove something, and to what "standard" they are required to prove it. The burden of proof in a jury trial is exactly the same as it is in a bench trial. The prosecutor is required to show "beyond a reasonable doubt" that in fact, you are guilty of the crime or crimes charged.[397] The burden never "shifts" to you to prove your innocence. The defendant in a criminal case has no burden to prove anything, whatsoever.

While the burden never completely shifts to the defense, the burden of persuasion may shift to the defense on some "evidentiary" matters. For example, if the prosecutor is able to overcome all of your attorney's objections to admissibility of your breath test result of 0.10; it is up to your attorney to put up some evidence to cast doubt on the test's results accuracy and/or reliability. Usually, even the best cross-examination of the State's breath test personnel will not gain an acquittal of a per se OWI charge, unless you have expert testimony that can refute or cast doubt on the result.

15.11.1. Affirmative Defenses—the Burden to Disprove may Eventually be on the State.
Once you have claimed an affirmative defense (like justification or entrapment), you and your attorney must "come forward" with your proof.[398] Then, the prosecutor can seek to disprove the affirmative defense, and in certain circumstances, is required to do so.

15.11.2. State's Burden to get Chemical Test Results Admitted, then the Burden Shifts to Defendant to Rebut or Explain why an Error Exists.
For any chemical test that was used to determine your blood alcohol level (either blood or breath) or that you had drugs in your system (blood or urine), the prosecutor is first required to prove that the tests were performed according to Michigan's administrative rules in a valid and proper manner.[399] However, once the prosecutor has met this burden, it is then up to your attorney to prove to put forth evidence these results should not be accepted as being reliable by the judge. In the alternative, your attorney may have a way to argue that the results are totally inadmissible.

Another possible approach might be for your lawyer to show why the prosecutor, while meeting his or her burden of admissibility, has not actually presented sufficient evidence to prove the results are reliable. This is because of the distinction between admissibility and reliability. This distinction may be lost on a judge who has decided, long ago, that admissibility is commensurate with reliability. These are the judges who "presume" that breath and blood testing is accurate.

15.11.3. Presumptions and Inferences.
The biggest and most important presumption in any trial is that you are innocent until proven guilty.[400] This is different than on an appeal of a guilty verdict, where the verdict is presumed to be correct.[401] The presumption of innocence requires that the evidence be viewed in the light most favorable to you. Regarding chemical tests, once a test result is admitted, a presumption arises that the law enforcement officer did his or her duty and that these duties were performed correctly, until

the contrary is shown.[402] This presumption should not apply, however, if the administrative rules were not followed.

15.11.4. Who gets to Benefit from Inferences. In most states, an inference in your favor will arise if your test results are at 0.05 grams or below (and you are over 21 years of age). Most state statutes that deal with these "low" numbers state that "it shall be inferred" (or "it shall be presumed") that the driver was not impaired. Similarly, many states have inferences that give the prosecutors an edge when the "number" is 0.08 grams or more. The state law may state that an inference of impairment would then exist, but that this is subject to being rebutted by the defendant.

Prior to 2003, Michigan drivers benefited from such presumptions. However, when Michigan's intoxicated driving laws were rewritten in 2003 to comport with the national 0.08 standard, these presumptions were removed. Now, no matter how low your chemical test results, you are not protected from prosecution or conviction. Thus, if your chemical test is 0.03 and the prosecutor can prove you were OUIL, he or she may be able to gain a conviction against you.

A new inference was also added as a part of the 2003 changes. This new inference is that the chemical test result at the time of the test is the same as at the time of your driving.[403] This inference almost always benefits the prosecutor, as it makes a rising blood defense all the more difficult to establish.

15.11.5. No Presumptions for OWI Drugs. There is no matching statutory presumption in most states (including Michigan) of being under the influence of drugs if your blood or urine tests reveal a certain number (nanograms per ml or cc) of a particular chemical or drug. There is such a presumption in Virginia for certain levels of cocaine, methamphetamine, 3,4- methylenedioxymethamphetamine and PCP.[404]

However, in Michigan there is the OWI crime of OUID (operating under the influence of drugs) or the combination of drugs and alcohol. If the drug in question is a prescribed drug, then the standard is "substantially lessened." On the other hand, if the drug in question is a controlled substance, then the crime is "zero tolerance," meaning if the drug is present in your system while you are driving, then you are guilty regardless of it the drug impacted your ability to drive. The "zero tolerance" controlled substances are defined by statute.[405] They are called "Schedule 1" drugs. Zero tolerance is not the same thing as a presumption. If it were, it would be an "irrebuttable" presumption, and in criminal cases, these kinds of presumptions are not allowed.[406]

Finally, in Michigan, the refusal to take a blood test can be admitted against you but cannot be considered evidence creating an inference that the test would have shown the presence of a prohibited substance.[407] Thus, it cannot be considered as evidence of guilt.

15.12. Motion for Directed Verdict of Acquittal. A motion for directed verdict of acquittal may be requested by your attorney once the prosecutor "rests" (ends the presentation of evidence). If granted, this is a ruling by the judge that the evidence demands a verdict of not guilty.[408] This motion is proper where the prosecutor totally fails to present any evidence providing one or more critical aspect(s) of one or more of the charges against you. In an OWI trial, such a motion might be granted if (in a per se alcohol case) your attorney is able to obtain a legal ruling in the middle of your trial that the test result cannot be considered by the jury. In these cases, the judge takes the decision about guilt or innocence away from the jury and instructs or directs an acquittal (not guilty) on that charge (or charges, if more than one of them have been challenged).

15.12.1. Winning a Directed Verdict by Exclusion of Evidence. In an OWI trial, a directed verdict might occur if for some reason all evidence of your blood test result or breath test result prohibited from being considered as evidence. This prohibition would likely come about in the middle of your trial because your attorney successfully made a legal argument that this evidence must be excluded.

15.12.2. Judge can Decide Issue, with or without Permitting Argument. In instances where a directed verdict is requested by your OWI attorney, the judge can make an immediate ruling without hearing arguments from either attorney. Usually both sides get to argue their respective positions. If the judge grants this motion, this issue or "count" of the accusatory document is taken away from the jury's final decision. Acquittal of that charge is declared by the judge due to a lack of evidence.

15.13. Judge Cannot Direct Jury to Return Verdict of Guilty. In a jury trial, it is the jury who determines the question of your guilt or innocence. If a judge were to direct a jury to return a verdict of guilty, this would be impermissible and excellent grounds for an appeal.[409] Only a few judges ignorant of the law would make such an overt error. Your OWI specialist, however, must be watchful that a pro-prosecution judge does not "communicate" his or her desire or belief that you are guilty of the OWI offense. This type of "telegraphing" of how he or she thinks is usually very subtle. This is true despite the fact that the jury will be told by the judge at the conclusion of your trial that he or she has no opinion about how the case should be decided. Furthermore, the jury is told that if the members of the jury believe that the judge has such an opinion, the jury should disregard it.[410]

15.13.1 Must the Jury Ever Return a Verdict of Guilty? There is no dispute that jurors have the right and responsibility of judging the facts in a criminal trial. But what about the law? Should they also be allowed to judge a law or societal practice that they believe to be unjust by returning a not guilty verdict when, perhaps, all of the elements of a crime have been proven?

A typical jury instruction in a criminal case will instruct that the jury may only decide questions of fact, and must take the law as the judge gives it. They are instructed that they can only decide the truth and weight of the facts of the case, and apply the judge's law to these facts.

When a jury fails to follow this instruction, this act of defiance is call "jury nullification." Jury nullification is the refusal of jurors to convict a defendant despite their belief in the defendant's guilt. The jury is thus said to "judge the law," though more accurately the jury is judging the law's specific application, not its general validity. This divisive practice, once well-accepted, has become the unspoken secret of the American jury deliberation room. No longer may juries freely disregard laws that they believe to be unjust. This does not mean however that juries no longer nullify. For a more detailed explanation of this, and to learn how nullification might apply in your case see: "*Independent Juries: Liberty's Last Defense.*"[411]

15.14. What Happens if You are Acquitted? If you are acquitted your bond is returned and you walk out of the courtroom with no further legal concerns with regard to the charges you faced. The prosecutor cannot appeal an acquittal by a jury or ask for a mistrial after the verdict has been returned. If you are acquitted, it is almost as if you were never arrested.

15.15. What Happens if You are Convicted? If the jury or the judge comes back with a verdict of guilty, numerous issues arise. First, you are required to be sentenced by the judge who presided over your trial. Michigan law requires that you be screened by the court's probation department prior to sentencing.[412] The purpose of this probation interview is to have the court determine if you have an alcohol or drug abuse problem. Consequently, it is not usually possible to have the judge sentence you to your punishment at the same proceeding. Instead, sentencing is usually scheduled for several days or weeks after your trial.

Also, your lawyer may consider the value of possibly filing a motion of some type to request that the judge not accept the jury's verdict, or make the verdict the judgment of the court. Also, a motion for a new trial may be sought or a motion in arrest of judgment, as facts may dictate. If none of these post-trial motions are viable, your lawyer may simply file a motion to ask the judge to delay imposition of the sentence imposed until after an appeal can be taken. This motion is more likely to be granted if the appeal is simultaneously filed by your attorney with the court.

15.16. Sentencing. A minimum and maximum sentence is set by statute regarding any sentence you could receive for an OWI conviction.[413] The minimum and maximum sentence depends on whether this is your first or subsequent OWI conviction. If you have prior OWI convictions, regardless of age, the jail sentence you face is likely to be greater, and if the prior offenses are within the "enhancement" periods (7 years for second/ lifetime for 3rd offense felony), then the minimum and maximum sentences are essentially required to be higher.

Nevertheless, the judge has some discretion in determining the appropriate sentence. Part of this discretion is based on the crime and the offender. In other words, the judge must "individualize" your sentence. Factors to be considered in determining an appropriate sentence include: 1) the reformation of the offender; 2) the protection of society; 3) the disciplining of the wrongdoing; 4) the deterrence of others from committed like offenses.[414] Keep in mind that even if the prosecutor does not know about prior offenses, and even if they are not used for criminal enhancement, a judge can still consider them for sentencing. In this case the increased sentence is discretionary rather than mandatory.

The sentence you will receive for a second or subsequent OWI conviction will almost include jail time. Not all first offenders go to jail, but some judges and some particular counties do make a practice of sending everyone convicted of intoxicated driving to jail. Often times such factors as jail overcrowding are an issue. In addition to jail time, there is also a term of probation, crime victim rights fees, screening fees, costs of prosecution, the imposition of fines and costs, some number of hours of community service, treatment, and alcohol and drug assessment.. There is also possible forfeiture or immobilization of your vehicle, and you may be allowed to drive only with an ignition interlock device.

In addition to the sentence of the court, the Michigan Department of State will impose a driver license sanction. These sanctions are not "individualized," meaning they are the same for everyone. The length and terms of any driver license sanction depends only on the number of alcohol convictions during the appropriate enhancement periods, which again are 7 and 10 years. Finally, there is a driver responsibility fee of either $500.00 or $1000.00 payable for the first two years after your conviction.

15.17. Mistrial can be Raised by Either Attorney or at the Judge's Initiative. A mistrial is the termination of your trial before its normal conclusion due to a procedural error, improper statements by a witness, judge or attorney which prejudice your jury, or an act or misconduct by a juror such as conducting his or her own investigation of some aspect of your case.[415] A mistrial can also occur when there is a deadlock by a jury without reaching a verdict after lengthy deliberation (a "hung" jury).

When situations like this arise, the judge, either on his or her own initiative or upon the motion (request) of one of the parties can "declare a mistrial." If granted, this causes dismissal of the jury. Unless the mistrial was caused by the prosecutor's intentional or inexcusable error, the criminal prosecution will be set for trial again, starting from the beginning.

A mistrial is only available once a trial has begun, which means after the jury has been impaneled and sworn in.[416] A mistrial is not available once the verdict has been rendered. Your experienced litigator will know all the applicable legal issues relating to Michigan's rules on mistrials, and will be able to posture your case for the best possible result on appeal or retrial.

15.18. Is a Motion for a New Trial Possible After Your Trial? Depending on what errors may have been committed during trial, your attorney may recommend asking for a new trial or appealing the guilty verdict to a higher court. A motion for a new trial is based on a guilty verdict which is contrary to the evidence, and the principles of justice and equity are strongly and decidedly against the weight of the evidence.[417] It is more common for a motion for a new trial to be sought by the defense following a jury trial. In Michigan, this motion must typically be filed within 60 days of the entry of the judgment against you.[418]

Although a motion for a new trial is rarely granted, if your attorney believes that the prosecutor or judge committed legal error or that his or her own actions during trial have constituted "ineffective assistance of counsel," a motion for a new trial may be filed and might even be granted.

Because it is the judge in a bench trial who makes the decision of guilt based on the evidence presented at trial, it is unlikely to believe that the same judge would change his or her mind. It may happen more often if new evidence is discovered that was unavailable or unreachable prior to the trial. Plus, another reason for requesting a motion for a new trial after a non-jury verdict of guilt could be that your attorney (or a new attorney) may raise the issue of your trial attorney's ineffective assistance of counsel.

15.19. Is Appeal Possible After Your Trial? If a motion for a new trial is not appropriate, or has been made and denied, the next step is to file an appeal. In almost every OWI case, opportunities for appellate error will occur more often in jury trials than in bench trials. Because a trial judge is typically required to answer dozens of questions of law, a good trial attorney (by raising numerous issues during trial) can create many more opportunities for appeal in a jury trial rather than a bench trial.[419] In deciding whether or not to appeal your case, keep in mind that appellate courts are primarily concerned with questions of fairness, not whether in fact you are guilty. This is because only issues of law can be appealed. Also, appellate courts generally do not directly dismiss cases. If an error is found in the lower court's processes, the Court of Appeals may simply order that the process be repeated correctly.

There are advantages and disadvantages to the appellate process, and you should consider these with your attorney before deciding how to proceed. The biggest disadvantage of an appeal is the time and expense. While you can ask to have your sentence "stayed" during your appeal, such stays are rarely granted, and the appeals process can literally take years. Thus, you may have long since finished your sentence before you receive a ruling from the appeals courts.

In almost every OWI case, opportunities for appellate error will occur more often in jury trials than in bench trials. Because a trial judge is typically required to answer dozens of questions of law, a good trial attorney (by raising numerous issues during trial) can create many more opportunities for appeal in a jury trial rather than a bench trial.[420] For a conviction in a bench trial to be reversed, the trial judge has to have made an error admitting evidence at trial that should not have been admitted. If you win either type of trial, the State cannot appeal.

15.20. If You Appeal After Your Trial, is Your Punishment Deferred? It is possible to apply for a supersedeas bond following a trial.[421] This is a surety bond from you required to delay punishment until conclusion of the appeal. In Michigan, such procedures are usually available in misdemeanor cases, with any "abuse of discretion" by the trial judge being appealable. In unusual situations, your attorney may need to ask for involvement by an appeals court. Be aware that felony convictions will not have the same "automatic" avenue of appeal while holding off the punishment until your appeal is completed.

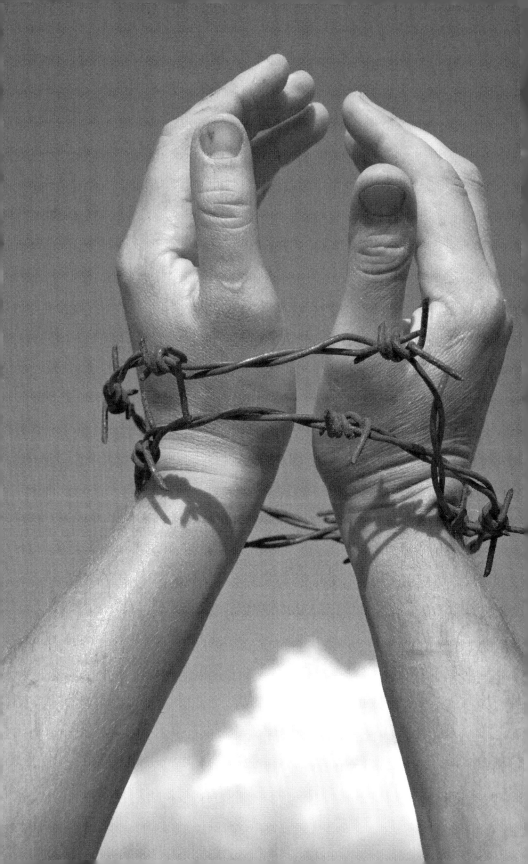

Chapter 16:

The Verdict: Acquittal or Conviction? Issues Related to Jail, Probation and Loss of License

16.0. The Purpose of this Chapter. At the end of your trial you will receive a verdict from the court. Based on this verdict, you may be finished with the legal aspects of your case, or you may be facing punishment. In rare cases you may be required to undergo an entirely new trial. This chapter discusses everything that happens from the time the verdict is announced in open court through the possible imposition of punishment.

16.1. Verdict Rendered by Jury (or Judge). A verdict is the decision of guilty or not guilty by a judge or jury after a trial.[422] A jury verdict must be accepted by the trial judge to be final, and then is made an "order" of the court. If the jury verdict is not in the correct form, the judge may reject the verdict.[423]

Usually, the single most important question the jury decides in an OWI criminal trial is whether or not you are guilty. A judgment is different than a verdict. A judgment is a determination of guilt or innocence by a judge sitting without a jury.[424] A "special verdict" is a decision by the jury on the factual questions in the case, leaving the application of the law to those facts to the judge, who makes the final judgment.[425]

A "directed or instructed verdict" is a decision made by the trial judge (following a motion made by your defense counsel) that there is insufficient evidence of guilt on any particular charge.[426] A "chance verdict" (decided by lot or the flip of a coin) and a "compromise verdict" (based on some jurors voting against their beliefs to break a deadlock)[427] are both improper, and if uncovered, will result in a mistrial (having the verdict thrown out by the judge) or cause for reversal of the judgment on appeal.

16.1.1. Read and Published in Open Court. When the jury reaches a verdict as to your guilt or innocence, they notify the judge and present them with the written and signed form upon which their verdict was rendered. The judge ensures that the form is filled out correctly and signed, then directs the foreperson of the jury (or a bailiff) to read the decision aloud to everyone present in the courtroom.[428] Usually, the judge will ask you to stand and receive the verdict of the jury. In the law, publication is anything made public by print, orally, or by broadcast (radio, television). When the verdict is read by the foreperson in open court, this is known as the verdict being read and "published".

16.1.2. Judge Must Accept the Verdict and Make it the Order of the Court. Once the verdict has been read and published by the foreperson, the judge must generally accept the decision of the jury. (In rare instances the judge may disregard a guilty verdict and find for the defense. A judge cannot overturn a "not guilty" verdict). The judge typically makes the verdict of guilt or innocence the "order" of the court, meaning that under the legal authority of the court. The judge will require that this order be filed with the clerk of the court and complied with.

An order is every direction or mandate of a judge or a court that is not a judgment or legal opinion (although both may include an order) directing that something be done or that there is prohibition against some act. By having to accept the decision of guilt or lack of guilt from the jury, the judge then must enter an order confirming or mandating your guilty or not guilty status. In essence, based totally on the verdict of the jury, the judge is ordering the rest of our society to accept that you are either guilty or not guilty of the crime(s) charged.

16.1.3. Polling the Jurors, by Either Side. Once the verdict of the jury has been read and published, either the prosecution or defense can ask for the jury to be "polled."[429] This means each juror will have to individually answer that the verdict reached was his or her vote. This process was put into place to allow jurors who might feel they were forced, pressured or coerced into "going along with the others" to have an avenue to let this be known, and to ensure that the form the foreperson puts forth accurately represents the opinion of the entire jury, not just the foreperson. Although extremely rare, this process will occasionally cause a juror to recant, and the verdict becomes a "mistrial" (meaning that the jurors could not unanimously agree).

16.2. Three Possible Outcomes for Each Count (each separate charge against you). In a criminal trial, there are only three possible outcomes for each count: not guilty; guilty; and no decision. Each count or criminal charge against you is considered separately. It is not unusual if you have been charged with multiple counts to receive more than one of the possible outcomes in the same overall verdict. Jurors usually resolve charges with "guilty" or "not guilty," but occasionally will be unable to unanimously agree. If a jury cannot unanimously agree to a verdict, this is called a "hung" jury and this results in a "mistrial" of such counts of the case.

16.2.1. Not Guilty – Judge Discharges You from the Case, Orders Bond Released. If you are found not guilty on all charges (or some), the judge discharges you from criminal liability for such offense(s). If you had a bond placed so that you could remain out of jail while you were waiting for their trial, this bond is released at this time by order of the judge. The security given for the bond is returned or released. If you are found not guilty, the prosecutor cannot appeal this decision, nor force you to face a new trial.

16.2.2. Guilty – Sentencing will Follow by the Judge. If the verdict of the jury or the judgment from the judge is that you are guilty on one, several or all of the counts in a trial, sentencing is usually done several days or weeks later. Sentencing is not immediate because Michigan law requires that you be screened by the court's probation department prior to sentencing in all OWI cases.[430] The purpose of this probation interview is to help the court determine if you have a drug or alcohol abuse problem. The probation department will also "recommend" a sentence to the court. The judge will review and consider the probation report and recommendation, listen to you and your attorney, and will then impose the sentence.

16.2.3. Mistrial Declared by Judge because the Jurors Cannot Reach Unanimous Verdict. In OWI trials, the jury is required to reach a unanimous verdict.[431] If the jurors cannot entirely agree on either a guilty or not guilty verdict on any of the counts, they may be considered by the judge to be "deadlocked." If this happens, the judge usually gives them a chance to break the deadlock by bringing them into court and reminding them of the importance of reaching their verdict. This statement by the judge will be in the form of a specific jury instruction drafted just for this purpose. The name of this jury instruction is the "Allen" charge.[432] If after being read the Allen charge the jury still cannot agree on a verdict, the judge may declare a mistrial. It is up to the judge to decide how long the jury must deliberate before he or she declares a mistrial. If a mistrial is declared, then this may lead to another trial, or may create a stronger negotiating position for your attorney to get a reduced charge, or a dropping of the still disputed charge(s) by the prosecutor.

16.3. Sentencing (if Convicted on Any Count) is Required to be Done. A "sentence" is both the act of imposing the punishment on a person convicted of a crime as well as the actual verbalization of what punishment is handed down.[433] A sentence is ordered by the judge, based on the verdict of the jury (or the judge's decision if there is no jury) within the possible range of minimum and maximum punishments set by Michigan law (or federal law in convictions for a federal crime). In every day jargon, "sentence" refers to the jail or prison time ordered after conviction, as in "his sentence was 30 days in the county jail." Technically, a sentence includes all fines and costs, alcohol and drug assessment and treatment, community service, restitution or other punishment, and terms of probation. If you are convicted of an OWI offense, then you are required in Michigan to have a pre-sentence report by a probation officer based on an investigation of background information and circumstances of the crime.

Michigan statutes also specifically require that you be screened to uncover any possible alcohol or drug problems.[434] This substance abuse evaluation is usually in the form of a "NEEDS" assessment, which is a 130 question multiple choice test. Based on your score on this test, and the personal interview, the probation department then prepares a "pre-sentence" report containing a recommendation to the judge as to the amount of treatment he or she believe is appropriate, and also sometimes, the degree of punishment.[435] After reading the recommendation of the probation department, your attorney will be allowed to suggest changes relative to both punishment and treatment. In urging the court to deviate from the recommendations of the probation department, he or she will point out to the court "mitigation" issues on your behalf. You also have an absolute right to be heard before the court imposes its sentence. This is called your right to "allocution."[436] During allocution, a defendant may then speak in defense of a belief or apologize for their actions and humble themselves before the court. If a defendant did not have a trial and wishes to bring up matters of integrity and realization that are more sincere from their mouth than that of their attorneys, this may sway the Judge just as a statement by a victim my sway a Judge in another direction. If one plans to do this, they should consult their attorney beforehand, as this may backfire if found insincere or merely giving excuses.

A "concurrent sentence" is a sentence for one count in the verdict that is served at the same time as the sentence for another count and only lasts as long as the longest term. A "consecutive sentence," is a rare instance where the judge "stacks" the jail terms, for each to be served one after another. Under some circumstances, you may receive a "suspended sentence," which means the jail portion of the punishment is not imposed if you do not get into trouble (i.e. violate probation) for a given period of time. It is also possible for a portion of your sentence to be suspended, as where the judge gives you a jail term of 93 days, but orders that only the first 30 days be served immediately. This period of suspension is usually the term of your probation. Thus, if you are placed on probation for one year, your sentence, or a portion of your sentence, will be suspended or held in abeyance during this 12 month period. An "indeterminate" sentence" is one in which the actual release date is not set and will be based on review of prison conduct. In OWI practice, such sentences are extremely rare, but may occur if your case was a felony involving death or serious injury.

16.3.1. Merger with the OWI offense? "Merger" can have several meanings with regard to OWI offenses. Certain criminal offenses are integral parts of greater offenses. If you are convicted of the greater offense, you cannot also be sentenced for the lesser offense as well. This is not always true in Michigan with OWI charges. In an OWI trial, if you are found guilty of a second degree homicide, the lesser misdemeanor of the OWI causing a death may not be merged into the punishment for the homicide.[437] The more typical scenario though is where you are found guilty of the principal charge of OWI. You could not then be punished also for the "lesser" offense of OWVI (operating while visibly impaired).

16.3.2. Evidence in Aggravation. "Evidence in aggravation" refers to factors which in some instances could not be introduced by the prosecutor at trial in the determination of guilt, but which may be presented by the prosecutor at sentencing and considered by the court in imposing a fair punishment. Examples of generally admissible aggravating factors include a particularly high chemical test result, injury to any party as a result of your actions, having children in the vehicle you were driving. Examples of non-admissible aggravating factors are any prior criminal record or possibly facts surrounding your actions after you were confronted by the police or after placed in custody by the police. Thus, while it is usually improper for the prosecution to tell the judge or the jury about your prior OWIs during the trial itself, your prior criminal offenses are fair game during sentencing after conviction.

16.3.3. Evidence in Mitigation. "Mitigating circumstances" in criminal law, are facts, conditions or circumstances which do not excuse or exonerate the defendant's criminal conduct, but which may be considered by a judge in deciding what would be fair punishment. Your attorney can present this evidence and may do so in the form of a sentencing memorandum that he or she files with the court prior to sentencing. For example, such a memorandum might explain how you made elaborate plans to use a designated driver and the plans fell apart, leading you to attempt to get home from a remote location. These events would not be a legal defense to your case, but they might carry some weight with some judges relative to determining an "individually appropriate" sentence in your case.

Stated differently, mitigating factors are a type of information that might not be relevant in the determination of a defendant's guilt, but which may be important in a determination of a fair punishment. In an OWI sentencing, other types of evidence in mitigation may include proof of regular attendance at Alcoholics Anonymous or SMART recovery meetings, witnesses on your behalf such as a "sponsor," voluntary submittal to alcohol abuse counseling, performing community service hours as a form of penance, and possibly making restitution for property damage or loss. These facts do not relate to the particular offense, but instead demonstrate how you responded appropriately to being arrested for OWI.

16.3.4. Attacks on Prior Conduct. In OWI Sentencing, Your Prior Criminal Conduct can almost always be considered as a Part of Sentencing.[438] In other words, if you have a prior conviction, for a previous alcohol related offense such as MIP (minor in possession),[439] or OWI or even a "deferred plea", and you are convicted for a second OWI offense at a later time, it is likely the sentence for the second offense will be more severe because of the first conviction or the "deferred adjudication." One avenue of attacking the more severe sentence for the second offense is to either seek to vacate (to remove) or to attack the first offense, if possible.

Bear in mind, however, that Michigan courts have made such "collateral" attacks on prior convictions increasingly difficult. As a general rule, in order to successfully attack a prior conviction, you must show two things; first that you did not have an attorney for the prior case, and second, that you spent time in jail as a result of this "uncounseled" conviction.[440] If your prior offense was out-of-state, it is then important for your attorney to check the other state's law to determine if it is "substantially similar." If it is not, then it cannot be used for enhancement. These challenges are rare, but can result in saving your driving privileges and possibly reduce the jail time you face by many days or even months.

16.3.5. Incarceration. This means time in custody, whether in a jail, under house arrest or some other form of detention. It means the State controls your freedom of movement. If convicted of an OWI offense, many jurisdictions require that you be led in handcuffs from the courtroom by deputies if the sentence includes jail time Some courts, however, will delay imposition of the jail sentence. For example, if your incarceration is going to be particularly disruptive to your employment, your attorney can request that you not begin your jail term until the following Friday, allowing you to "tie up your affairs." This request can always be made, but is not always granted. A judge also may or may not allow you to serve your jail sentence on "work release." Also, an appeal may delay imposition of jail time.

You will receive credit for any time previously served as a result of your arrest and inability to make bond, but the judge is not required to give you credit against your sentence for any house detention served as a condition of your bond (such as if you were on a home alcohol tether), or for any time served at an in-patient substance abuse treatment center.

16.3.5.1. Maximums and Minimums. For an OWI (which is typically a misdemeanor), the maximum period of incarceration is 93 days for a first offense, (180 days if found guilty under "super-drunk" statute), and twelve months for a second offense.[441] However, if convicted of multiple criminal counts from a single driving episode, one or more of which are OWI offenses, the total amount of incarceration can extend (due to consecutive sentences being "stacked") to more than one year, even if all counts are misdemeanors. If this is your third OWI offense your repeat OWI offense is a FELONY, and the statutory maximum period of incarceration is five years in jail.[442] Previously, the statute of limitations was 10 years, but under "Heidi's Law" as enacted there no longer is a statute of limitations for third offense OWI. There is a question if in some instances this law is an ex post facto violation. Enhancement periods between OWI offenses are 7 years in regards to second offense OWI and no limit in regards to third offense OWI. These periods are set by Michigan statute.[443] Prior OWI offenses outside the enhancement period of seven years cannot be used to increase the statutory minimum sentence of a second offense OWI but can still be considered by the judge in determining your sentence, and might still result in increased periods of incarceration.

There is no minimum amount of time you must spend incarcerated if convicted of a first OWI offense. If this is your second OWI conviction within 7 years, then the minimum period of incarceration is 5 days. There is also an alternative minimum sentence for second offenses only of 30 to 90 days of community service. If this is your third OWI, then the minimum sentence is 30 days, at least 48 hours of which must be served consecutively. How much additional time you have to serve (beyond what was served when arrested) at the time of sentencing depends on these statutory minimums and the judge's sentencing practices. Most jurisdictions give credit for time in jail on the night of your arrest.

16.3.5.2. Alternatives to Regular Jail Time. There may be alternatives to regular jail time that a judge might consider in your case. However, because sentencing alternatives tend to be very jurisdiction specific you should always consult with your OWI specialist regarding the specific alternatives that may be available in your particular court. Any "alternative" is at the discretion (choice) of the judge, not your defense attorney. If sentenced to one of these alternatives, the period of incarceration is typically longer than what might have been required for "regular" jail time. This period is intended to offset the special benefit of obtaining the alternative sentence and is sometimes thought of as necessary by a judge who thinks he or she must always be mindful of the need to adequately punish the wrongdoer.

All of these alternatives to jail time have significant "compliance" requirements and "accountability requirements." For example, a judge may require phone monitoring or order that an ankle bracelet be utilized to make sure that the conditions imposed are in fact followed. Another option is for a judge to require regular drug and alcohol screening. A violation of **any** of these requirements or any of the criteria imposed likely means that you violated the terms of your sentence and consequently a loss of these privileges. Such violations usually result in significant jail time being added to the existing sentence.

Another sentencing alternative might be "work-release," although this option is not available in all Michigan counties. In this case, you are allowed some time off on a daily or regular basis so that you can go to work, but must report to the jail to be kept locked up every evening. Defendants who are allowed this option will typically be tested regularly for alcohol and drugs as a condition of this type of incarceration. Plus, the rules of the work release facility are strict. A court may allow work release for defendants who are otherwise at low risks to commit further crimes and who have regular jobs that would likely be lost if they were to serve regular jail time. Many judges try not to harm your dependents, if possible.

A weekend jail sentence is also sometimes available. With this alternative you are allowed to work all week, and stay at home all week, then report only to the jail for service of jail time on the weekends. This is very uncommon for OWIs due to the limited bed space at jails throughout Michigan.

House arrest is another alternative to formal incarceration. In this situation, you must physically stay in your home where you remain subject to frequent and random confirmation by the State. You might be required to wear a form of electronic monitoring device such as an ankle bracelet to verify your whereabouts. Other jurisdictions use technology such as Vis-a-tel (phone camera plus breathalyzer) to assure compliance. Others use a device that continuously monitors sweat from your skin to detect any use of alcohol. This device is known by the acronym "SCRAM," which stands for Secure, Continuous, Remote, Alcohol Monitor. As with other forms of incarceration alternatives, a positive test for alcohol while wearing this device usually means a return to jail for a now longer period of incarceration.

Finally, there are a variety of court-specific treatment plans or "drug courts" in which you may qualify to participate. These programs stress addiction treatment over punishment. The idea here is that rehabilitation in the form of sobriety is more important or beneficial and will protect society better in the long run. Many jurisdictions and states are setting up courts specializing in perceived origins and stressors contributing to the offense. There are now numerous mental health courts. Recently, many individual counties in Michigan have veterans' courts specializing in helping current and former military personnel. There is currently a law likely to be passed streamlining these courts across state guidelines. Veterans' courts will be specialized in that individuals will be within their cohort of other military individuals. They will have mentors of a military background helping them cope through the process. Specialized courts often have the prosecutor, judge, and defense attorney work on a treatment plan for the convicted individual and have close supervision and frequent discussions regarding successes and areas to improve. Another benefit of specialized courts is that if the party that pled guilty successfully completes their probation they may have certain records expunged. However, in Michigan, intoxicated driving violations can never be expunged.

16.3.5.3. Sobriety Court. Ever since the sweeping changes to Michigan's intoxicated driving law in 1999, repeat offenders have faced lifetime license revocation. If you had one prior offense within 7 years then you would be eligible for a review of the revocation after one year, and depending on the circumstances, if you had two prior convictions within 10 years the wait for a review could be as long as five years. Of course there was no guarantee of success at this license review, and if you were not successful, then you would have to wait another year for each subsequent review hearing.

For many repeat offenders, however this will be the old paradigm. Effective January 1, 2011, a new paradigm changing law, entitled "Restricted license; DWI/sobriety court interlock pilot project," has significantly changed these revocation periods. This new law amends seven sections of Michigan's OWI law,[444] and adds one additional section. The additional section grants new privileges, procedures, and corresponding sanctions for repeat offenders. Most significantly, after an initial 45 days of suspension, qualifying repeat offenders will also be able to obtain restricted driving privileges with a breath alcohol ignition interlock device provided they have successfully participated in a sobriety court program. You should discuss with your lawyer whether or not sobriety court is a possibility for you. Also, review the article *"Michigan's New Sobriety/DWI Court Law"* for more detailed information.[445]

16.3.6. Fines. A fine is a monetary punishment that is paid to the court either immediately or over a period of time. Minimum and maximum fines are established by statute, although the judge usually has some discretion in the amount of the fine within this specific range. The amount of these minimums and maximums depends on whether this is your first OWI, super dunk, or if there is a prior OWI conviction within the year enhancement periods or a third one in a lifetime.[446]

If the fine cannot be paid all at once, then you may be able to make payments over time. Keep in mind however that the Michigan court rules require all fines and costs to be paid at the time of your sentencing.[447]

If you make every good faith effort to pay the fine, yet fail due to economic misfortune or family obligations, then the judge might convert the fine to an appropriate number of community service hours. Do not count on this concession because any modification to your sentence is strictly at the judge's discretion. Be sure to contact your attorney (or probation officer) if you need to request such a modification.

16.3.7. Probation. Probation is a chance to remain out of jail but on "community supervision." Significant and restrictive terms and conditions are always added to and are a part of your probationary sentence. For OWI offenses, a typical condition would be the non-use of alcohol or non-prescription drugs. Even if you have never used drugs, random drug urine or blood analysis is likely. A sentence to probation is given by a judge as an alternative to ordering that you be sent to jail or prison. Another way to end up on probation would be when you are placed on probation following any jail time imposed.[448] A violation of any of the terms or conditions to your probation will usually result in your being sent to jail for all or part of the remaining "probation" term. Repeat criminals are sometimes not eligible for probation. Probation is not the same as "parole," which is a term describing "conditional" freedom under certain restrictions given to convicted felons at the end of their imprisonment.

Probation can be either "reporting" or "non-reporting." Reporting means you must maintain regular contact. Usually this means physical, in person contact with your probation officer, although the contact can occasionally be made by phone or by mail. Non-reporting means you are officially still under supervision by the court but do not have to make this regular contact with a probation officer. Some reporting probation can be converted to non-reporting after a period of time such as where the conditions specified by the court are met.

"Intensive probation" is a term used to describe very strict and harsh reporting and compliance. Many courts are starting to utilize intensive probation to control every aspect of a repeat OWI offender's lives. In this way, some offenders are essentially set up to fail because compliance with all of these terms is extremely difficult. This usually occurs with "sobriety courts" specific to substance abuse offenders. It may include home visits by a probation officer, increased random drug and/or alcohol testing at ANY time, as well as routine visits to discuss your compliance with a judge.

16.3.7.1. Conditions of Probation. Since jail time is nearly always a very real possibility for all OWI offenders, probation with no jail time should be thought of as a gift given by the judge. Consequently, probation is a non-jail alternative only as long as you comply with all of the many terms and conditions imposed by the judge. These terms and conditions usually include that you pay fines and costs and comply with the other terms and conditions imposed such as community service, alcohol education or treatment, complete non-use of drugs and alcohol, maintain or seek employment, and not violate any criminal laws while on probation. Of course, you must also report regularly to your probation officer. It is important that you maintain a friendly relationship with your probation officer at all times. They have the power to make you take a drug test whenever you meet with them. If you are required to go to three "meetings" per week, they have the power to let you make up time another week if you are ill, or to force you to go even while sick. They can recommend early release from probation to a judge if you are compliant. Further, it is important not to volunteer too much information, even if positive, to your probation officer. If you mention, for example, that you are taking classes at a college, it is possible they will then make it a part of your probation.

16.3.7.2. Community Service. This part of the probation is done under supervision by the probation department which assigns you to various public or non-profit service programs. It will be up to your probation officer to approve the type of service done.[449] While it is discretionary, almost any public or non-profit program may be accepted, such as church, school or community programs. Before you begin such community service, however, you should make sure such programs are pre-approved by the probation officer. Otherwise, your long hours may not count toward the sentence.

The types of service typically accepted range from picking up trash, to building homes for the poor, to working in a state facility. It is often best to call charities you are interested in and make a list for approval from your probation officer. It may mean the difference between spending countless hours mopping a floor to doing something less tedious. Just in case a question arises from the court, it is very important for both you and the probation officer to independently keep track of the hours spent. Written verification signed by the community service provider is almost always mandatory.

16.3.7.3. Probation Supervision Fee. In addition to fines and costs, you will also be required to pay a monthly probation supervision fee. These fees typically range between $30 and $50 per month. Regardless of the reason, a failure to pay these fees can result in the court revoking your probation and ordering you to spend all or part of the remainder of your sentence in jail.

16.3.7.4. Restitution. Restitution is the legal term identifying the repayment to a "victim" of a crime for any costs incurred as a result of the criminal behavior. For example, where an accident is caused by an OWI defendant, the court may order that the monetary value of any loss be paid back by the defendant. In OWI cases, restitution also may include lost wages for an injured person, medical bills, or both. Restitution for property damage is also a common "sentence" condition. Restitution may be a condition of granting you probation or giving you a shorter sentence than otherwise.

Although not strictly restitution, Michigan law also provides that OWI defendants be required to reimburse the costs of prosecution.[450] These costs typically range between $200 and $400, and are payable directly to the arresting police department. There have also been instances when prosecuting attorneys have attempted to "tax" their costs onto the defendant's "legal bill" to the court, but this is unusual.

16.3.8 Victim Impact Panel. You will likely be assigned to attend a Victim Impact Panel run by M.A.D.D. These are usually offered once a month and they do charge a fee. In general, someone from M.A.D.D. will talk about the dangers of intoxicated driving, followed by a film which often includes gory visual images, and then a speech from a victim of intoxicated driving.

16.3.9. Impact Weekend. For first and second OWI offenders, this is a three day course paid for by the defendant. It involves over 20 hours of classroom discussion as well as community service.

16.4.10. "Creative" Probationary Requirements. Rarely, some judges impose unique penalties. This may include a requirement to attend an autopsy and subsequent discussion by a coroner, viewing a specific film, or reading a specific book and giving a report about it.

16.4.11. Probation Revocation. If you violate any of the terms of your probation, the probated sentence can be revoked. All or part of this revocation is done at a "show cause" hearing before the judge who sentenced you. At this hearing, evidence of the violation must be presented. If you dispute this violation, you can also present evidence or testimony at this hearing. The amount of proof at these probation revocation hearings is much less than for a criminal conviction. "Preponderance of the evidence" or enough evidence to be "probative" of your guilt, rather than "proof beyond a reasonable doubt" is all that is required.[451] If you lose this hearing, you may spend the remaining time of your probated sentence in jail. It is also possible for you to spend more time than with your original sentence. As with most sentencing issues, this determination is discretionary with your judge.

16.4.12 License Suspension. As a part of the 1999 changes to Michigan's intoxicated driving laws, the court no longer has the authority to suspend your drivers' license. Now, the driver license sanction is handled only and completely by the Michigan Department of State's office. These sanctions are not "individualized," meaning they are the same for everyone. The length and terms of any driver license sanction depends only on the number of alcohol convictions during the appropriate enhancement periods. The Department of State will also collect a "driver responsibility" fee of either $500 or $1000, and this amount is payable for the first two years after the conviction. The court may also require that an ignition interlock device be installed on any vehicle the defendant will drive. This type of device checks your breath alcohol before ignition.[452] The suspension or revocation of your license is mandatory. This is a relatively immediate and unchangeable function of Michigan's statutes and is based solely on the number of OWI convictions. The judge is totally powerless to "grant" any type of limited driving privileges. However, if one is enrolled in sobriety court they may drive a vehicle with interlock device after 45 days.[453] After your conviction, the court will notify the Department of State. This is called "abstracting the conviction." Once they learn of the conviction, they will then track your master driving record and impose the appropriate sanction. You will be notified of this sanction by mail. The Department of State notice will include a "to" and "from" date, and instructions on how to obtain or attempt to obtain driving privileges at the conclusion of the revocation period.

16.4.13. Judge Sentences – Issues to Consider. Judges are supposed to know and follow the law. Every day, they are faced with people who are accused of breaking the law, and pass judgment on them. They see people accused of OWI every week, if not every day. An experienced OWI lawyer knows each judge's tendencies and "peculiarities," and on this basis, may recommend to you that you have a substance abuse evaluation performed by a competent therapist, or that you begin attending AA meetings or start community service. In fact, your attorney will probably recommend these things long before he or she has accessed your likelihood for success at trial.

While you may believe that this type of activity is an admission of guilt, you should understand that this is being recommended because your attorney believes that it will have a positive influence on your case. In making such a recommendation, your attorney is considering what factors may influence the judge (if you are later convicted) to give you a more lenient sentence. The ultimate goal is to help you avoid the maximum penalty. When handing down a sentence, judges appreciate your "taking the initiative" to get treatment and to seek to "change your behavior." Even though you may consider yourself not to be guilty of any crime, if you ultimately are convicted, prior preparation may save your job or may mean the difference between significant jail time and probation.

Becoming involved in treatment can also have a positive influence on plea negotiations. Prosecutors are much more likely to agree to a significant reduction or some other unusual result if they believe that you are making an earnest effort to address any underlying drug or alcohol abuse problem. Both judges and prosecutors are concerned with protecting society and the perception that they are being soft on drunk drivers. Treatment can often be the cover they need to justify an atypically lenient plea or sentence bargain.

Chapter 17:
Appeals and New Trials

17.0. Purpose of the Chapter. Once your trial is over and you have been found guilty by a judge or jury, important dynamics will be set in motion. Aside from possible jail time, the next most serious potential consequence is the loss of your driving privileges. This loss will take place within a matter of 2 to 3 weeks, as it will take some time for the Michigan Department of State to be notified by the court that you have been convicted of OWI, and then some additional time for them to notify you of the applicable driver license sanction. You will only be able to obtain a restricted license or work permit if you have no other alcohol convictions within the prior 7 to 10 years.[454] If an administrative license suspension or revocation is already in place, this new suspension or revocation will likely will result in additional "904" suspensions,[455] but in other situations, it is possible for the two sanctions to run coterminous.

The "appearance bond" that was posted at the time of your arrest terminates upon a conviction. However, you will remain on bond until you are "remanded" (turned over) to the custody of the sheriff to serve any jail time called for by your sentence. Unless you have been convicted of a serious alcohol felony, such as where a death or a serious injury is involved, it is likely you will remain on bond and won't be sentenced for at least several days, and perhaps not for weeks. At this point, there are several options available to your attorney, and some of these options may delay or prevent any immediate jail sentence.

You may decide to take no further steps to fight your case and merely accept the conviction and penalty placed on you, complete the conditions of your sentence including jail time, and move on with your life. Nevertheless, it may be necessary for you to ask your attorney to request that you be allowed to defer your jail sentence for some brief period of time based upon some personal or business need.

Another option is for your attorney to file a motion for a new trial. In making such a motion your attorney is arguing that there was significant legal error that made your conviction unfair or unjust. Your trial judge will review the specific legal issues raised in the motion and will determine if errors were made that justify "vacating" (removing) the conviction and starting over with a new trial. Motions for a new trial will be discussed fully in this chapter.

In rare cases, other motions may be pursued by your attorney. These motions are based upon the specific facts of your case and legal issues that your attorney raised during your trial. If successful, such motions may actually convince the judge to make a ruling that tantamount to these facts and issues, you **NOT** be convicted at all. A ruling of this nature would likely be due to the prosecutor's failure to either meet all of his or her required proof at your trial or the prosecutor's failure to properly prove the charges against you.

A fourth option is to appeal your case to a higher court. If this is done, some courts will allow your attorney to file an application for an appeal bond that lets you stay out of jail Be aware, however, that in Michigan appeal bonds are rarely granted. This chapter discusses all options available to your attorney if you decide not to accept your guilty verdict and forego appealing further.

17.1. Having Paperwork Ready, if an Appeal Bond will be Permitted. In some courts it is possible to apply for a supersedeas bond immediately after your conviction is entered by the court.[456] The word "supersedeas is Latin for "you shall desist." This is an order (a writ) issued after your conviction by the trial court that instructs the sheriff to "hold off" enforcement of most aspects of your punishment, most importantly, jail time. The use of a supersedeas bond will also prevent the imposition of other "punishment" while the merits of your appeal are reviewed by the appellate court. Hence, mandatory terms of punishment such as community service or alcohol assessment and treatment can be deferred until the appeal has been decided upon.

Because the driver license sanctions in Michigan are imposed by the Department of State, such a bond does not delay or prevent the imposition of a license suspension or revocation. The only way to accomplish this result would be to somehow persuade a court to notify the Department of State a second time to remove the original "abstract of conviction." This is unlikely to occur, so you may end up on bond but with no ability to work because you have no license.

Most experienced OWI attorneys will have all the standard appeal documents prepared for immediate filing in the event you lose the case. This is important because it may take months for an appeal to be prepared and briefs written and argued. Then, several more months may pass before you receive a ruling by the appeals court. If the proper paperwork is not timely filed, and the bond granted, you could be fully punished BEFORE the appeals court has a chance to review the errors by the trial court and possibly overturn your guilty verdict.

17.2. Deciding whether to Appeal or File a Motion for New Trial or Motion in Arrest of Judgment. Everyone is familiar with the concept of an appeal; that is, the concept of having a lower court's decision or verdict reviewed by a higher court. However, there are less familiar tactical choices that might be sought by your attorney either before or as an alternative to a more formal appeal. Pursuing these "other" options will usually have no effect on your right to pursue a later appeal.

A motion in arrest of judgment is a special form of post-conviction pleading. It is generally only filed when a jury has found you guilty and some flaw or missing component in the State's case dictates to the trial judge that he or she must overturn your conviction. Although motions in arrest of judgment are rarely available, if granted, your OWI conviction would be "vacated" (undone) and you would be acquitted of the OWI. A successful motion of this type ends with the judge declaring that the State failed to prove or properly accuse the OWI offense fully, and therefore that the jury's verdict cannot stand.

A motion for a new trial is a more common pleading that, like the motion in arrest of judgment, is filed at the trial level. Such a motion allows the trial judge the opportunity to "correct" the improper verdict before an appellate court has the chance to review the case. A motion for a new trial is based on a guilty verdict which is contrary to the evidence, and the principles of justice and equity are strongly and decidedly against the weight of the evidence.[457] It is more common for a motion for a new trial to be sought in a jury trial rather than a bench trial.

Trial level courts have a variety of names, and these names may depend on the physical location of the court. In Michigan, the court of primary or general jurisdiction is the "circuit" court. This is where the more serious crimes such as felonies are heard. The "district" court is considered a lower court, and its jurisdiction is "carved out" of the circuit court's larger jurisdiction. So, if your case is a misdemeanor, it will always be heard in the district court. The first appeal from the district court is to the circuit court. After an unsuccessful appeal to the circuit court, the final appeal is to the Michigan "Court of Appeals."

If your OWI case is a felony, then your first level of Michigan appellate courts is to the "Court of Appeals." In that case, your final appeal would be to the highest state court which is, of course, called the "Supreme Court." Your experienced OWI specialist will help you review Michigan's courts that handle appeals so you can see what avenues of appeal may exist.

17.2.1. Appeals. In Michigan, you only have the right to one trial, but you can opt for either a bench or a jury trial. You also have a right to at least one appeal.[458]

Appellate courts are generally in place to review the actions of the lower court that handled your trial. In an appeal of a criminal conviction you no longer have a presumption of innocence as you did at trial.[459] On appeal, the evidence is reviewed with an inference that the verdict reached was correctly rendered.[460] Appellate courts utilize different "standards of review" in considering a multitude of different types of appellate errors that a trial judge may have committed. Your experienced OWI attorney will know all these "standards of review."

Appellate courts are primarily concerned with questions of fairness and the proper application of law, not whether you are in fact guilty. Thus, the focus of an appeal is not to look at issues of "guilt" or "innocence." Instead, the purpose of an appeal is to review rulings of the trial court that led to a failure of justice or a misapplication of state law or procedure. Since this is the "focus" of an appeal, an appellate issue is only "preserved" and thus subject to appeal where timely objections or challenges were made at or before your trial. Such challenges might be raised relative to the form or the nature of testimony received during your trial, or may allege certain evidence, such as your breath test result, was improperly admitted. Your attorney may also argue that the jury was given improper advisements on the law. The essential argument is that since the trial judge improperly instructed the jury or allowed evidence to be wrongfully heard by the jury, the jury's verdict was tainted and should not stand.

As indicated, any rulings that were made at any pre-trial or mid-trial motions are also subject to appeal. Hence, your attorney's written motions, oral objections or motions, jury challenges for "cause" (meaning that your attorney sought to exclude a juror who was obviously biased) are all possible places that the judge made erroneous rulings that may cause your conviction to be ultimately overturned.

A trial transcript can be from several hundred to more than a thousand pages in length. This transcript contains the "record" of all that was done in the case. In reviewing your case, the court of appeals will confine its review only to what is contained in the transcript. Legal challenges made at any stage in your case can potentially offer a chance for appellate review, and it is these rulings of law by the judge that form the basis of most appeals.

Once your trial is concluded, your attorney generally has a very limited time in which to file an appeal on your behalf. Once this time limit has passed, very rarely will the appellate court hear your challenges made "out-of-time." Instead, the appellate court will simply rule that your appeal is too late. One form of late appeal that is available in Michigan is a "6.500" motion. Where appropriate, you should discuss whether or not such a motion is available in your case.

Once your notice of appeal has been filed, your attorney must obtain the transcript of your trial or hearing. The preparation of this record is generally your expense. After obtaining the "record," your attorney will thoroughly examine it to look for errors of law. Your attorney must also obtain the clerk's "record" of all documents that were filed before, during and after your trial. This is a certified account of every document filed in the case, including the date and time of filing. This will also carry a fee for preparation, and this cost will generally be passed on to you.

Once an appeal is correctly and timely filed, it typically takes anywhere from nine to twenty-four months for the appellate court to render its decision. Your attorney may or may not be asked to present an oral argument to the appellate judges to assist them in making their decision. The trend today is that most appellate courts prefer to only receive written argument, not oral arguments. While it is true that only 10-15% of the cases that are appealed get favorable results from the court, "deals" are sometimes cut while the appeal is pending that could result in a reduction in the original charges, or a reduction in the sentence.

If the appellate court decides against you, you may still have the opportunity to bring a form of request for further review to the Michigan Supreme Court. This court not only looks at the possible errors of law, but may also review the legal reasoning given by the intermediate appellate court. Usually, the request for review by the Supreme Court is a matter of "discretion" and not mandatory. Generally, the Supreme Court gets to choose which cases it hears, and more importantly, which it will not.

Once the Michigan Supreme Court has either accepted your petition for further review or refused to take the case on certiorari(an order directing a lower court to send the record in a given case for review), almost all cases are at the end of the final "review" stage. In rare circumstances, a federal or state "habeas corpus" proceeding may be sought. However, this is almost never done in OWI cases.

17.2.2. Motion for a New Trial. A motion for a new trial may be granted if the verdict is contrary to the evidence, or if the principles of justice and equity are decidedly and strongly contrary to the jury's guilty verdict.[461] Your OWI defense attorney may also be able to convince the trial court judge that one or more critical rulings made at trial were incorrect, thereby justifying a new trial. In other words, the trial judge has the discretion to decide that based on the evidence (or lack of evidence) presented at trial, or based upon the judge's erroneous rulings during trial, that the jury's verdict needs to be vacated (removed) so that a new trial can be heard again without such "error" (or errors) being part of the presentation of evidence. This motion must typically be filed within 60 days of the entry of the judgment against you.[462]

17.2.3. Motion in Arrest of Judgment. A motion in arrest of judgment is asking the trial judge to not allow the entry of any judgment of you due to a serious technical problem with the evidence that has been produced or possibly a problem with a defective accusatory document that the state produced at trial. To sustain a motion in arrest of judgment, it must typically be based upon the court in question lacking jurisdiction or that the evidence presented at trial is in some respect fatally deficient or defective and (therefore) legally insufficient to support a judgment.[463]

17.3. Extraordinary Motion for New Trial, Based on Newly Discovered Evidence. The granting of a new trial based on newly discovered evidence is very rare. Numerous well-established criteria must ALL exist and be shown to have occurred by the party seeking the extraordinary motion before a new trial will be granted.[464] Failure to show *even one of these requirements* is sufficient to authorize the judge to deny the extraordinary motion for a new trial.

In a nutshell, this "newly discovered" evidence must not only be "new" but must also be of such a nature that the new evidence was not known, or could not have been known, to the party bringing the motion. The new evidence cannot be merely repetitive or cumulative of what was already presented at the original trial. The new evidence cannot be merely information that will impeach the credibility of a witness who testified at the original trial. The granting of this extraordinary motion for a new trial is left to the discretion of the trial judge, and no appellate relief will be granted to overturn the trial judge's ruling except upon an "abuse of discretion."

17.4. What can the Appellate Court Consider in the Appeal, and what can they (or will they) not Consider? There are two basic types of appeals, "final" appeals and "interlocutory" appeals. With an interlocutory appeal, your attorney is able to bring the appeal before a verdict has been received, and sometimes before a trial is even begun. Your attorney would also usually bring a motion for stay of proceedings while your interlocutory appeal is heard. Such stay is, of course, discretionary with the court. However, if it is not granted, then it may make little sense to pursue an interlocutory appeal. Instead, the issue can be "preserved" for appeal after the verdict has been rendered.

Unless the issue is brought as an interlocutory appeal, appellate courts will usually only consider final judgments or decisions.[465] A final judgment is one that disposes of all claims affecting all parties that were brought before the court.[466] Except in extraordinarily rare circumstances, the appellate court will not retry your case, will not weigh evidence, or review the jury's (or the trial judge's) determinations of fact (like guilt or innocence).

Appellate courts are quick to point out that they are not seeing and hearing the actual witnesses. Instead, they review the "record" (the transcript and pleadings filed at or before trial). They will seldom review any of the physical evidence presented at trial, including any video tapes. The focus of the appellate courts is to look for erroneous trial court rulings of law that somehow affected the outcome or were so significant to the evidence being considered by the jury that without it, there may not have been a conviction.

As mentioned above, the appellate court only reviews decisions on legal issues made by the trial court. These rulings usually involve the admission of evidence, or the refusal to admit evidence. Sometimes, these rulings involve the granting or denial of oral or written motions, or the overruling or sustaining of objections made by your attorney or the prosecutor in the midst of the trial. Improper jury instructions are also a very common issue. For you to have any chance on appeal, you must have a skillful trial lawyer who has the innate ability to seamlessly create a proper record of numerous challenges to the evidence and instructions offered at trial.

The form of the decision by the appellate court can take many forms. The appellate opinion may briefly review the arguments and "**affirm**" (uphold) your conviction. This means the appellate court believes that the trial court either "got it right" or was close enough that any error didn't affect the verdict. The appellate court may also rule that an error was made by the trial judge, and that the error was of a type that will cause a "new trial" to be ordered, free of the erroneous prior ruling. If the prior conviction is overturned, then this last type of ruling is the most common appellate result. The appellate court may also review the "challenged" rulings from lower court and find that the rulings were of such a nature that justice was denied. In that case, you walk free of all of the charges. It is very unusual for this to occur, and in the best case scenario, you usually end up after the successful appeal in exactly the same position you were in just before your trial began.

The appellate court may **modify** a lower court's verdict, and change it somewhat to better fit with the law as determined by the appellate court. This, however, is rare in OWI cases and other criminal law concerns. If the appellate court believes that the trial court did something wrong and this error was significant, then what they may do is to instruct the trial court not to allow the evidence or the instructions to be heard by the jury for your next trial. In order to make such a ruling, the appeals court must believe that such improper evidence or instructions are likely to have had an impact on your jury's verdict of guilty. In such cases, the appellate court will return the case or **remand** it with appropriate instructions to the lower court for your retrial.

An appellate court might decide that the "legally admissible" evidence was insufficient to sustain a conviction. This can result from the trial judge overruling objections by your criminal defense attorney or the trial judge not granting a motion for directed verdict of acquittal. In such a case, the appellate court will **reverse** your conviction. In some cases, the reversal will also contain language that constitutes an "acquittal," due to the fact that (without the erroneous evidence being introduced) the remaining evidence was insufficient to support the OWI charge. In a smaller number of "reversals" of convictions, the case cannot be retried. This means that after the appellate court makes a finding that your rights were so significantly violated that you cannot be tried again so you win your freedom from the OWI charge.

17.5. Is Your Punishment Held in Abeyance During Your Appeal? Maybe. The availability of a supersedeas writ or bond is a function of Michigan's laws.[467] If it is available, your sentence (or most aspects of it) will be delayed until the appeal is finalized. If not, you will begin your sentence at the discretion of the trial court. In most misdemeanor OWIs, you have a specific right to be released from jail after posting a reasonable bond pending your appeal. Your knowledgeable OWI defense attorney will know about the availability of an appeal and deferral of the imposition on punishment in your state.

17.6. Is Your Probation Oversight or Delayed Totally Until the Case is Finalized on Appeal. If you are convicted of an OWI offense, and an appeal is sought along with a supersedeas writ or appeal bond application, you may be required to have a probation officer assigned to your case until your appeal is finalized. You may have to report periodically, either in person or by mail. The probation officer may not need to see you all the time, but may check the state crime information computer weekly or monthly to make sure that you have not violated any new laws. You may need to be monitored through some means of electronic detection, such as through an alcohol monitoring ankle bracelet or an alcohol detection and monitoring system on your home phone. All of this occurs, however, while you remain free on bond.

17.7. License Loss is Usually Immediate, even if other Punishment is Held Off. No matter what other punishment might be delayed due to the start of an appeal process or as a result of filing a motion for a new trial, the loss of your drivers' license is not usually held off. Since October 1, 1999, the driver license sanctions are generated automatically by the Michigan Department of State, and are, based upon receipt of conviction information and a review of your master driving record.[468] This conviction information is sent to the Department of State by the court where your case is pending. You are then notified some time later about the specifics of the driver license sanction, including when it begins and when it ends.

In spite of an appeal or motion for a new trial, your license will usually remain suspended. The determination of when reinstatement can occur depends on Michigan's laws. Usually, you remain suspended until: (1) you are either found not guilty at a new trial; (2) or the appellate court reverses your original conviction; (3) or the period of suspension or revocation (as set by state law) is completed and all conditions for reinstatement have been met by you.[469] These conditions vary significantly depending on if your license was suspended or revoked. With a simple suspension, you will probably only be required to pay a reinstatement fee. However, with a revocation, you will be required to have a successful restoration hearing before the Michigan Administrative Hearings Section. Also, if your license was revoked, you will be required to install an ignition interlock device as a part of your driving privilege.

17.8. Expungement of a Conviction is Controlled by Statute and by Michigan's Decisional Authority. For crimes other than OWI, Michigan allows for your record to be cleaned of any first misdemeanor offense after five years and assuming you commit no other criminal offenses.[470] Also, if your conviction of a Michigan law has violated your civil rights, then a federal district court likely has the power to expunge your criminal records.[471] Regardless, the federal government almost NEVER totally clears all records and computer notations to your criminal arrest record.

Unfortunately, Michigan does not allow expungment of any OWI crimes under any circumstances.[472] Michigan has also made it much more difficult to attack the legal sufficiency of prior convictions. This is called a "collateral" attack, and is rarely an option in Michigan.

Because you will never be able to remove your Michigan OWI from your record, if you apply for a security clearance in the future, possibly on a job application, it is usually best to inform your potential employer about your prior circumstances rather than to chance them finding the record of your conviction. Deception on a job application is usually considered to be worse than the old record of having made a mistake in your past. Clearly, the best report you can make to a prospective employer is that you were merely accused of OWI, but found NOT GUILTY. Hence, the value of having a top-notch OWI defense specialist is of paramount importance. A good OWI specialist will know the options available to you and can help you in whatever process is available. Do not expect your attorney to be able to correct a matter that is totally beyond his or her control.

17.9. If a New Trial is Granted by the Trial Judge or Your Case is Reversed and Remanded After an Appeal, will a New Trial be Required? Possibly. When an appellate court reverses (takes away the conviction) and remands (sends the case back to the trial court), they are saying that the trial court made one or more significant errors of law at your trial. This means that your conviction cannot be upheld. Often, the evidence that was allowed (incorrectly) to be introduced will either be excluded at your new trial or no longer available for use at the new trial. Hence, the prosecutor may not have enough evidence to proceed to a new trial. Under these circumstances, a dismissal or a reduction of charges may be mandated.

The prosecutor may also consider that his or her office already took their best shot at you, and is now faced with starting over. This is expensive, and often their witness or witnesses may no longer be available. Plus, your defense attorney will have the benefit of using the detailed, sworn testimony of the police officers at your first trial to impeach these officers at any new trial. Such facts may give your attorney powerful leverage to negotiate with the prosecutor to either dismiss the OWI charges or seek to reduce the charges to a lesser offense.

Chapter 18
Michigan Driver License Restoration

18.0. General Purpose to this Chapter. In Michigan, the term "habitual violator" does not have the same meaning and is not used the same way as it is in other states. Michigan does, however, have criminal enhancements for repeat OWI offenders, and this topic has been discussed in prior chapters. Michigan's Department of State also broadly applies the concept of a habitual violator when conducting the administrative hearing that is required when a repeat OWI offender attempts to regain driving privileges after a license revocation. In these driver license restoration hearings, the repeat offender must rebut the "presumption" that he or she is a habitual violator of Michigan's intoxicated driving laws.

It is also helpful to understand that in other states, multiple OWI offenders may have their driver's license permanently withdrawn. In these states, once a driver has been declared a habitual violator because of OWI convictions (or other serious driving offenses in some jurisdictions); it becomes illegal for him or her to operate a motor vehicle, even if they somehow obtain a driver's license.

This chapter discusses what is required for you to be considered a "habitual violator" in other states, and perhaps more importantly, what might make you subject to similarly enhanced penalties in Michigan. Also discussed in this chapter are the ramifications of having been placed in this unenviable habitual violator legal status.

18.1. Statutory Wording. Although there is no statutory definition of a "habitual violator" in Michigan, the courts have recognized a very similar status for repeat OWI offenders. A habitual violator in Michigan is essentially any person who has been arrested and convicted within the United States two or more times (of serious driving offenses like OWI) within seven years.[473] It does not matter if your two OWI convictions were each in different states.[474] If you meet this definition, then your driver's license will be revoked. This means a permanent loss of your driver's license and the privilege to operate a motor vehicle. After the minimum period of revocation (1 year or 5 years), you may re-apply for a license and try to prove that you will be a safe driver in the future. After conducting an appropriate hearing, the Department of State may deny or grant a restricted license.

Michigan has added other highly dangerous driving convictions other than OWI to the list of "HV" offenses that can count toward two violations within this time period. Examples of these are any felony where a motor vehicle was used, negligent homicide, manslaughter or murder where a vehicle was used and reckless driving.[475]

18.2. The State's Burden of Proof. The facts that led to your driver license revocation are of no consequence when you are found behind the wheel of a motor vehicle without a driver's license.[476] Once your driver's license has been revoked, if you are caught driving or operating any vehicle, the State is not required to address any collateral attacks that your attorney may raise as to why you originally received multiple convictions. As a general rule, the legitimacy of your prior convictions will not be considered in your current driver license action.

18.3. Habitual Violator Status Differs from "Recidivist" Status. A recidivist is a repeat criminal offender who is convicted of a crime after having been previously convicted of this same crime. If you are considered a recidivist, your penalty for the second conviction for the same crime may be significantly greater because of the existence of a prior offense. All that is required to become a recidivist is to break the law a second time. For example, you would be considered a recidivist if you received a second OWI conviction at any time in your life.

It is a crime for anyone to drive while intoxicated. Unless you are under 21 years of age, it is legal in Michigan to drive after drinking. If you are driving with an ignition interlock device on your car, of course you cannot consume any alcohol and drive. In this way, you are prohibited by law from doing something which other people can legally do. If your license is revoked, it is a crime for you to **operate any motor vehicle**, whether sober or intoxicated, for any reason, even though doing so would not be illegal for anyone with a license. Simply stated, having your license revoked makes you totally ineligible to operate **ANY** vehicle for any purpose, at any time, until your privilege to drive has been legally restored in accordance with state law.

18.4. Procuring a License from other State does not Cure Revoked Status. Once you have had your license revoked, if you operate a motor vehicle, you can be convicted of driving in violation of your revoked license even if you somehow obtain a driver's license from another state.[477] Your legal right to drive has been revoked by the state government and procuring a license by any means from another state will not restore your right to operate a vehicle. Your revoked status is typically uncovered when your full name, fingerprints, date of birth, social security number or other identifying information is entered into the state's computer database.

18.5. The Origin of Predicate Offenses Leading to "Revoked" Status. You can have your license revoked based upon a second or subsequent conviction for OWI or any of the other serious alcohol related offenses proscribed by Michigan, such as homicide by vehicle or by any similar violation of the laws of any state.[478] A conviction based on a plea of nolo contendere is considered in Michigan as a prior offense, and can be used for enhancement purposes just as if you were otherwise found or plead guilty. The enhancement periods in Michigan for the imposition of driver license sanctions/revocation are two OWI related offenses within seven years, or three OWI related offenses within 10 years.[479] Although the revocation period for a second offense is often said to be one year, and for a third offense, five years, it is more accurate to say that Michigan has lifetime revocation. If you have two priors within 7 years you may request a hearing within either 1 year or 5 years, depending on if you've had a prior revocation within the prior 7 years. Either way, if you lose your hearing, you can't make another request for at least another year. The fact of the matter is, once your license has been revoked, there is no guarantee that you will <u>ever</u> get your license back. See section 18.11, *infra*, for more details about revocation periods.

18.6. A Driver License Restoration is not a Criminal Proceeding. Unlike the underlying criminal OWI case, the driver license restoration hearing is civil in nature. This means that the burden of proof is slightly lower, and you do not benefit from the rights of the criminally accused, such as the presumption of innocence. In fact, the exact opposite is true. Instead of benefitting from a presumption as you do when faced with a criminal charge, at the driver license restoration hearing, the Department of State starts out with the assumption that they will not be giving you your license back. In fact, the rules say that they "shall not" give you your license back unless you show by clear and convincing evidence that you are of low or minimal risk to repeat offend.

18.7. Constitutional Considerations. One reason you do not have any criminal protections for the driver's license restoration hearing is that the United States Supreme Court has determined that taking away your driver's license is not denying you any of your State or U.S. Constitutional rights.[480] Having a driver's license is only a privilege, not a constitutional or statutory entitlement. This privilege can be continuously reviewed by the State that gave it to you. For good cause, this privilege can be taken away from you. However, the

State cannot take your license away without reason, or without notice and an opportunity to be heard.[481]

Courts across America have recognized a driver's right to due process of law in being able to challenge the legitimacy of the license revocation or the declaration of "HV" status.[482] When taking away your license for repeat OWI convictions, the State acts under its police powers for the protection of the public. So, while the right to hold driving privileges in your state is not guaranteed, nor protected by your legal rights, certain procedural and due process rights still are available.

18.8. The Quantum of Proof Required. Once your license has been revoked in Michigan, if you ever desire to again have a driver's license, it is up to you to provide "clear and convincing evidence" that you meet the statutory standards to get another license.[483] A revocation is imposed for multiple OWI convictions. Revocation means the permanent loss of your driver's license and privilege to operate a motor vehicle. After a minimum period of revocation (1 year or 5 years), you may re-apply for a license and try to meet your burden of proof.

The applicable statute starts out with the assumption that you are not going to obtain a driver license. In other words, it's just the opposite of a criminal case like intoxicated driving where you are protected by the presumption of innocence and you cannot be convicted unless and until the state meets it's burden of proof. The actual burden of proof is "clear and convincing evidence" which basically means the hearing officer must be left with a definite and firm conviction that your substance abuse problem is under control and likely to remain under control and that you are at low or minimal risk for repeat behavior.

Because the burden of proof is so high, and because the hearing officer is supposed to start out with the assumption that you are not going to obtain a license, he or she will be looking for any reason to deny your application. Here is part of what you need to show: (i) That your alcohol or substance abuse problems, if any, are under control and likely to remain under control; (ii) that the risk of your repeating past abusive behavior is a low or minimal; and (iv) that the you have the ability and motivation to drive safely and within the law.

18.8.1. Preparing for Your License Restoration Hearing. Once you are able to seek license restoration, in order to seek and be successful at a hearing you must have a substance abuse evaluation, passed a 10 panel drug screen, three or more notarized testimonial letters and community proof, and be prepared to give your own testimony

Your substance abuse evaluation must be current and prepared by a qualified professional. It must also be complete and accurate. To that end, you must be completely open and honest with the evaluator. You must ensure that he/she is aware of all of your past convictions/treatment/relapses/etc. The Secretary of State will hold you responsible for any deficiencies in the evaluation or discrepancies between the information in the substance abuse evaluation and other evidence presented. You should also provide along with the substance abuse evaluation an original copy of laboratory results of a 10-panel urinalysis drug screen report, including readings of the two integrity variables, most often creatinine and specific gravity.

If you obtain a substance abuse evaluation and it reports anything other than a good or excellent prognosis DO NOT submit it. You are looking for a report containing the therapist's opinion that you are in sustained remission as well as containing a good or excellent prognosis. Anything other than that can kill your chances for a license. The most important part of your appeal is the evaluation. Do not save money and go to someone that is inadequate because their evaluation is your argument. Go to someone who is at least an M.S.W. or PhD/M.D.

Once you have obtained the evaluation from your therapist, scan it for anything inconsistent with you actual past recovery or criminal history. Some errors you can correct yourself on your appeal paper and affidavit, but if it is bad enough, such as a wrong reporting on a blood alcohol levels, substance abuse history, convictions dates or months or years in recovery, you should go to your evaluator and have THEM change their report. Otherwise, if they make errors on your report it hurts you in that the hearing officer will consider your evaluator's overall prognosis was based on insufficient and wrong evidence provided by yourself. Again, these errors could KILL your chances of obtaining a license.

If you are under any medical care or attending counseling, then along with the substance abuse evaluation you should provide progress reports from care givers. If any medications are prescribed, you must provide the reason for them, the date they were prescribed, any changes in dosage, and the expected period that they will need to be taken should be specified. The report should indicate whether the medications are addictive or habit-forming and, if they are, that the prescribing doctor is aware of your prior substance abuse history. Therefore, you should have a letter from your doctor that your medications do not have implications regarding your ability to drive.

If you have a psychological ailment such as Bi-Polar disorder, anxiety or depression you should have your psychiatrist write a letter stating that your psychological ailment is under control. Hearing officers have in the past and continue to reject people's application based on their psychological conditioning if in ANY way that influenced drinking patterns.

If you are currently on an addictive drug this weakens your case. If you have a "marijuana" card this practically destroys your case. If you have one and want your license back, tear it up and forget it. Remember, if you are pulled over and they test you for marijuana it's an additional strike. You can go to prison if you have previously had two priors.

Regarding your community proofs including testimonial letters – your proofs must verify abstinence from alcohol, "non-alcoholic beer" and/or illegal drugs. There must be at least 3 witnesses and/or recent letters that conform to the directions contained in Form DAAD-66– They must be are very specific about length of any abstinence, and from a cross-section of the community, such as from work, family, friends, and support groups– they should not be just from AA or support group attendees. Hearing officers are looking for people that know you well. Letters from people stating that they have been to your residence and see no signs of alcohol, i.e. empty bottles, are a plus. Also, statements that you do not go to establishments that serve alcohol with them, i.e. "wet places" will help you.

Proof of weekly attendance and participation in an established, structured substance abuse support group – Such groups include Alcoholics Anonymous (AA), Narcotics Anonymous (NA), SMART RECOVERY, Alcoholics for Christ, or SOS (Secular Organizations for Sobriety, also known as Save Our Selves) and/or regular participation in a recognized substance abuse treatment and/or counseling program.

18.8.2. Minimum Requirements and Timing of License Restoration Hearing. The minimum necessary to request a DLR hearing is the substance abuse evaluation including the test instruments and a signed petition for license reinstatement. Common test instruments are the MAST test, the SASSI test, Addiction Severity Index, among others. Your therapist will select the appropriate instruments for your substance abuse evaluation. As of this writing, you need to have participated in and be graded on at least TWO tests and scored. This is part of your diagnosis. Timing is an important element of the entire process; the substance abuse evaluation must be dated no more than 90 days from our submission date, while the letters should not be older than 90 days at the time of the hearing. In a perfect world, every client would have would have a second evaluation/urinalysis and a second set of letters completed a few days prior to the hearing. Obviously time and monetary constraints will not make this possible for every client. However, it illustrates the importance that the Department of State puts on establishing a pattern of consistent testimony and evidence of sobriety.

18.8.3. Requirement for Complete Abstinence from Alcohol and Drugs. You will not be successful at your hearing for license restoration unless you can show COMPLETE abstinence from alcohol or drugs. This is an absolute requirement, which means total abstinence. In other words, telling the hearing officer that you had a Champagne toast last New Year's Eve will surely result in the loss of your hearing. This loss will have the monumental effect of your having to wait another year to even request another hearing. We always recommend that you be capable of testifying under oath that you've had no alcohol or drugs of any kind for at least 12 months before you request your hearing. If you can't show 12 months of absolute sobriety, then we recommend that you wait before contacting us.

18.8.4. How to Request a Hearing. Once you have accomplished a minimum period of sobriety, obtained a substance abuse evaluation and have begun working on your "community proofs," then you may submit your request for a hearing to the Michigan Department of State. Be mindful that your substance abuse evaluation must be "current" which means dated not more than 3 months before the date it will be received by the Department. Make sure your letters include the full address and phone numbers of those that have written them.

In most instances your attorney will file your petition, and it is strongly recommended that you obtain a lawyer. The form for the substance abuse evaluation may be obtained at the department of state web site[484] and when properly completed can be sent to: Michigan Department of State, Administrative Hearings Section, P.O. Box 30196, Lansing, MI 48909-7696. **It is STRONGLY recommended that you send your application through certified mail.**

18.9. Penalty. If your license has been revoked and you are caught operating a motor vehicle, you likely face a potentially significant punishment which may include incarceration for up to 93 days for a first offense. The penalty is even greater for repeat offenses.[485] A punishment only becomes "excessive" and unconstitutional if it either is nothing more than a purposeless and needless imposition of pain and suffering or it is grossly out of proportion to the severity of the crime.[486] In that light, an imposition of significant mandatory jail time (without the possibility of any of this spent on probation or parole) for driving with a revoked license is neither barbaric nor excessive.[487] Often, courts justify lengthy sentences based upon the clear danger that a two or three ton guided missile poses when driven by a chronically dangerous driver who has received clear notice of the lack of any legal right to do so. Furthermore, the time period to appeal your revocation is increased to the initial amount (1 to 5 years).

18.10. Novel Punishment within Trial Court's Discretion. Because the purposes of probation include a trial judge's duty to protect society and to rehabilitate the probationer, in states that have looked at this question other than Michigan, the court's discretion to impose other forms of punishment outside of the norm will not be questioned in the absence of express authority to the contrary.[488]

18.11. Habitual Violator and Administrative License Loss. In Michigan, your license will be revoked for one year if you have two OWI convictions within seven years and for five years if you have three OWI convictions.[489] During these periods you cannot even apply to have this status ended.[490] However, with a five year revocation, you can apply to again be allowed to drive after the first year if you have no prior revocations within the prior seven years. Also, if you fail to meet your burden of proof at your hearing, you cannot apply for another year. Thus, a one year revocation can easily turn out to be a two year revocation.

It is your burden of proof to show two things by clear and convincing evidence. First, that your substance abuse problem is under control and likely to remain under control. Second, you must show that you are at low or minimal risk for repeat behavior. If you are successful you will be given a restricted driver's license with an ignition interlock device. After one year you do have the option of requesting another hearing. Currently, this can be a "paper" hearing where one does not have to go before a hearing officer in person or via closed circuit television. The "paper" hearing is usually more favorable than the first in person hearing. If one is denied, they can then opt for an in-person hearing or go to circuit court for an appeal if they feel the ruling against them has been arbitrary and capricious.

Chapter 19:
Boating Under the Influence and Other Related "Impaired Operation" Laws

19.0. Purpose of this Chapter. Michigan has one of the highest per capita rates of boat ownership. This should come as no surprise due to the State's many navigable lakes and rivers. There can be no question that boating is important to Michigan's economy. Nevertheless, operating a boat while under the influence of drugs or alcohol is illegal in Michigan and carries penalties that are similar to the crime of OWI. There are also some important differences between drunk driving and drunk boating. This chapter discusses these similarities and differences, as well as the ramifications of flying while intoxicated. If you have any question, consult your OWI specialist who can likely give you best information.

19.1. Boating Under the Influence or Boating While Intoxicated (BUI-BWI). The drunken boating provision is in the Marine Safety portion of the Natural Resources and Environmental Protection Act.[491] The boating violation has not been "updated" to a 0.08 BAC level as have the driving provisions, and still references a 0.10 BAC. Otherwise, boating under the influence (BUI) or boating while intoxicated (BWI) is treated much like OWI in most situations.[492]

There are different ways you can be charged with BUI-BWI. One form of BUI-BWI is a "visibly impaired" offense, where you just have to be adjudged to be visibly impaired to the extent that it is less safe for that person to operate any moving vessel because of alcohol.[493] The determination of whether or not alcohol caused your ability to be impaired is a fact question for the judge or jury. Another form of BUI-BWI is a per se offense, that is it is automatically illegal for you to operate a boat if your blood alcohol level is at a 0.10 grams per 100 milliliters of blood level or higher.[494] As with automobile offenses, however, the prosecutor must still be able to show that the test result is admissible, and that the result is reliable.

Another form of BUI-BWI is a "visibly impaired" offense where you just have to be adjudged to be visibly impaired because of drugs while operating a boat.[495] The presence of drugs is usually determined by a blood test, and would therefore be defendable in the same manner as a drugged driving automobile case. Yet another form of BUI-BWI is a "less safe" offense where you just have to be adjudged to be less safe because of any combination drugs while operating a boat.[496]

There is little case law on the subject, because few trials go on to an appeal which would be recorded so as to establish case law. However, because of the similarities between BUI-BWI and OWI it is likely the courts would apply the same thought process and legal reasoning to both situations.

19.2. "Presumptions" (Inferences) Arising from Test Results. In 2003, the Michigan Legislature removed the presumptions from the OWI automobile statute.[497] However, no change was made to the drunk boating statute. Thus a presumption arises of your guilt or innocence if the State can or cannot prove specific blood levels of alcohol. If there was at that time less than 0.07 grams per 100 milliliters of alcohol in the person's blood, it shall be presumed that you were not impaired by alcohol at the time of the alleged offense.[498] If there was at that time 0.07 grams of alcohol or more, but less than 0.10 grams in your blood, no presumptions arise that you were or were not under the influence of an alcoholic beverage. If there was at that time 0.10 grams of alcohol in your blood, it shall be presumed that you were impaired by alcohol at the time of the alleged offense. Presumption does not equate to absolute proof. Attacks against this kind of presumption would likely either be against the fact that you were really operating the boat, or against the scientific accuracy of the test.[499]

19.3. Implied Consent. Similar to when you drive your vehicle on a public road, the term implied consent means that by operating a boat on any of Michigan's tributaries, you have implicitly and automatically given your consent to give a sample of your breath, blood or urine for chemical analysis if a law enforcement officer decides to arrest you for something occurring as a result of your operation of the boat..

19.4. Refusal Admissible into Evidence. If you are involved in a boating incident where a law enforcement officer requests that you undergo a breath, urine or blood test, and you refuse, this refusal can be used as evidence against you in virtually all cases.[500] While the implication may be obvious, the judge will instruct the jury that such evidence can only be used to prove a test was given, not as evidence of your guilt.

19.5. Underage Boating Under the Influence. Unlike in most other states, there is no Michigan statute against underage boating under the influence.

19.6. "Nolo contendere" or "Alford" Plea – are they Allowed? The ability of a person to be able to enter a plea of nolo contendere, or no contest, is dependent on other factors, but are generally allowed in Michigan only where there is an inability to remember what happened or where there is the risk of civil liability.[501] An "Alford plea" is a guilty plea where you do not admit that you did the act, yet you accept that the prosecution likely has enough evidence with which they could convict you. While there is a distinct scarcity of legal decisions regarding such pleas relative to BUIs, in general, under Alford, an individual accused of this crime may voluntarily, knowingly, and understandably consent to imposition of his sentence even if he is unwilling to admit his participation in acts constituting the crime.

19.7. Reckless Operation of Vessel or other Water Device. Simply being "reckless" in your boat is a violation of state law. Reckless operation can include, but it is not limited to, weaving through congested vessel traffic at more than idle speed; or jumping the wake of another vessel within two hundred feet of that vessel; or crossing the path or wake of another vessel when the visibility around the other vessel is obstructed; or maintaining a collision course with another vessel or object and swerving away in close proximity to the other vessel or object.[502]

19.8. Homicide by Vessel. If someone dies as a result of your operation of a boat, this is likely considered a homicide.[503] Like almost all other homicides, this is typically a felony offense, meaning the punishment can be more than a year in prison and severe fines.

19.9. Serious Injury by Vessel. Michigan has an additional serious (felony) criminal offense if you cause a serious injury through your use of a vessel. What constitutes a serious injury is considered on a case-by-case basis, but likely includes depriving another person of a member of his or her body, by rendering a member of his or her body useless, by seriously disfiguring his or her body or a member thereof, or by causing organic brain damage which renders the body or any member thereof useless.[504]

19.10. Implied Consent Warnings. The implied consent advisements must include your right to an independent test of your blood, breath or urine, that you have the right to refuse the test (although the officer can get a forced test with a court order), and that your refusal carries with it an automatic suspension of your right to operate a vessel in Michigan for 6 months.[505] Readers may note that the implied consent suspension for an automobile offense is 1 year. This was changed from 6 months to one year as a part of the other changes made to the OWI laws in 2003. The drunk boating statute was not similarly changed in this regard. The most important thing is that you inform your attorney if anything was read to you regarding your implied consent and what exactly was told to you by the law enforcement officer before any blood, breath or urine samples were taken from you.

19.11. Administrative Suspension/Revocation of Boating (and Possibly Driving) Privileges for Refusing to Submit to Testing. In Michigan, if you refuse to undergo a breath, urine r blood test at the request of a law enforcement officer following some boating incident, a six month automatic suspension of your boating privileges applies. This is similar to the automatic driver's license suspension for a refusal to take a similar test if stopped while driving a car, but obviously is for half as long.[506]

Additionally, all violations of the drunk boating statute are abstracted to the Department of State, and every conviction carries with it various court-ordered restrictions on your boating privileges, ranging from suspension to revocation. However, there are no ramifications to your automobile driving privileges from a boating violation.

19.12. Requesting a Hearing – Timing and Letter Requirement. Much like the qualified right you have to a driver's license, the qualified right you have to operate a boat cannot typically be taken away without you having notice and an opportunity to be heard. This is not a criminal hearing. It usually only affects whether or not you lose your right to operate a boat, not any punishment for any crime.

19.13. Term of Suspension. The length of this revocation or suspension of boating privileges for a BUI-BWI conviction can be for up two years for a first offense, although the typical suspension is 6 months.[507] Suspensions are typically longer for subsequent offenses.[508]

19.14. Penalties if Convicted. The penalties you face if convicted of BUI-BWI depend on if this is your first or a subsequent offense. For first offenses, you typically face up to 45 days of community service, up to 93 days in jail and or a fine of up to $500.[509] Subsequent offenses within 7 years may lead to up to a year in jail, a fine of up to $1000 and up to 90 days of community service.[510]

19.15. What Constitutes Reasonable Suspicion to Stop a Boat, Versus Stopping a Motor Vehicle on the Highway? The level of your activity for a police officer to have "reasonable cause" in order to legally stop you while you are in a boat appears to be less than or the same as what is needed for this same officer to stop you if you were driving your car.[511] The officer may also request a preliminary breath sample from you as a part of his or her investigation.[512]

19.16. Is Reasonable Suspicion even Required to Stop a Boat? In Michigan, some "reasonable cause" is needed to stop you in a boat.[513] It is likely safest to assume that unlike your home, the police may stop your boat at any time and inspect you and the contents for illegal activity. Boaters are also regularly stopped in Michigan waters for "safety" inspections. Such stops do not require any just cause or reasonable suspicion at all.

19.17. Flying Under the Influence. Similar to driving or boating under the influence of either drugs or alcohol, it is against Michigan law to fly while under the influence. It is also specifically against federal law to operate an aircraft while under the influence of either alcohol or drugs.[514] The Michigan statute reads that it is unlawful for any person to operate an aircraft in the air or on the ground or water who has 0.02 percent or more, by weight, of alcohol in his or her blood.[515] Take notice of the much **LOWER** alcohol standard that applies to everyone, regardless of the age of the pilot.

19.18. Federal Law also has Jurisdiction: Possible Double Judicial Proceedings Because of Two Sovereigns. Many of Michigan's waterways (rivers, lakes, great lakes and canals) form state, national and international boundaries. Consequently, you could be prosecuted in two or more different courts in two states for the same act of drunken operation of a boat or an aircraft. It is even possible for you to face prosecution in two different countries. Just as many flights might originate in one state or country and might overfly or land in a different one, because of Michigan's many great lakes and international waterways, it is possible for a boating trip to start in one state or country and end up in a different one. Also, because many of Michigan's waterways are considered "international waterways, they are subject to federal law enforcement and oversight.

Due to this ability to become subject to the laws of multiple jurisdictions, a "drunk" boater could potentially face multiple trials and sentences for any one continuous boating action. This is because each state and the Federal government are separate sovereigns, meaning they are independent governments. The concept of double jeopardy prohibiting multiple prosecutions for the same offense only applies when the multiple prosecutions occur within the same sovereign. Thus, if you commit a possible criminal offense like boating or flying while intoxicated, any state may attempt to prove that you violated the law within or above its boundaries when you were boating or flying after drinking or using drugs AND the federal government each could potentially prosecute you for the same actions. These same rules can apply to boating in more than one state's waters.

Chapter 20:
Snowmobiling and Off-Roading Under the Influence

20.0. Purpose of this Chapter. Michigan is known to have some of the nicest trials for snowmobiling and off-roading, so it is no coincidence that so many Michigan residents own snowmobiles and off-road vehicles (ORVs), such as ATVs, dirt bikes, and dune buggies. Because of this, laws have been passed in Michigan to regulate drinking while operating these "vehicles." Many of the laws are similar to the Motor Vehicle Code's section regarding drinking and driving.

20.1.0. Snowmobiling Under the Influence. Even though we would not think of a snowmobile as an automobile, the State may charge an intoxicated snowmobiler under both the Snowmobile Act as well as the Motor Vehicle Code.[516] Any violations and points you receive for operating a snowmobile will be placed on your driving record.[517] Therefore, any points that you received for driving a snowmobile intoxicated may result in having your driver's license becoming suspended or revoked.

20.1.1. Penalties Involved – Operating Snowmobile While Intoxicated. If you are charged with a first offense of operating a snowmobile while intoxicated, then you face a number of possible penalties. You may face up to 93 days of imprisonment, up to 45 days of community service, and/or fines ranging from $100 to $500.[518] If you are sentenced to perform community service under this statute, you must reimburse the government for the cost of supervision as a result of your activities if ordered by the court.[519] In addition, you may have your snowmobile operating privileges revoked for six months to two years.

As mentioned, Michigan courts recognize a snowmobile as a "vehicle" to which the Motor Vehicle Code can apply. Therefore, if you are convicted under this statute, you will receive six points on your driving record. And since the points are added to your driving record, you will have to pay a $1,000 Driver Responsibility fee for two consecutive years.[520]

If you receive a second conviction within seven years, the penalties are increased. You will face 10 to 90 days of community service and imprisonment of up to one year, or up to 90 days of community service and imprisonment for two days to one year. In addition to one of these penalties, you will receive a fine ranging from $200 to $1,000.[521]

Your snowmobile operating privileges will be completely revoked, and you will receive six points on your driving record. Due to the added points, you will be responsible for the $1,000 Driver Responsibility fee for two consecutive years.[522]

A third snowmobile OWI conviction within 10 years of two or more prior convictions means you will be guilty of a felony and face imprisonment ranging from one year to five years, or a fine of $500 up to $5,000.[523] Like with the second offense, you will have no snowmobile operating privileges. The felony also carries with it six points on your driving record, in turn, having to pay the $1,000 Driver Responsibility fee for two consecutive years.[524]

If you caused a serious impairment as a result of operating a snowmobile under the influence, you will be charged with a felony. You can face up to five years imprisonment and fines ranging from $1,000 to $5,0000.[525] A situation where death has resulted is also classified as a felony, punishable by imprisonment up to 15 years and/or a fine ranging from $2,500 to $10,000.[526] Both of these convictions carry six points on your driving record and a $1,000 Driver Responsibility fee for two consecutive years.[527]

20.1.2. Penalties Involved –Operating Snowmobile While Visibly Impaired. Like the automobile charge, the snowmobile statute also contains a charge of operating while visibly impaired. If you are guilty under this charge, you face up to 93 days of imprisonment, 45 days of community service, and fines up to $300. You will not be able to operate a snowmobile for 90 days to one year. In addition, four points will be added to your driving record.[528]

If you receive a second offense of operating while visibly impaired within seven years, you will face 10 to 90 days of community service and jail up to one year, or up to 90 days of community service and jail for two days up to one year.

Fines are increased, ranging from $200 to $1,000. Under this charge, you will not be able to operate a snowmobile for six months to two years, and will have four points added to your driving record.[529]

20.1.3. Allowing an Intoxicated Person to Operate a Snowmobile. Since snowmobiling is done mostly for recreation, many people allow their friends or family to join in and operate their snowmobile. It is important to note, however, that the "allowing an intoxicated person to operate" statute also applies to a snowmobile that you own or are in control of. A person who is convicted of allowing an intoxicated person to operate a snowmobile under their ownership or control is guilty of a misdemeanor. They will face up to 93 days of imprisonment and/or a fine ranging from $100 to $500.[530]

20.2.0. Off-Roading Under the Influence. Michigan law treats a driver of an off-road vehicle (ORV) quite similar to a driver of an ordinary automobile. Open containers of alcoholic beverages are not allowed to be transported or carried on an ORV unless it is in a compartment separate from that of the operator.[531] Also like in the Motor Vehicle Code, an operator is considered to have given his or her implied consent to chemical tests for a BAC level.[532] An ORV driver is treated so similar to an automobile driver that Michigan courts have ruled that an ORV was a "vehicle" for purposes of the Motor Vehicle Code, and so any person operating an ORV on a public highway while intoxicated can be charged and prosecuted under the Motor Vehicle Code or under the ORV act.[533]

The ORV statute states that you may be arrested for operating an off-road vehicle under the influence of intoxicating liquor or a controlled substance, or both, or for having a blood alcohol content of 0.10 or higher.[534]

20.2.1. Penalties Involved – Operating an ORV While Intoxicated. If you are convicted of operating an ORV while intoxicated, you will be found guilty of a misdemeanor, punishable by up to 93 days imprisonment and/or a fine ranging from $100 to $500. The statute also states that you will have to pay for the costs of the prosecution against you. As part of your sentence, you will be ordered not to operate an ORV for at least six months or up to two years.[535]

A second offense within seven years means you will be facing another misdemeanor; however, this one has increased penalties. The court may impose imprisonment up to one year and/or a fine up to $1,000. Your ORV operating privileges will be suspended for at least one year, up to a maximum of two years.[536]

A third or subsequent conviction within a 10 year period is a felony, punishable by a minimum of one year imprisonment, up to five years, and/or a fine ranging from $500 to $5,000. Your ORV operating privileges will be suspended for at least one year, up to a maximum of two years.[537]

The ORV statute mirrors the snowmobile statute for situations where serious impairment or death occurs as a result of operating an ORV while intoxicated. In a case where serious impairment has resulted, you will be charged with a felony and will face up to five years imprisonment and fines ranging from $1,000 to $5,000.[538] A situation where death has resulted is also classified as a felony, punishable by imprisonment up to 15 years and/or a fine ranging from $2,500 to $10,000.[539]

If you are convicted under any of the above mentioned ORV offenses, the Department of State will automatically add six points onto your driving record. And since the points are added to your driving record, you will have to pay a $1,000 Driver Responsibility fee for two consecutive years.[540]

It is also important to note that the court may order you to perform community service for a period up to 12 days. The statute also clearly states that you must reimburse the government out of your pocket for any cost of insurance incurred by them as a result of your activities under this section.[541] The payments don't stop there though. Before the court hands down your sentence, they will order you to undergo a screening and assessment to determine whether you would benefit from a rehabilitative service, an alcohol or drug treatment program, or some type of alcohol or drug education program. In doing so, you will be ordered to pay for the cost of the screening, the assessment, and the rehabilitative service.[542]

You should also know that before you accept any plea of guilty under the ORV statute, the court must advise you of the possible statutory consequences of a guilty plea in respect to your suspension of your right to operate an ORV, as well as the penalty imposed for violating the section.[543]

Something else you should be aware of is that the ORV statute contains a section that explicitly states that the court must prepare and immediately forward an abstract of the court of record to the Department of State for every case that violates the statute.[544]

20.2.2. Penalties Involved – Operating an ORV While Visibly Impaired. Like the Snowmobile Act, the ORV statute includes the operating while visibly impaired charge. It is a misdemeanor punishable up to 93 days imprisonment and/or a fine of up to $300, including the costs of prosecution. You will be ordered not to operate an ORV for a period of 90 days to a year.[545]

A second visibly impaired conviction within seven years has an increased penalty of up to one year imprisonment and/or a fine up to $1,000. You will lose your ORV operating privileges for a period of six to 18 months. A first or second visibly impaired conviction results in four points being added to your driving record.[546]

20.2.3. Penalties Involved – Allowing an Intoxicated Person to Operate an ORV. Like snowmobiles, ORVs are used mostly for recreation, and because of that people allow their friends and family to drive theirs. As in the snowmobile statute, you may be charged with allowing an intoxicated person to operate an off-road vehicle that you are in charge of or that you own.[547]

Chapter 21
Enhanced Intoxicated Driving Cases and Those Involving Injury or Death

21.0. Purpose of this Chapter. As mentioned, a drug or alcohol charge is not always a simple intoxicated driving. There are many particulars of intoxicated driving incidents that can not only affect the severity of your charge, but the charge itself. Many people do not realize how certain factors can impact an intoxicated driving stop – amount of drugs or alcohol consumed, certain passengers in the vehicle, causing the injury or death of others and even on ownership of the vehicle.

This chapter discusses some of the alternative alcohol related charges that Michigan lawmakers have come up with aside from the typical intoxicated driving offenses. Some of the charges are entirely different than the OWI statutes; others are similar and include harsher punishments.

21.1 The Super Drunk Law. A new law in Michigan has raised the stakes for drunk driving, toughening penalties for first-offense drunk drivers with a bodily alcohol content of .17 or higher.[548] This law is commonly referred to as the "high BAC" or "super-drunk" law.

The super-drunk law was made for the purpose of punishing those drivers who operate a vehicle with a "high" BAC much harsher than the typical drunk driver. The difference between a typical drunk driving and a super-drunk driving will turn on the result of your BAC. Prior to this law, you could receive a drunk driving charge for operating a vehicle with any level above at or above .08. With the super-drunk law, you are categorized as being "super-drunk" once your BAC is at .017 or higher.

21.2. What are the Potential Penalties Involved with the Super Drunk Law? The super-drunk law carries with it far more aggressive penalties. In some respects, it is similar to a second offense OWI due to the alcohol rehabilitation and ignition interlock device requirements.

21.2.1. Jail Time. The maximum jail sentence for a typical drunk driving case is 93 days in jail; however, if you are charged under the super-drunk law, that maximum jail sentence is increased to 180 days.[549]

21.2.2. Fines. The fines associated with the super-drunk charge have been increased as well. The typical drunk driving fees range from $100 up to $500. The super-drunk fees are higher, ranging from $200 up to $700.[550]

21.2.3. Driving Consequences. Your driving privileges will be seriously affected if you are convicted under the super-drunk law. The driving suspensions under this law are far stricter than those of a typical drunk driving. Not only is the license suspension period increased from six months to one year, the super-drunk law also demands a 45-day mandatory suspension before you can even attempt to receive a restricted license.

21.2.4. Ignition Interlock Device. If you are eligible to receive a restricted license, you must install an ignition interlock device in your vehicle for a minimum of one year.[551] This device would require you to blow into it in order to start your vehicle. As of now, this device also requires you to blow into while you are driving. Currently, there are different devices with different qualities as to how they are used. It is in your interest to compare devices and to do thorough research before electing which one to have installed in your vehicle. If the interlock device registers an alcohol level of 0.025 or higher, your vehicle will refuse to start, and moreover, you will have violated the ignition interlock rules.[552] A violation will result in a revocation of your restricted license, suspending it for one year, and that includes the mandatory 45-day day period in which you will not be able to receive a restricted license.[553] The super-drunk law has provisions that make it illegal for someone who has an ignition interlock order to drive a vehicle that does not have an interlock device.[554]

You will also have to incur the costs associated with the interlock device.[555] An ignition interlock device must be bought or rented from a company, which may charge you up to $100 a month to maintain. However, if you are indigent you can file papers and seek to have the cost reduced. Many companies also charge additional fees for installation, calibration, and security deposit as well as the final interlock report when you seek your full license.

21.2.5. Alcohol Treatment. If you are convicted under the super-drunk law, the court will order you to successfully complete one or more appropriate rehabilitative programs for a minimum of one year as part of your sentence. These treatment plans are prepared for you from an assessment performed by a person approved by the court. You will have to pay for the cost of the screening, the assessment, and the rehabilitative services.[556]

A drunk driving charge should never be treated as an open and shut case; rather, it may turn on a number of variables. A BAC level is one of those variables, especially when it comes to a super-drunk charge. Your potential penalties may depend on the amount of alcohol that a device registers. With so much emphasis being placed on a BAC result, you will need an attorney with experience and expertise in dealing with devices used to calculate bodily alcohol content.

21.3. Child Endangerment. Many states have laws that make it a crime to endanger the health or life of a child by certain negligent or reckless acts. Michigan law states that you may be charged with child endangerment if you drive intoxicated or impaired with a child under the age of 16 years old in your vehicle.[557]

21.3.1. Misdemeanor Charge. If you are found guilty of endangerment of a child under this law, you face the possibility of imprisonment ranging from 5 days up to a year, or 30 to 90 days of community service. You will also have to pay a fine ranging from $200 to $1,000. It is important to note that the court may also order your vehicle to be immobilized under this same charge.[558]

21.3.2. Felony Charge. If you have a second child endangerment charge within seven years, or if it is a third child endangerment charge (regardless of years), it will be considered a felony.[559] Along with having a felony record, you will also face possible imprisonment ranging from one to five years, or a period of probation ranging from 30 days to a year along with 60 to 180 days of community service. In addition, you will be ordered to pay a fine ranging from $500 to $5,000. The same vehicle immobilization statute applies to the felony convictions as well.[560]

21.4 Allowing an Intoxicated Person to Drive. The laws of intoxicated driving not only place responsibility on you to not operate a vehicle while intoxicated but also on allowing an intoxicated person to operate. More specifically, the law in Michigan states that you have a responsibility to not allow an intoxicated person to operate a vehicle that you own or control.[561]

If you become involved in a situation where you are a passenger in a vehicle that has been pulled over, you need to be aware that even though you are not the driver, you should not admit to things that you do not have to. Many passengers, either out of a feeling of guilt or an attempt to get leniency by police, will state that they should not have let the driver drive. However, this may be used against you if you later get charged with allowing an intoxicated person to drive. Furthermore, your vehicle is subject to possible immobilization or forfeiture. The general rule of thumb applies. Never confess anything to a police officer, keep your mouth shut and specifically invoke your rights against self-incrimination. The police are never your friends in these circumstances.

21.4.1. What the Prosecutor Must Prove. It is important that you never state that you knew the driver was intoxicated or impaired. The prosecutor must establish certain elements in the case against you, one of them is whether you knew that the driver was intoxicated or visibly impaired. The next thing that the prosecutor must prove is that the vehicle belonged to you or was in your control. If so, the prosecutor will try to show that you allowed an intoxicated driver to operate the vehicle.

21.4.2. What are the potential penalties for an allowing charge? If you are convicted of allowing an intoxicated or visibly impaired driver to operate a vehicle in your control or ownership, you will be guilty of a misdemeanor punishable by imprisonment up to 93 days and/or a fine ranging from $100 to $500.[562]

If the driver caused a serious injury as a result of driving drunk, then you too will be held responsible if you "allowed" the driver to operate the vehicle, as defined by the statute. The offense is increased from a misdemeanor to a felony. As far as the punishment, the court may hold you equally responsible and you may face up to five years imprisonment and/or a fine ranging from $1,500 to $10,000.[563]

The same policy is applied to an incident where the driver's actions result in death. Under the "allowing" statute, you can be held responsible and may face a felony, punishable by imprisonment up to two years, and/or a fine ranging from $1,000 to $5,000.[564]

21.5. Something to Consider When Dealing With Alternative Charges. Many people are not familiar with these charges because they are either new laws in Michigan or because they are less common than the typical intoxicated driving charges. It is because of that unfamiliarity that it is in your best interest to hire an experienced and well-informed OWI attorney.

A knowledgeable and experienced OWI attorney will know how to handle the case whether it goes to trial or to simply see if your incident even meets the elements of the crime. He or she will know how certain prosecutors and judges handle the type of crime you are being charged with. Moreover, you will want to know if you are receiving a good plea bargain by the prosecutor. An attorney not well versed in these laws won't know what type of deal to push for, let alone whether the deal being offered is even fair.

21.5 Intoxicated Driving Causing Serious Injury. If you operate a motor vehicle while impaired or intoxicated by either alcohol, drugs or any intoxicating substance, and by the operation of that motor vehicle cause a serious impairment of a body function of another person is guilty of a felony punishable by imprisonment for not more than 5 years or a fine of not less than $1,000.00 or more than $5,000.00, or both. By definition, the following injuries are included in this crime; "loss of a limb or loss of use of a limb, a foot, hand, finger, or thumb, an eye or ear, substantial impairment of a bodily function, serious visible disfigurement, a skull fracture or other serious bone fracture, subdural hemorrhage hematoma, or loss of an organ. Also, an accident that causes the victim to be in a comatose state that lasts for more than 3 days, or have measurable brain or mental impairment."

21.6. Intoxicated Driving Causing Death. If you are under the influence of alcohol, drugs or any intoxicating substance while driving, by operation of your car there is an accident, and a death occurs, then you are facing a felony punishable by up to 15 years in prison and a fine of between $2,500 and $10,000. If the death is a police officer or firefighter then the penalty is increased to 20 years.

If you are charged with OWI causing death, then you should expect very aggressive prosecution. In fact, OWI causing death is one of the most aggressively prosecuted crimes in Michigan. Additionally, meaningful plea and/or sentence bargains are exceptionally difficult to obtain, making a plea straight up or a trial on the merits the only remaining options. Thus, effective representation nearly always requires a knowledgeable and creative defense strategy. Armed with such a strategy which is then put forward by a top OWI defense lawyer you are far more likely to obtain justice in the courtroom.

21.6.1. Second Degree Murder a Possible Charge When Death Has Occurred. The trend over the last twenty years, and something that has intensified in the last five to ten years, is for courts and legislatures to reduce, if not eliminate, the amount of intent required to be convicted of OWI causing death. If there are any exacerbating circumstances, anything that can raise the negligence to gross or willful and wanton, then the prosecutor may try to further increase the penalty to second degree murder. In order to enhance the penalty from 15 years to life, as it is with OWI causing death, to life imprisonment, as it is with second degree murder , the essential elements that must be established beyond a reasonable doubt are: (1) a death, (2) caused by an act of the defendant, (3) with malice, and (4) without justification or excuse. The element of malice can be satisfied by establishing that you intended to do an act in wanton and willful disregard of the likelihood that the natural tendency of such behavior is to cause death or great bodily harm.

While not every case in which intoxicated driving leads to death constitutes second-degree murder, when the evidence establishes a level of misconduct that goes beyond that of intoxicated driving a conviction for second-degree murder can be sustained. Examples might be having a high BAC and traveling at an excessive speed, such as 87 mph in a 25 mph speed zone. The pre-eminent case that initiated second degree murder from drunk driving implies that if someone previously drove drunk they should understand it to be inherently dangerous and also know that the likely possible result is the death of another. This imputed knowledge satisfies the "intent" requirement. This means that even though you did not wish to harm or kill another person, if you previously were convicted of impaired or intoxicated driving, and therefore "knew" that driving while intoxicated was dangerous, on this basis alone the prosecutor can seek to have your OWI causing death charge raised to second degree murder.

21.6.2. Causation Element in Causing Death Cases. By the very nature of an accident causing death, there is often some question as to whether or not the accident was or must be the actual cause of the death. For example, what if it was not your intoxication that caused the accident? What if, instead of intoxication something unforeseeable occurs, and this unforeseeable event breaks the chain of causation? The legal term for this is "proximate cause." Michigan law relative to this sort of causation is not totally clear, but a leading case says that "proximate causation," in the criminal context, is a legal construct designed to prevent criminal liability from attaching when the result of the defendant's conduct is viewed as too remote or unnatural." This is an issue of foreseeability and ordinary negligence is considered reasonably foreseeable, and it is thus not a superseding cause that would sever proximate causation in the criminal context. Gross negligence" or "intentional misconduct" on the part of a victim is considered sufficient to break the chain of proximate causation between the defendant and the victim, in the criminal context, because it is not reasonably foreseeable. While a victim's negligence is not a defense in a criminal case, it is an important factor to be considered by the trier of fact in determining whether proximate cause has been proved beyond a reasonable doubt.

21.6.3. Is the Victim's Intoxication Relevant or Admissible? In an OWI causing death case it is not unusual for the victim to have drugs or alcohol in his/her system at the time of the accident. Michigan courts have struggled with whether or not evidence of the victims blood alcohol content (BAC) or the results of a drug test are admissible at trial. One recent case held that evidence of victim's BAC was admissible as relevant to issue of causation and whether victim was grossly negligent. In other words, the probative value of victim's BAC was not substantially outweighed by danger of unfair prejudice or jury confusion. An unpublished case however says that our Legislature has essentially created a presumption that a defendant-driver's intoxication while driving constitutes gross negligence. But, that no such presumption has been established as to victim-drivers' illegal intoxication. The court therefore declined to create a bright-line rule linking a particular blood alcohol level to gross negligence on the part of a victim driver.

21.6.4. Emotional Turmoil is Normal Where a Death Has Occurred. It is important to understand that when a death has occurred, you and your family will be experiencing intense emotions. There is a great deal of guilt and remorse experienced when processing the fact that you may have caused a death, and again, this difficulty in part relates to the randomness of the event and the lack of intent to do anything wrong. Add to this the fact that the victim's family is often out for vengeance and have no interest in listening to an apology or expressions of remorse and you may feel as if you have nowhere to go with those emotions. If there is a conviction, the sentences are almost always quite long, often measured in terms of a decade or more and this results in your family also losing a family member. It is very helpful to seek the assistance of a professional to assist you with dealing with these emotions whenever you are charged with OWI causing death. As much as you may wish to do so, it is important not to contact the family and admit guilt.

21.6.5. The Destruction of Evidence in Causing Death Cases. The biggest difficulty you will face is the potential destruction of the evidence from the accident scene. Sometimes this can happen simply due to the passage of time and the more time that passes from the accident itself, the more evidence will become less and less valuable. For example, if there are any skid marks that were left on the road, the state's expert will be measuring this, and using it as part of the causation determination. If by the time your traffic accident expert has been retained the skid marks are gone, then he or she will not be able to perform proper measurements. Similarly, if debris has been removed, either purposely or because of the weather or traffic conditions, then that is also going to play into the integrity of your expert's opinion. The same may be true for other evidence such as the condition of your car ad that of the victim, both of which will be kept for evidence. It is not unusual, however, for these to be eventually destroyed, thereby again depriving your expert from investigating and evaluating this valuable evidence. Depending on the police of the lab where the blood tests were conducted, a separate sample may or may not be available for independent testing by you and your attorney. All of this again demonstrates the need to act quickly and to obtain assurance from the prosecutor and perhaps the judge that such evidence will be available and not destroyed.

21.6.6. A Rushed Discovery Period in Causing Death Cases. Another handicap you sometimes face is also related to the emotions felt by the victim and the victim's family. They may be putting pressure on the prosecutor for a quick resolution and in turn sometimes the judge. Their response is to fast track the case and to propose a correspondingly rushed period of discovery. This might perpetuate an overall feeling that defending the case is a waste of everyone's time. Unfortunately, this is the acrimonious environment within which these cases are often litigated.

21.6.7. Deciding on a Case Strategy in Causing Death Cases. Once you have been debriefed by your attorney, and the discovery obtained and thoroughly understood, then your lawyer can begin settling on the best of the available legal theories to defend your case. In most instances these theories will broadly address either the intoxication or the causation elements of the crime. The case must ultimately be viewed through the eyes of a juror who will not have the same level of legal or scientific knowledge as you or your attorney. Be sure to have your lawyer use your experts not to further increase the complexity of the case, but rather to simplify the explanation of the issues to the jury.

21.6.8. A Final Note: Where Death Has Occurred Obtaining The Best DUI Defense Lawyer is Your Top Priority. A Michigan OWI causing death case is perhaps the most complicated case any lawyer can handle. Not only is the law exceedingly complex, it changes rapidly. In addition to complicated laws, there will nearly always be two blood tests, the one taken from you at the hospital, known as a serum blood test, and the one collected by the police and tested at the forensic laboratory in Lansing. Thus, your lawyer will need to be well-versed in both enzymatic reagent testing (serum) and gas chromatography (whole blood) testing. Inevitably there will also be an accident reconstruction, and your lawyer must also be facile with the science behind this as well.

Additionally, there are the delicate considerations of the political environment in which these cases are litigated. There will be an aggressive and usually very experienced and skilled prosecuting attorney assigned to the case. Pushing the prosecutor and calling for retribution will be victim's family, and presiding over your case will be a judge thinking about the next election. It is within this cauldron that your case will be defended.

The only way that you can hope to obtain any semblance of justice is simply to hire the best DUI defense lawyer you can find and afford. Make sure he or she has the right combination of skill, knowledge and experience handling intoxicated driving causing death cases. By finding the right lawyer you will maximize your opportunity for the best possible result. Doing so might save you from spending additional years in prison.

Bonus *Champion Reprint:* Independent Juries: Liberty's Last Defense[1]

By Patrick T. Barone & Brittani N. Baldwin

There is no dispute that American jurors have the right and responsibility of judging the facts in a criminal trial. But what about the law? Should they also be allowed to judge a law or societal practice that they believe to be unjust by returning a not guilty verdict when, perhaps, all of the elements of a crime have been proven?

A typical jury instruction in a criminal case may instruct that the jury may only decide questions of fact, and must take the law as the judge gives it. Jurors are instructed that they can only decide the truth and weight of the facts of the case, and apply the judge's law to these facts.

When a jury fails to follow this instruction, this act of defiance is called "jury nullification."[1] Jury nullification is the refusal of jurors to convict a defendant despite their belief in the defendant's guilt.[2] The jury is thus said to "judge the law," though more accurately the jury is judging the law's specific application, not its general validity. This divisive practice, once accepted, has become the unspoken secret of the American jury deliberation room. No longer may juries freely disregard laws that they believe to be unjust.

Jury Nullification: A Prominent Component of Early American Criminal Law

What options do jurors have when they disagree with a law, but recognize that the legal elements have been met? At the birth of

---

[1] Reprinted with permission; originally published in Champion Magazine (December 2012), Copyright is owned by the National Association of Criminal Defense Lawyers.

the United States, the Founding Fathers asked themselves this very question, and although "jury nullification" had not yet been named, the concept easily became an integral part of the American criminal justice system.

When the Founding Fathers convened at the Constitutional Convention of 1774, 12 of the states represented had already drafted state constitutions.[3] Of the various provisions included in these constitutions, the only one that had been included in all was the right of a criminal defendant to a trial by jury.[4] Given the role that juries had played in resisting English authority, this was hardly surprising at the time.[5]

During the pre-Revolutionary period, it was not uncommon for juries to act as the voice of the people, using their implied authority of nullification to free defendants who opposed involvement of the British and convicting those who sympathized with it.[6] In fact, it might be persuasively argued that jury nullification was the raison d'être of the constitutional right to trial by jury.

The unrest of the people in those pre-Revolutionary times was clearly evidenced by a series of trials involving seditious libel. In the most famous of those trials, none other than Andrew Hamilton represented accused printer John Peter Zenger.[7] Zenger was the printer of the *New York Weekly Journal*, a politically charged publication. In one edition, Zenger criticized the governor for arbitrarily revoking defendants' right to trial by jury.[8] During Zenger's trial, Hamilton had this to say to the judge, who insisted that the jury may only determine the issues of fact[9]:

> I know ... the jury may do so; but I do likewise know they may do otherwise. I know they have the right beyond all dispute to determine both the law and the fact, and where they do not doubt of the law, they ought to do so. ... [L]eaving it to the judgment of the Court whether the words are libelous or not in effect renders juries useless.[10]

The enduring conviction of the people to retain trial by jury was again made clear in 1776 when the Declaration of Independence listed a grievance against King George III for "depriving us ... of the benefits of trial by jury."[11] Fifteen years later, with the ratification of the Sixth Amendment to the U.S. Constitution, "the right to a speedy and public trial, by an impartial jury"[12] finally and irrevocably became available to those accused in a criminal prosecution.

This right to trial by jury was held so dear that of all the rights the Constitution guarantees to the people, it is the only one that appears in both the original Constitution and the Bill of Rights.[13] Additionally, three of the amendments in the Bill of Rights make mention of trial by jury.[14] Yale Constitutional Law professor Akhil Reed Amar has accurately noted that "juries were at the heart of the Bill of Rights."[15]

It is clear that jury nullification was an important component of early American litigation.[16] The importance of this right was certainly recognized by the Founders[17] and, for a time, echoed vigorously by the Supreme Court.[18]

Proponents of the concept have struggled to understand what made it such an integral part of early American law, only to become a pariah of modern litigation. Some believe that it was simply a matter of necessity — lawyers and even law books were in short supply. Later, however, it seems that that this power of the jury became a symbol of trust in the public's sense of justice.[19]

Early in its history, the U.S. Supreme Court heard a very small number of jury trials. One of them, in 1794, was *Georgia v. Brailsford*.[20] In *Brailsford*, jurors were told that they were presumed to be the best judges of fact while judges were presumed to be the best judges of the law.[21] However, they were also told that "it must be observed, that by the same law, which recognizes this reasonable distribution of jurisdiction, you have nevertheless a right to take upon yourselves to judge of both, and to determine the law as well as the fact in controversy."[22]

Jury Nullification Through the Ages

Andrew J. Parmenter interestingly explains the history of jury nullification in the United States by describing various centuries of fluctuation.[23] Parmenter's description is based on a review of the case law during each period. Thus, the period of 1789–1895 is called "The Century of the Jury."[24] Parmenter explains that "if there was any doubt about the jury's right to judge the law after the adoption of the Sixth Amendment, this doubt was quickly laid to rest in the Supreme Court decision of *Georgia v. Brailsford*, where Chief Justice John Jay instructed that juries have the right to determine the law as well as the fact in controversy."[25]

The decision in the 1895 case, *Sparf & Hansen v. United States*,[26] brought with it an end to "The Century of the Jury," and ushered in "The Century of the Judge (1886-1990)."[27] In *Sparf*, Justice Harlan ended almost a hundred years of relatively free exercise or jury nullification by holding that the court's determination of the law and the jury's determination of the facts "cannot be confounded or disregarded without endangering the stability of public justice, as well as the security of private and personal rights."[28]

After the decision written by Justice Harlan in *Sparf*, the use of jury nullification decreased drastically.[29] Courts seemed eager to end what many considered an "archaic, outmoded, and atrocious" practice.[30] But perhaps a more careful interpretation of *Sparf* was in order. The holding of the Court did not preclude judges from giving nullification orders in all circumstances; it only stated that it was not reversible error for an attorney to instruct the jury that it would be wrong to disregard the court's instruction of law.[31]

Parmenter goes on to describe the 1990s as "A Decade of Debate," citing nullification verdicts handed out in the Rodney King,[32] O.J. Simpson,[33] and Jack Kevorkian[34] cases. In the Simpson case, the defendant's attorney, Johnny Cochran, was well aware that the *Sparf* holding did not expressly prevent jury nullification, and he pleaded with the jury to send a message:

You … police the police. You police them by your verdict. You are the ones to send the message. Nobody else is going to do it in this society. They don't have the courage. Nobody has the courage. They have a bunch of people running around with no courage to do what is right, except individual citizens. You … are the ones in war; you are the ones on the front line.[35]

It would be very difficult to say with certainty whether the jury acquitted O.J. Simpson because the prosecution failed to prove its case, or if it was an example of "symbolic" nullification. The decision of the case was so polarizing that many people remember where they were when they heard the verdict. It might well be argued that the O.J. Simpson verdict was the most well-known example of jury nullification in recent times.

So We Know Juries Nullify, but Why?

In addressing the issue of jury nullification, young lawyer Arie Rubenstein observed that nullification can and does happen for any number of reasons.[36] He recognized and classified the most common. "Classical" jury nullification is, perhaps, the type that first comes to mind when a lawyer considers the concept. Classical jury nullification occurs when the jury believes that the law itself, or perhaps the mandated punishment, is not just.[37] "As applied" jury nullification is a little bit different. Jurors do not believe that the law itself is unjust, just its application in the case at bar.[38] Most people have a sense of how they believe their laws should be applied, and deviation from these preconceptions does not always sit well with juries. The most extreme example of this in the realm of jury nullification is "symbolic" nullification. When this happens, the members of the jury do not necessarily disagree with the law or its application; their decision, instead, is intended solely to send a message. This message may be directed at the court participants, the government, or society in general. Oft-argued as an example of symbolic jury nullification is the acquittal of O.J. Simpson.[39] It is believed by some that the intent of the jury was to send a strong message opposing improper police conduct.[40]

Early in U.S. history, jury nullification was at the very heart of the desire to maintain the right to trial by jury. Nullification was seen as a way to unhitch the yoke of British tyranny from the necks of the colonists. But as the United States grew secure in its own laws, jury nullification became less significant. And while a jury's power to nullify may currently be on the wane, a jury yet has the power to render a verdict "in the teeth of both law and facts."[41]

As a Nation "For the People, by the People," Jury Nullification Is Still Necessary

It is common knowledge that juries are responsible for returning the verdict, but it is usually the province of law schools to teach attorneys the rules that jurors must follow to reach that verdict. How often do lawyers think about, much less really understand, the constitutional role the jury is fulfilling? Furthermore, why did the Founders consider the right to a jury trial so essential to a properly limited government?

To answer these questions, it is helpful to remember that the U.S. government is made up of three co-equal entities — the judicial, executive, and legislative branches.[42] A system of checks and balances ensures that these branches do not grow too powerful or otherwise abuse their powers.[43] The jury system is one of these checks and balances.

Because the government exists to serve the people, there has always been a question of what role citizens may directly play in their own governance. On this topic, Thomas Jefferson wrote:

"Were I called upon to decide, whether the people had best be omitted in the legislative or judiciary department, I would say it is better to leave them out of the legislative. The execution of the laws is more important than the making of them."[44]

It would seem that the final act in this "execution" of the criminal law happens when the jury returns its verdict. Thus, as Jefferson suggested, jury service is a way for citizens to directly participate in the execution, rather than the making, of laws. If Jefferson's premise is accepted, it seems that criminal juries are a sort of hybrid, possessing the ability to judge the law and in doing so determine its appropriate execution. So how much influence can, or should, the judiciary have in limiting or otherwise influencing the jury's right to nullify? Said differently, as "keepers of the law," what role do judges have in explaining or denying nullification?

Proponents of jury nullification feel that it should be permissible to inform the jury of their right to nullify,[45] especially in cases where defendants may be technically guilty but are morally blameless.[46] Those opposed to jury nullification have argued that juries are not savvy enough to make findings of law. But research suggests that juries are more sophisticated than the court might assume.[47]

One of the foremost proponents of jury nullification is Michael Dann, a retired Arizona judge. Judge Dann feels that jury instructions are currently designed to prevent juries from exercising their prerogative to vote their conscience.[48] In fact, a recent study found that 75 percent of Americans polled would indeed vote their conscience if they felt that following jury instructions would lead to an unjust verdict.[49] Juries are instructed that they must convict if the applicable standard of proof is attained,[50] but this is not the only option. Juries have extraordinary latitude in the making of their decisions. There would be no legal consequence to them returning a not guilty verdict.[51]

Why then, when jury nullification has had such an enduring and accepted role in criminal trials, has it fallen so drastically out of favor with the courts? Today, juries will not be told that they have the power to nullify the law. Lawyers and judges in the modern era must agree on the law that is to be applied; agree to a general meaning of that law; and, through jury instructions, convey both to the jury. It is vehemently argued that there should be no mention to members of the jury of their ability to consider the option of nullification. Any deviation from this model is met with, at the very least, apprehension. And sometimes the reaction is much more hostile.

In 2011, New Jersey resident Julian Heicklen was indicted on charges of jury tampering for handing out pamphlets on the steps of the courthouse and telling passersby about the option of jury nullification.[52] The 78-year-old retired Pennsylvania State University chemistry professor made clear that he never targeted actual jurors in ongoing cases.[53] Instead, Heicklen would simply stand on the steps handing out literature to anyone who wanted it, hoping that there might be jurors among them.[54] While the prosecutors on the case refused to comment, one former prosecutor stated that Heicklen's activities could confuse and mislead jurors.[55]

Maintaining Ethics When Using Jury Nullification: It Can Be Done

To see the harm that reckless jury nullification can cause, one need only look back 50 or 60 years. The Civil Rights Era became a clear and resounding example of jury nullification at its worst, when racist Southerners refused to convict defendants who had perpetrated heinous crimes against civil rights activists. There can be no argument that care must be taken when considering nullification, because juries can be used to enhance and augment the power of the elite rather than to limit it.

With this proviso, however, jury nullification can be a critical and necessary limitation on a legislative branch of government bent on promulgating, and a judiciary bent on enforcing, ever more overreaching criminal laws — including an increasing plethora of intentless crimes and those in which the government attempts to proscribe behavior that is not obviously seen by the public at large as dangerous or criminal.

Determining a jurisdiction's position on the issue of whether to instruct jurors of their ability to exercise nullification is often as simple as typing a few words into Lexis or Westlaw. It is more difficult, perhaps, to know if and when it is ethical.

It would be rash for a defense attorney to argue that nullification is appropriate in every case. It is a practice that must be used and considered only in the factual context of a particular case or defendant. Consider, for example, an article written by law professor Paul Butler. In his article entitled *Racially Based Jury Nullification: Black Power in the Criminal Justice System*,[56] Professor Butler argued that "the race of a black defendant is sometimes a legally and morally appropriate factor for jurors to consider in reaching a verdict of not guilty or for an individual juror to consider in refusing to vote for conviction."[57] While the article did seem to have the benefit of bringing the issue of nullification to the attention of courts across the country, it was met with a great deal of apprehension. Fearful, perhaps, of its reckless application, courts became eager to establish precedent that nullification would not be tolerated. In *United States v. Thomas*, the court made clear that "[n]ullification is, by definition, a violation of a juror's oath to apply the law as instructed by the court."[58]

Since nullification has been considered a "violation of a juror's oath,"[59] and it is well known that "neither the court nor counsel should encourage jurors to violate their oath,"[60] practitioners must take care when attempting to utilize jury nullification. A lawyer's attempt (often in closing argument) must strike a perfect balance between not "mak[ing] arguments calculated to appeal to the prejudices of the jury"[61] and fulfilling the foremost obligation to the client — "actin[ing] with commitment and dedication to the interests of the client and with zeal in advocacy upon the client's behalf."[62]

Because there are very few states that allow affirmative nullification arguments or instructions, informing members of the jury of their ability to nullify must be done with some finesse. When appropriate, it is the zealous advocate's obligation to inform the jury that improper or even immoral prosecutions do not have to be tolerated. They must be told that the decision of what is improper or immoral can be their decision to make.

In a Senate hearing held in October 2011, Supreme Court Justice Antonin Scalia was asked about his opinion of the jury in checking governmental power. He responded that it would not be inappropriate for jurors to "ignore the law" if the law "is producing terrible results."63 The people of the United States, in their role as jurors, have found that on a number of occasions, "terrible results" were indeed being produced. Jury nullification has continued, throughout history, to right society's perception of wrong. Northern jurors used their authority to nullify when they refused to convict runaway slaves under the fugitive slave laws. Later, jurors were largely responsible for the end of Prohibition. More recently, American jurors have "judged the law" criminalizing homosexual conduct by refusing to convict citizens based on consensual conduct that happened in one's home. In such cases nullification ought to be embraced. Armed with this historical perspective, defense counsel can help members of the jury understand that they are indeed liberty's last defense.

Index of Authorities

Chapter 1

1. M.C.L. 257.625(1)(c)
2. P.A. 1917, No. 164; C.L.1948, § 257.625; P.A.1949, No. 300, § 625, Eff. Sept. 23.
3. P.A.2003, No. 61; M.C.L.257.625.
4. C.L.1948, § 257.625c; P.A.1949, No. 300, § 1, Eff. Sept. 23, added by P.A.1967, No. 253, § 1, Eff. Nov. 2, 1967.
5. http://www.sadd.org/ accessed 11/6/2012

Chapter 2

6. M.C.L. 257.625a.
7. M.C.L.
8. M.C.L. 257.625(1)(a).
9. M.C.L. 333.7210 et. seq.; M.C.L. 333.7216.
10. M.C.L. 257.625(25).
11. http://www.hpus.com/ accessed 2/7/2013
12. http://desimd.com/list-of-drugs/H?drug_type[human-prescription]=human-prescription&drug_type[human-otc]=human-otc&drug_type[homeopathic]=homeopathic&drug_type[animal]=animal&drug_type[remainder]=remainder&page=120 accessed 2/7/2013
13. http://www.pharmqd.com/node/85781/lesson accessed 2/7/2013
14. http://www.pbm.va.gov/NationalFormulary.aspx accessed 2/7/2013
15. No person ... shall be compelled in any criminal case to be a witness against himself... **U.S.C. Const. Amend. V.**
16. **U. S. ex rel. Young v. Follette,** S.D.N.Y.1970, 308 F.Supp. 670; **U.S. ex rel. Parker v. McMann,** D.C.N.Y.1969, 308 F.Supp. 477; **U. S. v. Smith,** 31 F.R.D. 553 (D.D.C 1962).
17. **Miranda v. Arizona,** 86 S.Ct. 1602, 384 U.S. 436, 16 L.Ed.2d 694, (1966).
18. **Malloy v. Hogan,** 84 S.Ct. 1489, 378 U.S. 1, 12 L.Ed.2d 653 (1964).
19. **U. S. v. Henry,** 604 F.2d 908 (1979); **U.S. v. Brooks,** 284 F. 908 (1922).
20. **Smith v. Fairman,** 862 F.2d 630 (1988).
21. **Waldrop v. Thigpen,** 857 F.Supp. 872 (1994).
22. **Hiibel v. Sixth Judicial Dist. Court of Nevada,** Humboldt County, 542 U.S. 177, 124 S.Ct. 2451, 159 L.Ed.2d 292 (2004).
23. **People v. Burrell,** 417 Mich. 439, 339 N.W.2d 403 (1983).
24. Kwasnoski, John B., Stephen, John, & Partridge, Gerald, *Officer's DUI Handbook*, Lexis Publishing (1998) at 3.
25. Fenella Sanders, *Straight Talk - R&D - News of science, medicine, and technology*, Discover Vol. 21, No. 10 (Oct. 2000).
26. NHTSA 1995.

[27] http://www.nhtsa.dot.gov/people/injury/pedbimot/motorcycle/610DWIMotorcyWeb/images/Motorcyclists.pdf. Accessed 11/6/2012
[28] **Whren v. United States,** 517 U.S. 806, 116 S.Ct. 1769, 135 L.Ed.2d 89 (1996).**Ohio v. Robinette,** 519 U.S. 33, 117 S. Ct. 417, 136 L. Ed. 2d 347 (1996); **Atwater v. City of Lago Vista,** 532 U.S. 318, 121 S.Ct. 1536, 149 L.Ed.2d 549 (2001); **Hiibel v. Sixth Judicial Dist. Court of Nevada, Humboldt County,** 542 U.S. 177, 124 S.Ct. 2451, 159 L.Ed.2d 292 (2004); **Illinois v. Caballes,** 543 U.S. 405, 125 S.Ct. 834, 160 L.Ed.2d 842 (2005).
[29] **Terry v Ohio,** 392 US 1, 88 S Ct 1868, 20 L Ed 2d 889 (1968).
[30] **State v. Despain,** 74 P.3d 1176 (Utah Ct. App. 2003).
[31] M.C.L. 257.625a(2)(d).
[32] Due Process clauses of the Vth Amendment, IVX Amendment, U.S.C.
[33] M.C.L. 257.625f(1)(a).
[34] M.C.L. 257.625g.
[35] M.C.L. 257.323c.
[36] M.C.L. 257.323c.
[37] M.C.L. 257.625d.
[38] **Schneckloth v. Bustamonte,** 412 U.S. 218, 93 S.Ct. 2041, 36 L.Ed.2d 854 (1973).
[39] **Breithaupt v. Abram,** 352 U.S. 432, 1 L. Ed. 2d 448, 77 S. Ct. 408 (1957); M.C.L. 257.625a(6).
[40] M.C.L. 257.625a(6).
[41] M.C.L. 257.625d.
[42] **People v. Hanna,** 223 Mich.App. 466, 567 N.W.2d 12 (1997).
[43] M.C.L. 257.625f(1)(a).
[44] **Atwater v. City of Lago Vista,** 532 U.S. 318, 121 S.Ct. 1536, 149 L.Ed.2d 549 (2001)
[45] You have the right to remain silent. Anything you say can and will be used against you in a court of law. You have the right to have an attorney present during questioning. If you cannot afford an attorney, one may be appointed for you. **Miranda v. Arizona,** 384 U.S. 436, 86 S.Ct. 1602, 16 L.Ed.2d 694 (1966).
[46] M.C.L. 257.625c.
[47] **People v. Borchard-Ruhland,** 460 Mich. 278, 597 N.W.2d 1 (1999).
[48] **People v. Green,** 260 Mich.App. 392, 677 N.W.2d 363 (2004).
[49] M.C.L. 257.625a(6)(b).
[50] **People v. Dicks,** 190 Mich.App. 694, 476 N.W.2d 500 (1991).
[51] **People v. Anstey,** 476 Mich. 436; 719 N.W.2d 579 (2005).
[52] M.C.L. 257.625d.
[53] M.C.L. 257.625(7)(B)(ii).
[54] Id.

Chapter 3

[55] No person …shall be compelled in any criminal case to be a witness against himself…U.S.C. Const. Amend. V.
[56] M.C.L. Const. Art. 1, § 17.
[57] **Miranda v. Arizona,** 86 S.Ct. 1602, 384 U.S. 436, 16 L.Ed.2d 694 (1966).
[58] **Malloy v. Hogan,** 84 S.Ct. 1489, 378 U.S. 1, 12 L.Ed.2d 653 (1964).

Index of Authorities | 351

[59] **U. S. v. Henry,** 604 F.2d 908 (1979); **U.S. v. Brooks,** 284 F. 908 (1922).
[60] **Smith v. Fairman,** 862 F.2d 630 (1988).
[61] **Waldrop v. Thigpen,** 857 F.Supp. 872 (1994).
[62] MCR 8.110(c).

Chapter 4

[63] Makins, Bird, Root, *Making Star Teams Out of Star Players,* Harvard Business Review, (January-February 2013), pg. 74
[64] Id.
[65] www.google.com.
[66] www.bing.com.
[67] www.ncdd.com/.
[68] www.nacdl.org/public.nsf/freeform/publicwelcome?opendocument.
[69] www.martindale.com/xp/Martindale/home.xml.
[70] www.abanet.org/barserv/stlobar.html.
[71] www.abanet.org/legaled/approvedlawschools/alpha.html.
[72] Health Insurance Portability and Accountability Act of 1996 {HIPAA}. 42 U.S.C. § 1320d et. seq

Chapter 5

[73] **People v. Veling,** 443 Mich. 23, 504 N.W.2d 456 (1993).
[74] M.C.L. 257.904a.
[75] M.C.L. 257.322(6)(a); M.C.L. 257.625k.
[76] M.C.L. 257.323c.
[77] M.C.L. 257.319(8)(b)
[78] M.C.L. 257.319 8(g)(h)
[79] M.C.L. 257.303(1)(c).
[80] M.C.L.S. 257.903.
[81] M.C.L. 257.302a.
[82] M.C.L. 257.625; M.C.L. 257.323c.
[83] M.C.L. 257.319.
[84] M.C.L. 257.625.
[85] M.C.L. 257.625b.
[86] M.C.L. 257.732a.
[87] M.C.L. 257.625 et. seq.
[88] M.C.L. 257.625.

Chapter 6

[89] http://dictionary.law.com/default2.asp?typed=defense&type=1&submit1.x=49&submit1.y=12.
[90] **Cochran v. United States,** 157 U.S. 286
[91] M.C.L. Const. Art. 1, § 20; 21A Am. Jur.2d Criminal Law § 979.

[92] **Spencer v. State of Tex.**, 385 U.S. 554, 87 S. Ct. 648, 17 L.Ed.2d 606 (1967); M.C.L. Const. Art.1, § 20.
[93] The right of the people to be secure in their persons, houses, papers, and effects, against unreasonable searches and seizures, shall not be violated, and no Warrants shall issue, but upon probable cause, supported by Oath or affirmation, and particularly describing the place to be searched, and the persons or things to be seized. **U.S.C. Const. Amend. IV.**
[94] **People v. Tracy,** 186 Mich.App. 171, 463 N.W.2d 457 (1990).
[95] http://dictionary.law.com/default2.asp?typed=search+warrant&type=1&submit1.x=52&submit1.y=7.
[96] **Michigan Dept. of State Police v. Sitz,** 496 U.S. 444, 110 S.Ct. 2481, 110 L.Ed.2d 412 (1990).
[97] **Sitz v. Department of State Police,** 443 Mich. 744, 506 N.W.2d 209 (1993).
[98] **Delaware v. Prouse,** 440 U.S. 648, 99 S.Ct. 1391, 59 L.Ed.2d 660 (1979); **People v. Nelson,** 443 Mich. 626, 505 N.W.2d 266 (Mich. 1993).
[99] **People v. Shabaz,** 424 Mich. 42, 378 N.W.2d 451 (1985).
[100] **People v. Rizzo,** 243 Mich. App. 151, 622 N.W.2d 319 (2000).
[101] The right of the people to be secure in their persons, houses, papers, and effects, against unreasonable searches and seizures, shall not be violated... **U.S.C. Const. Amend. IV.**
[102] **Berkemer v. McCarty,** 468 U.S. 420, 104 S.Ct. 3138.82 L.Ed.2d 317 (1984); **People v. Zahn,** 234 Mich.App.438, 594 N.W.2d 120 (1999).
[103] **People v. Green,** 260 Mich. App. 392, 677 N.W.2d 363 (2004).
[104] **People v. Dunbar,** 264 Mich. App. 240, 690 N.W.2d 476 (2004); **United States v. Jackson,** 652 F.2d 244
[105] **Stansbury v. California,** 511 U.S. 318, 114 S. Ct. 1526, 128 L.Ed.2d 293 (1994); **Berkemer v. McCarty,** 468 U.S. 420, 104 S.Ct. 3138.82 L.Ed.2d 317 (1984)
[106] **People v Roark,** 214 Mich. App. 421, 423; 543 N.W.2d 23 (1995).
[107] **People v. Stephen,** 262 Mich. App. 213, 685 N.W.2d 309 (2004).
[108] **People v. Rizzo,** 243 Mich. App. 151, 622 N.W.2d 319 (2000).
[109] The right of the people to be secure in their persons, houses, papers, and effects, against unreasonable searches and seizures, shall not be violated... U.S.C. Const. Amend. IV. See also, **People v Chambers,** 195 Mich. App. 118, 123; 489 N.W.2d 168 (1992).
[110] **Florida v. Royer,** 460 U.S. 491, 103 S.Ct. 1319, 75 L.Ed.2d 229 (1983); **People v. Dunbar,** 264 Mich.App.240, 690 N.W.2d 476 (2004).
[111] **Illinois v. Caballes,** 125 S.Ct. 834, 160 L.Ed.2d 842 (2005).
[112] **Illinois v. Andreas,** 463 U.S. 765, 103 S.Ct. 3319, 77 L.Ed.2d 1003 (1983);
[113] **People v. Kazmierczak,** 461 Mich. 411, 605 N.W.2d 667, 674 n.13 (Mich. 2000); **Edmond v. State,** 951 N.E.2d 585, 593 (Ind. Ct. App. 2011)
[114] **New York v. Belton** 453 U.S. 454, 101 S.Ct 2860, 69 L.Ed.2d 768 (1981).
[115] **Whren v. U.S.,** 517 U.S. 806, 116 S.Ct. 1769, 135 L.Ed.2d 89 (1996);
[116] **Arizona v. Gant** 556 U.S. 332 129 S. Ct. 1710 173 L. Ed. 2d 485 (2009)

[117] **Mich. Const. 1963, art 1, § 17; Paramount Pictures Corp. v. Miskinis,** 418 Mich. 708, 344 N.W.2d 788 (1984).
[118] **Miranda v. Arizona,** 384 U.S. 436, 86 S.Ct. 1602, 16 L.Ed.2d 694 (1966); **People v. Burton,** 252 Mich.App.130, 651 N.W.2d 143 (Mich. App. 2002).
[119] **Berghuis v. Thompkins** 560 US ___; 130 S.Ct. 2250; 176 L. Ed. 2d 1098 (2010).
[120] **People v. Burton,** 252 Mich. App. 130, 651 N.W.2d 143 (2002).
[121] **Berkemer v. McCarty,** 468 U.S. 420, 104 S.Ct. 3138, 82 L.Ed.2d 317 (1984); **Hughes v. State,** 259 Ga. 227, 378 S.E.2d 853 (1989).
[122] **People v. Burhans,** 166 Mich. App. 758, 421 N.W.2d 285 (1988).
[123] In all criminal prosecutions, the accused shall enjoy the right... to have the Assistance of Counsel for his defense. U.S.C. Const. Amend. VI.
[124] **Escobedo v. State of Ill.,** 378 U.S. 478, 84 S.Ct. 1758, 12 L.Ed.2d 977 (1964).
[125] **Messiah v. United States,** 377 U.S. 201, 84 S.Ct. 1199, 12 L.Ed.2d 246 (1964).
[126] **People v. Mullen,** 282 Mich. App. 14, 762 N.W.2d 170 (2008), and **People v. Berger,** 217 Mich. App. 213, 551 N.W.2d 421 (1996).
[127] Id. *and see* **People v. Coy,** 258 Mich.App.1, 669 N.W.2d 831 (2003).
[128] **People v. Mullen,** 282 Mich. App. 14, 762 N.W.2d 170 (2008), and **People v. Berger,** 217 Mich. App. 213, 551 N.W.2d 421 (1996).
[129] **People v. Berger,** 217 Mich. App. 213, 551 N.W.2d 421 (1996).
[130] **People v. Berger,** 217 Mich. App. 213, 551 N.W.2d 421 (1996)
[131] **People v. Mullen,** 282 Mich. App. 14, 762 N.W.2d 170 (2008).
[132] **People v. Mullen,** 282 Mich. App. 14; 762 N.W.2d 170
[133] Barone, Crampton, *Do Standardized Field Sobriety Tests Reliably Predict Intoxication,"* Mich. Bar. J. July, 2005, http://www.michbar.org/journal/pdf/pdf4article882.pdf
[134] **People v. Sheldon,** 234 Mich. App. 68, 592 N.W.2d 121 (1999).
[135] MCR 6.201(A)(6).
[136] MCR 6.201(B)(2).
[137] MCR 6.201(A)(1).
[138] MCR 6.201(B)(3).
[139] MCR 6.201(B)(1).
[140] M.C.L. 257.625a(8).
[141] MCR 6.201(A).
[142] MCR 6.201(J).
[143] **People v. Johnson,** 197 Mich. App. 362, 494 N.W.2d 873 (1992).
[144] **People v. Greenfield,** 271 Mich. App. 442, 722 N.W.2d 254 (2006).
[145] M.C.L. 257.625a(6)(b).
[146] M.C.L. 257.625a(6)(b)(iv).
[147] **People v. Borchard-Ruhland,** 460 Mich. 278, 597 N.W.2d 1 (1999).
[148] **People v. Brady,** 2001 WL 651357 (Mich. App. 2001).
[149] **People v. Anstey,** 476 Mich. 436 (Mich., 2006).
[150] M.C.L. 257.625a(6).
[151] **People v. Anstey,** 476 Mich. 436 (Mich., 2006).
[152] M.C.L. 257.625a(6)(b)(ii).

[153] D. Shinar, E. Schechtman, R. Compton, *Drug identification on the basis of observable signs and symptoms.*, Accident Analysis and Prevention, 2005.
[154] **People v. Fosnaugh,** 248 Mich. App. 444, 639 N.W.2d 587 (2001).
[155] **People v. Hagadorrn,** 2007 Mich. App. LEXIS 1982
[156] **People v. Wujkowski,** 230 Mich. App. 181, 583 N.W.2d 257 (1998).
[157] M.C.R. 6.202
[158] **People v. Fosnaugh,** 248 Mich. App. 444, 639 N.W.2d 587 (2001).
[159] **People v. Fosnaugh,** 248 Mich. App. 444, 639 N.W.2d 587 (2001).
[160] **People v. Perry,** 2002 WL 31930765 (Mich. App. 2002).
[161] **People v. Fosnaugh,** 248 Mich. App. 444, 639 N.W.2d 587 (2001).
[162] **Bauer v. Veith,** 374 Mich. 1, 130 N.W.2d 897 (1964); **People v. Cords,** 75 Mich.App.415, 254 N.W.2d 911 (1977).
[163] **Morris, The Champion,** Pg. 12, May 2012.
[164] **Hunter v. State,** 55 A.3d 360. Del. Supr., (2012).
[165] Tavris, Aronson, *Mistakes Were Made (but not by me) Why We Justify Foolish Beliefs, Bad Decisions and Hurtful Acts,* Harvest Books (2007).
[166] Id. at pg. 13.
[167] ... nor shall any person be subject for the same offence to be twice put in jeopardy of life or limb... U.S.C. Const. Amend. V.
[168] **U.S. v. Jorn,** 400 U.S. 470, 91 S.Ct. 547, 27 L.Ed.2d 543 (1971); **People v. Williams,** 85 Mich.App.258, 271 N.W.2d 191 (1978).
[169] **People v. McEwan,** 214 Mich. App. 690, 543 N.W.2d 367 (1995).
[170] **United States v. Ursery,** 518 U.S. 267, 116 S.Ct. 2135, 135 L.Ed.2d 549 (1996).
[171] **United States v. Ursery,** 518 U.S. 267, 116 S.Ct. 2135, 135 L.Ed.2d 549 (1996).
[172] http://dictionary.law.com/default2.asp?typed=collateral+estoppel&type=1; **Ditmore v. Michalik,** 244 Mich.App.569, 625 N.W.2d 462 (Mich. App. 2001).
[173] Res judicata - http://dictionary.law.com/default2.asp?typed=res+judicata&type=1; **Labor Council, Michigan Fraternal Order of Police v. City of Detroit,** 207 Mich. App.606, 525 N.W.2d 509 (1994).
[174] M.C.L. 780.131; M.C.L. 780.133.
[175] M.C.L. Const. Art. 1, § 20; M.C.L. 768.1
[176] MCR 8.110(4)(5)
[177] **Barker v. Wingo,** 407 U.S. 514, 92 S.Ct. 2182, 33 L.Ed.2d 101 (1972); **People v. McLaughlin,** 258 Mich.App.635, 672 N.W.2d 860 (2003).
[178] **People v. Hubbard,** 115 Mich. App 73, 77;320 NW2d 294 (1982)
[179] **People v. Lemons,** 454 Mich. 234, 562 N.W.2d 447 (1997).
[180] http://dictionary.law.com/default2.asp?selected=597&bold=duress||
[181] Vosk, *Measurement Uncertainty,* Encyclopedia of Forensic Sciences, Chapter 324 (2nd ed. Elsevier, In Press).
[182] **People v. Thill,** 297 Ill.App.3d 7, 696 N.E.2d 1175, 231 Ill. Dec. 604 (Ill.App. 2 Dist. 1998); **Trillo v. State,** 165 S.W.3d 763 (Tex.App.-San Antonio 2005); **State v. Downie,** 117 N.J. 450, 569 A.2d 242, 90 A.L.R.4th 135 (N.J. Jan 31, 1990).
[183] **People v Bonutti,** 212 Ill 2d 182; 817 NE2d 489 (2002)

Chapter 7

[184] The right of the people to be secure in their persons, houses, papers, and effects, against unreasonable searches and seizures, shall not be violated... U.S.C. Const. Amend. IV.
[185] [N]or shall any State deprive any person of life, liberty, or property, without due process of law... U.S.C. Const. Amend. XIV.
[186] M.C.L. Const. Art. 1, § 11.
[187] **Whren v. U.S.**, 517 U.S. 806, 116 S.Ct. 1769, 135 L.Ed.2d 89 (1996).
[188] **Nardone v. United States**, 308 U.S. 338
[189] **Delaware v. Prouse**, 440 U.S. 648, 99 S.Ct. 1391, 59 L.Ed.2d 660 (1979); **People v. Green**, 260 Mich.App.392, 677 N.W.2d 363 (2004).
[190] **People v. Robinson**, 79 Mich. App. 145, 261 N.W.2d 544 (1977).
[191] **People v. Johnson**, 1996 WL 33347791 (Mich. App. 1996); **People v. Williams**, 236 Mich.App.610, 601 N.W.2d 138 (1999); M.C.L. 257.683.
[192] **People v. Williams**, 236 Mich. App. 610, 601 N.W.2d 138 (1999).
[193] **Sitz v. Department of State Police**, 443 Mich. 744, 506 N.W.2d 209 (1993).
[194] **People v. Jones**, 260 Mich. App. 424, 678 N.W.2d 627 (2004).
[195] **Alabama v. White**, 496 U.S. 325, 110 S.Ct. 2412, 110 L.Ed.2d 301 (1990); **Florida v. J.L.**, 529 U.S. 266, 120 S.Ct. 1375, 146 L.Ed.2d 254 (2000).
[196] **Crawford v. Washington**, 541 U.S. 36, 124 S.Ct. 1354, 158 L.Ed.2d 177 (2004).
[197] **People v. Green**, 260 Mich. App. 392, 677 N.W.2d 363 (2004).
[198] The right of the people to be secure in their persons, houses, papers, and effects, against unreasonable searches and seizures, shall not be violated... U.S.C. Const. Amend. IV.
[199] [N]or shall any State deprive any person of life, liberty, or property, without due process of law... U.S.C. Const. Amend. XIV.
[200] **People v. Williams**, 236 Mich. App. 610, 601 N.W.2d 138 (1999).
[201] **People v. Williams**, 472 Mich. 308, 696 N.W.2d 636 (2005); **People v. Parisi**, 393 Mich. 31, 222 N.W.2d 757 (1974).
[202] The right of the people to be secure in their persons, houses, papers, and effects, against unreasonable searches and seizures, shall not be violated... U.S.C. Const. Amend. IV.
[203] **People v. Williams**, 472 Mich. 308, 696 N.W.2d 636 (2005); **People v. Christie**, 206 Mich.App.304, 520 N.W.2d 647 (1994).

Chapter 8

[204] **Brady v. Maryland**, 373 U.S. 83, 83 S.Ct. 1194, 10 L.Ed.2d 215 (1963).
[205] **Strickler v. Greene**, 527 U.S. 263, 119 S.Ct. 1936, 144 L.Ed.2d 286 (1999).
[206] **Taylor v. Illinois**, 484 U.S. 400, 108 S.Ct. 646, 98 L.Ed.2d 798 (1988).
[207] Endnote to 1999-3.
[208] **People v. Thomas**, 174 Mich. App. 411, 436 N.W.2d 687 (1989).
[209] http://dictionary.law.com/default2.asp?typed=subpena&type=1; M.C.L. 767A.9.

[210] **Anti-Kalsomine Co. v. Adsit**, 120 Mich. 250, 79 N.W. 186 (1899).
[211] http://dictionary.law.com/default2.asp?typed=subpena+duces+tecum&type=1
[212] M.C.L. § 15.231 et. seq.
[213] M.C.L. § 15.231 et. seq.
[214] M.C.L. 15.243.
[215] MCR 6.201.
[216] MCR 6.201(B)(1).
[217] M.C.L. § 15.231 et. seq.
[218] MCR 6.201(A)(1).
[219] MCR 6.201(A).
[220] MCR 6.201(A)(6).
[221] **People v. Greenfield,** 271 Mich. App. 442, 722 N.W.2d 254 (2006).
[222] M.C.L. § 15.231 et. seq.
[223] M.C.L. 257.625.
[224] **People v. Wager,** 460 Mich. 118, 594 N.W.2d 487 (1999).
[225] MCL 257.625(6)(a); MSA 9.2325(1)(6)(a).
[226] M.C.L. § 15.231 et. seq.
[227] MCR 6.201(B)(2).
[228] M.C.L. § 15.231 et. seq.

Chapter 9

[229] **Underwood v. Department of State,** 181 Mich. App. 168, 448 N.W.2d 779 (1989).
[230] P.A. 1917, No. 164.
[231] P.A. 1949, N0. 300, §625a.
[232] C.L.1970, § 257.625c.
[233] M.C.L. 257.625a(b)(6).
[234] **People v. Willis,** 180 Mich. App. 31, 446 N.W.2d 562 (1989); **People v. Green,** 260 Mich. App.392, 677 N.W.2d 363 (2004).
[235] **People v. Anstey,** --- N.W.2d ----, 2006 WL 2129807 (Mich., 2006).
[236] M.C.L. 257.625a(6)(b); **People v. Green,** 260 Mich. App. 392, 677 N.W.2d 363 (2004).
[237] **South Dakota v. Neville,** 459 U.S. 553, 74 L. Ed. 2d 748, 103 S. Ct. 916 (1983).
[238] **People v. Snyder,** 181 Mich. App. 768, 449 N.W.2d 703 (1989); M.C.L. 257.625a(6)(b).
[239] **People v. Green,** 260 Mich. App. 392, 677 N.W.2d 363 (2004).
[240] **People v. Willis,** 180 Mich. App. 31, 446 N.W.2d 562
[241] **People v. Borchard-Ruhland,** 460 Mich. 278, 597 N.W.2d 1 (1999); **People v. Keen,** 396 Mich. 573, 242 N.W.2d 405 (Mich. Jun 03, 1976).
[242] M.C.L. 257.625a(6)(b).
[243] **State v. Morale,** 174 Vt. 213, 811 A.2d 185 (Vt. 2002)
[244] **South Dakota v. Neville,** 459 U.S. 553, 74 L. Ed. 2d 748, 103 S. Ct. 916 (1983)." \l 4tc "
[245] Michigan Standard Jury Instruction 15.9.
[246] M.C.L. 257.625f.
[247] MCL 625(a)(6)(iv).
[248] **Schneckloth v. Bustamonte,** 412 U.S. 218, 93 S.Ct. 2041, 36 L.Ed.2d 854 (1973).

[249] **People v. Hanna,** 223 Mich. App. 466, 567 N.W.2d 12 (1997).
[250] **California v. Trombetta,** 467 U.S. 479, 104 S.Ct. 2528, 81 L.Ed.2d 413 (1984).
[251] **People v. Keen,** 396 Mich. 573, 242 N.W.2d 405 (1976).
[252] **Holmberg v. 54-A Judicial Dist. Judge,** 60 Mich. App. 757, 231 N.W.2d 543 (1975).
[253] See generally, Debra T. Landis, Annotation, *Request Before Submitting to Chemical Sobriety Test to Communicate With Counsel as Refusal to Take Test Under Implied Consent Law,* 97 A.L.R.3d 852 (2005).
[254] **Hall v. Department of State,** 60 Mich. App. 431, 231 N.W.2d 396 (1975).
[255] M.C.L.257.625a(2).
[256] M.C.L. 257.625a(2)(b)(ii).
[257] Logan, *Ethanol Content of Various Foods and Soft Drinks and their Potential for Interference with a Breath-Alcohol Test,* Journal of Analytical Toxicology, Vol. 22, May/June 1998.
[258] M.C.L. 257.625a(6)(b).
[259] **People v. Blondia,** 69 Mich. App. 554, 245 N.W.2d 130 (1976).
[260] M.C.L. 257.625a(6)(b).
[261] **People v. Green,** 260 Mich. App. 392, 677 N.W.2d 363 (2004); **People v. Dicks,** 190 Mich.App.694, 476 N.W.2d 500 (1991).
[262] **People v. Anstey,** 476 Mich. 436; 719 N.W. 2d 579
[263] **Collins v. Department of State,** 19 Mich. App. 498, 172 N.W.2d 879 (1969).
[264] Mich. Admin. Code R. 325.2655(e).
[265] **People v. Boughner,** 209 Mich. App. 397, 531 N.W.2d 746 (1995).
[266] M.C.L. 257.625f(4).
[267] De Novo: Considering the matter anew, the same as if it had not been heard before and as if no decision previously had been rendered. **Ness v. Commissioner,** 954 F.2d 1495, 1497 (9th Cir. 1992).
[268] **People v. Hanna,** 223 Mich. App. 466, 567 N.W.2d 12 (1997).tc "
[269] M.C.L. 257.625c.
[270] M.C.L. 257.625a(6)(b).M.C.L.M.C.L.M.C.L.M.C.L. M.C.L.M.C.L.M.C.L.
[271] **People v. Anstey,** 476 Mich. 436; 719 N.W.2d 579 (2006).
[272] **Sheehan v. State,** 267 Ga. App. 152, 598 S.E.2d 873 (2004).
[273] **Butts v. City of Peachtree City,** 205 Ga. App. 492, 422 S.E.2d 909 (1992).
[274] **Reibel v. Curry,** 38 Ohio Misc. 71, 313 N.E.2d 26 (1974); **Huber v. Comm'r,** 382 N.W.2d 573 (Minn. App., 1986). For two emphysema cases, which should be adaptable to COPD or lung cancer patients, see **Burson v. Collier,** 226 Ga. 427, 175 S.E.2d 660 (1970); **Department of Public Safety v. Orr,** 122 Ga. App. 439, 177 S.E.2d 164 (1970).
[275] *See generally* Russell G. Donaldson, Annotation, *Sufficiency of Showing of Physical Inability to Take Tests for Driving While Intoxicated to Justify Refusal,* 68 A.L.R. 4th 776 (2005).

Chapter 10

[276] M.C.L. 257.625a(2).
[277] M.C.L. 257.625a(2)(b).

[278] **People v. Fosnaugh,** 248 Mich. App. 444, 639 N.W.2d 587 (2001).
[279] Mich. Admin. Code R. 325.2655(f).
[280] Mich. Admin. Code R. 325.2655 - table - from 0.01 to 0.04.
[281] **People v. Willis,** 180 Mich. App. 31, 446 N.W.2d 562 (1989).
[282] http://inventors.about.com/library/inventors/blair_bags.htm.
[283] M.C.L. 257.625a(8).
[284] **People v. Tipolt,** 198 Mich. App. 44, 497 N.W.2d 198 (1993).
[285] Mich. Admin. Code R. 325.2653(3).
[286] **People v. Tipolt,** 198 Mich. App. 44, 497 N.W.2d 198 (1993).
[287] **People v. Carter,** 78 Mich. App. 394, 259 N.W.2d 883 (1977).
[288] Barone, *Defending Drinking Drivers,* Chapter 2, Sec. 240, et. seq.
[289] Id.at Sec 244.
[290] Id.
[291] **People v. Cords,** 75 Mich. App. 415, 254 N.W.2d 911 (1977).
[292] **People v. White,** 208 Mich. App. 126, 527 N.W.2d 34 (1994); **People v. Stevens,** 88 Mich.App.421, 276 N.W.2d 910 (1979).
[293] M.C.L. 257.625a(6).
[294] M.C.L. 257.625a(6)(b)(ii); **People v. Hagelgans,** 1998 WL 1989997 (Mich. App. 1998).
[295] **People V. Koon** 296 Mich. App. 223; 818 N.W.2d 473; 2012 Mich. App. LEXIS 691
[296] M.C.L. 257.625.

Chapter 11

[297] M.C.L. 257.625f(1); M.C.L. 257.625g(1).
[298] M.C.L. 257.625f(2).
[299] **United States v. Ursery,** 518 U.S. 267, 116 S.Ct. 2135, 135 L.Ed.2d 549 (1996); **People v. Everard,** 225 Mich.App.455, 571 N.W.2d 536 (1997).
[300] **Bunce v. Secretary of State,** 239 Mich. App. 204, 607 N.W.2d 372 (1999).
[301] M.C.L. 257.625f(2).
[302] M.C.L. 257.322; **Wolney v. Secretary of State,** 77 Mich. App. 61, 257 N.W.2d 754 (1977).
[303] M.C.L. 257.625f.
[304] M.C.L. 257.625f.
[305] M.C.L. 257.625f(4).
[306] M.C.L. 257.323c(2); M.C.L. 257.625f..
[307] **People ex rel. Scodeller v. Clem,** 47 Mich. App. 517, 209 N.W.2d 689 (1973); **Tauriainen v. Secretary of State,** 69 Mich.App.318, 244 N.W.2d 462 (1976).

Chapter 12

[308] **People v. Edwards,** 55 Mich. App. 256, 222 N.W.2d 203 (1974); **People v. Burton,** 71 Mich.App.473, 247 N.W.2d 336 (1976).
[309] M.C.L. 257.625b(1).
[310] **People v. Carroll,** 396 Mich. 408, 240 N.W.2d 722 (Mich.1976).
[311] MCR 6.610.
[312] M.C.L. 257.625b(2).

[313] http://www.m w.com/cgi bin/dictionary?book=Dictionary&va=Compromise&x=11&y =16.

Chapter 13

[314] **People v. Cobbs,** 443 Mich. 276, 505 N.W.2d 208 (Mich. 1993).
[315] **People v Killebrew,** 416 Mich 189 (1992).
[316] M.C.L. 257.625b(3)
[317] Barone, *Defending Drinking Drivers,* Chapter 6, Sec. 604, et. seq.
[318] **Baldwin v. New York,** 399 U.S. 117, 90 S.Ct. 1914, 26 L.Ed.2d 446 (1970), M.C.L. Const. Art. 1, § 20.
[319] In all criminal prosecutions, the accused shall enjoy the right to a speedy and public trial, by an impartial jury of the State and district wherein the crime shall have been committed... U.S.C. CONST Amend. VI. [N]or shall any State deprive any person of life, liberty, or property, without due process of law; nor deny to any person within its jurisdiction the equal protection of the laws. U.S.C. CONST Amend. XIV; M.C.L. Const. Art. 1, § 20.
[320] **People v. Brewer,** 88 Mich. App. 756, 279 N.W.2d 307 (1979); **People v. Johnson,** 62 Mich.App.63, 233 N.W.2d 188 (1975).
[321] M.C.L. 257.625b(5).
[322] M.C.L. 257.625.
[323] M.C.L. 333.7411.
[324] M.C.L. 762.11.
[325] MCL 257.304(1)(b)
[326] MCL 257.304(2)(a) and (b)
[327] MCL 257.304(4)(a)-(d)
[328] MCL 257.304(4)
[329] MCL 257.304(5)
[330] MCL 257.304(5)(a) and (b)
[331] Kansas - K.S.A. § 8-1567(m)(5); Oregon - **State v. Young,** 196 Or.App. 708, 103 P.3d 1180 (2004); Delaware - 21 Del.C.§ 4177B; Florida - West's F.S.A. § 948.08.
[332] M.C.L. 780.621.
[333] M.C.L. 257.625b(3); M.C.L. Const. Art. 1, § 20.
[334] M.C.L. 780.621.
[335] M.C.L. Const. Art. 1, § 20.
[336] M.C.L. 257.625.

Chapter 14

[337] M.C.L. Const. Art. 1, § 20.
[338] M.C.L. 767.24.
[339] "In all criminal prosecutions, the accused shall enjoy the right to a speedy and public trial..." U.S.C. Const. Amend. VI. "In criminal cases, the defendant shall have a public and speedy trial by an impartial jury." M.C.L. 768.1; M.C.L. Const. Art.1, § 20.
[340] MR 6.004(C).

[341] http://dictionary.law.com/default2.asp?typed=motion+in+limine&type=1&submit1.x=68&submit1.y=5
[342] http://dictionary.law.com/default2.asp?typed=motion+in+limine&type=1&submit1.x=68&submit1.y=5
[343] **People v. Harris**, 86 Mich. App. 301, 272 N.W.2d 635 (1978).
[344] **People v. Randall**, 42 Mich. App. 187, 201 N.W.2d 292 (1972); **People v. Kinnebrew**, 75 Mich.App.81, 254 N.W.2d 662 (1977).
[345] **People v. Wingfield**, 2003 WL 22018389 (Mich. App. 2003); **People v. Wright**, 2001 WL 651353 (Mich. App. 2001).
[346] The right of the people to be secure in their persons, houses, papers, and effects, against unreasonable searches and seizures, shall not be violated... U.S.C. Const. Amend. IV; M.C.L. Const. Art.1, § 11.
[347] **Jackson v. Denno**, 378 U.S. 368, 84 S.Ct. 1774, 12 L.Ed.2d 908 (1964); **People v. Walker**, 374 Mich. 331, 132 N.W.2d 87 (1965).
[348] ... nor shall any person be subject for the same offence to be twice put in jeopardy of life or limb... U.S.C. Const. Amend. V; M.C.L. Const. Art.1, § 15.
[349] **People v. Dawson**, 431 Mich. 234, 427 N.W.2d 886 (Mich. 1988).
[350] **United States v. Ursery**, 518 U.S. 267, 116 S.Ct. 2135, 135 L.Ed.2d 549 (1996); **People v. Everard**, 225 Mich.App.455, 571 N.W.2d 536 (1997).
[351] M.C.L. 257.625.
[352] **Wayne County Prosecutor v. Recorder's Court Judge**, 406 Mich. 374, 280 N.W.2d 793 (1979).
[353] **Grady v. Corbin**, 495 U.S. 508
[354] **Dixon v. United States**, 509 U.S. 688 (1993)
[355] **Blockburger v. United States**, 284 U.S. 299 (1932)
[356] **People v. Matuszak**, 263 Mich. App. 42, 687 N.W.2d 342 (2004).
[357] **People v. Nelson**, 73 Mich. App. 395, 251 N.W.2d 602 (1977).
[358] MRE 404(b).
[359] MRE 405.
[360] MRE 403.
[361] **People v. Hicks**, 447 Mich. 819, 528 N.W.2d 136 (1994).
[362] **People v. Moler**, 2005 WL 1398338 (Mich. App.); **People v. Sampson**, 2005 WL 2323824 (Mich. App.).
[363] M.C.L. 768.37; **People v. Poyntz**, 2005 WL 1875584 (Mich. App. 2005).
[364] **People v Wilkins**, 184 Mich. App. 443 (1990).
[365] **City of Missoula v. Paffhausen**, 367 Mont. 80, 289 P.3d 141 (Mont., 2012).

Chapter 15

[366] **Baldwin v. New York**, 399 U.S. 117, 90 S.Ct. 1914, 26 L.Ed.2d 446 (1970), M.C.L. Const. Art. 1, § 20.
[367] In all criminal prosecutions, the accused shall enjoy the right to a speedy and public trial, by an impartial jury of the State and district wherein the crime shall have been committed... U.S.C. CONST Amend. VI. [N]or shall any State deprive any person of

life, liberty, or property, without due process of law; nor deny to any person within its jurisdiction the equal protection of the laws. U.S.C. CONST Amend. XIV; M.C.L. Const. Art. 1, § 20.

[368] **People v. Brewer,** 88 Mich. App. 756, 279 N.W.2d 307 (1979); **People v. Johnson,** 62 Mich.App.63, 233 N.W.2d 188 (1975); **People v. Redman,** 250 Mich. 334, 230 N.W. 196 (Mich. 1930).

[369] MCR 6.401.

[370] MCR 6.412(b).

[371] **People v. Martin,** 386 Mich. 407, 192 N.W.2d 215 (1971); **People v. Hall,** 48 Mich. 482, 12 N.W. 665 (1882).

[372] MCR 6.412(b).

[373] No person ... shall be compelled in any criminal case to be a witness against himself... U.S.C. Const. Amend. V; M.C.L. Const. Art.1, § 17.

[374] **People v. Page,**122 Mich. App. 80, 329 N.W.2d 541 (1982).

[375] **Carter v. Jury Commission of Greene County**, 396 U.S. 320, 90 S.Ct. 518, 24 L.Ed.2d 549 (1970).

[376] M.C.L. 600.1307a.

[377] M.C.L. 600.1307a(2).

[378] MCR 6.410.

[379] MCR 6.412(C).

[380] MCR 6.412(C)(2).

[381] MCR 6.412(D).

[382] MCR 2.511.

[383] MCR 2.511.

[384] MCR 6.412(D)(2).

[385] MCR 6.412(E).

[386] MCR 6.412(E)(1).

[387] MCR 6.412(E)(2).

[388] **Batson v. Kentucky,** 476 U.S. 79, 106 S.Ct. 1712, 90 L.Ed.2d 69 (1986); **Johnson v. California,** 125 S.Ct. 2410 (2005).

[389] **J.E.B. v. Alabama ex rel. T.B.,** 511 U.S. 127, 114 S.Ct. 1419, 128 L.Ed.2d 89 (1994).

[390] **People v. Daoust,** 228 Mich. App. 1, 577 N.W.2d 179 (1998).

[391] **Prosecutor's reference in opening statement to matters not provable or which he does not attempt to prove as ground for relief,** 16 A.L.R.4th 810 (1982-2005); **People v. Wolverton,** 227 Mich. App. 72, 574 N.W.2d 703 (1997).

[392] **Herring v. New York,** 422 U.S. 853, 95 S.Ct. 2550, 45 L.Ed.2d 593 (1975).

[393] **People v. Finley,**161 Mich. App. 1, 410 N.W.2d 282 (1987).

[394] **People v. Anstey,** 476 Mich. 436; 719 N.W.2d 579 (2006).

[395] MCR 6.410.

[396] M.C.L. 771.1 et. seq.

[397] MCR 6.610.

[398] **People v. Moler,** 474 Mich. 1055; 708 N.W.2d 438; 2006 Mich.); **People v. Sampson,** 2005 WL 2323824 (Mich. App. 2005).

[399] **People v. Tipolt,**198 Mich. App. 44, 497 N.W.2d 198 (1993).

[400] MCR 6.610.
[401] **People v. Fields**, 66 Mich.App.347, 239 N.W.2d 372 (1976); People v. Hill, 257 Mich. App.126, 667 N.W.2d 78 (2003).
[402] **Lamoreaux v. Ellis**, 89 Mich. 146, 50 N.W. 812 (1891).
[403] M.C.L. 257.625a(6)(a).
[404] Va. Code Ann. § 18.2-269(A)(4) - cocaine, methamphetamine, 3,4-methylenedioxymethamphetamine and PCP.
[405] M.C.L. 333.7210 et. seq.; M.C.L. 333.7216.
[406] M.C.L. Const. Art. 1, § 17; M.C.L. Const. Art.1, § 20.
[407] M.C.L. 257.625a(9).
[408] MCR 6.419.
[409] **City of Lansing v. Hartsuff**, 213 Mich. .App. 338, 539 N.W.2d 781 (1995).
[410] Michigan Standard Criminal Jury Instructions. [AMENDED] M Civ JI 3.08
"My comments, rulings, questions, [summary of the evidence,] and instructions are also not evidence. It is my duty to see that the trial is conducted according to the law, and to tell you the law that applies to this case. However, when I make a comment or give an instruction, I am not trying to influence your vote or express a personal opinion about the case. If you believe that I have an opinion about how you should decide this case, you must pay no attention to that opinion. You are the only judges of the facts, and you should decide this case from the evidence."
[411] Barone, Baldwin, *Independent Juries; Liberty's Last Defense,* Champion, Vol. 36, No. 10, Pg. 24 (Dec. 2012).
[412] M.C.L. 771.1 et. seq.
[413] M.C.L. 257-625.
[414] **People v. Snow**, 386 Mich. 586, 194 N.W.2d 314 (Mich. 1972).
[415] **People v. Alter**, 255 Mich. App.. 194, 659 N.W.2d 667 (2003).
[416] **People v. Tracey**, 221 Mich. App. 321, 561 N.W.2d 133 (1997); **People v. Pribble**, 72 Mich. App..219, 249 N.W.2d 363 (1976).
[417] M.C.L. 770.1.
[418] M.C.L. 770.2.
[419] **People v. Gay,** 149 Mich. App.. 468, 386 N.W.2d 556 (1986).
[420] **People v. Gay,**149 Mich. App.. 468, 386 N.W.2d 556 (1986).
[421] M.C.L. 600.2607; MCR 3.604.

Chapter 16

[422] MCR 6.420.
[423] **People v. McGee,** 247 Mich. App.. 325, 636 N.W.2d 531 (2001).
[424] **Johnson v. California,** 541 U.S. 428, 124 S.Ct. 1833, 158 L.Ed.2d 696 (2004); **People v. Martinez**, 193 Mich. App..377, 485 N.W.2d 124 (1992).
[425] **People v. Jackson,** 80 Mich. App.. 244, 263 N.W.2d 44 (1977); M.C.L. 257.625(18 and 19)
[426] MCR 6.419.
[427] **People v. Graves,** 458 Mich. 476, 581 N.W.2d 229 (1998).
[428] MCR 6.420(A).

429 MCR 6.420(D).
430 M.C.L. 771.1 et. seq.
431 MCR 6.410.
432 **Allen v. U.S.**, 164 U.S. 492, 17 S.Ct. 154, 41 L.Ed. 528 (1896).
433 MCR 6.425.
434 M.C.L. 257.625b(5).
435 MCR 6.425.
436 MCR 6.425(D)(2); **People v. Petit**, 466 Mich. 624, 648 N.W.2d 193 (Mich. 2002).
437 **People v. Baker**, 216 Mich. App.. 687, 551 N.W.2d 195 (1996); M.C.L. 257.625(4).
438 MCR 6.425(A)(1)
439 Mich. Crim. L. & Proc. § 111:33A.
440 **People v. Reichenbach**, 459 Mich. 109, 587 N.W.2d 1 (Mich. 1998).
441 M.C.L. 257.625(7).
442 M.C.L. 257.625(7)(a)(ii).
443 M.C.L. 257.625(7).
444 The sections of 257. 625 that were amended include 219, 303, 319, 625n, 626, 732a, and 904d.
445 Barone, *Michigan's New Sobriety/DWI Court Law,* Mich. Bar. J. (Jan. 2012), www.michbar.org/journal/pdf/pdf4article1976.pdf
446 M.C.L. 257.625(7).
447 MCR 6.425
448 M.C.L. 257.625(7).
449 M.C.L. 257.625(7).
450 Mich. Crim. L. & Proc. § 22:144.
451 **People v. Staley**, 127 Mich. App..38, 338 N.W.2d 414 (1983).
452 M.C.L. 257.625(24).
453 MCL 257.304

Chapter 17

454 M.C.L. 257.319b.
455 M.C.L. 257.323.
456 W.D. Mich. LCrR 57; MCR 3.604.
457 M.C.L. 770.1.
458 M.C.L. 770.3.
459 MCR 6.610.
460 **People v. Fields**, 66 Mich. App..347, 239 N.W.2d 372 (1976); **People v. Hill**, 257 Mich. App..126, 667 N.W.2d 78 (2003).
461 M.C.L. 770.1.
462 M.C.L. 770.2.
463 M.C.L. 769.26.
464 **People v. Grant**, 470 Mich. 477, 684 N.W.2d 686 (2004); **People v. Barbara**, 400 Mich. 352, 255 N.W.2d 171 (1977); M.C.L. 770.1.
465 **People v. Pickett**, 391 Mich. 305, 215 N.W.2d 695 (1974).

[466] **Dean v. Tucker,** 182 Mich. App.. 27, 451 N.W.2d 571 (1990).
[467] W.D. Mich. LCrR 57; MCR 3.604.
[468] M.C.L. 257.319.
[469] M.C.L. 257.323c.
[470] M.C.L. 780.621.
[471] 42 U.S.C. § 1983, **United States v. Sumner,** 226 F.3d 1005, 1012 (9th Cir. 2000); **State v. Ambaye,** 616 N.W.2d 256 (Minn. 2000).
[472] M.C.L. 780.621; **Siegel v. Hare,** 30 Mich. App.. 189, 186 N.W.2d 80 (1971).

Chapter 18

[473] M.C.L. 257.303(2)(b).
[474] M.C.L. 257.303(2).
[475] M.C.L. 257.303(2)(b).
[476] **Bunce v. Sec. of State,** 239 Mich. App.. 204, 607 N.W.2d 372 (2000).
[477] M.C.L. §257.904.
[478] M.C.L. 257.303(2)(b).
[479] M.C.L. 257.625(7)(a)(ii).
[480] **South Dakota v. Neville,** 459 U.S. 553, 103 S.Ct. 916, 74 L.Ed.2d 748 (1983).
[481] Fifth Amendment, Fourteenth Amendment, U.S.C.
[482] **Bunce v. Sec. of State,** 239 Mich. App.. 204, 607 N.W.2d 372 (2000).
[483] **Bunce v. Sec. of State,** 239 Mich. App.. 204, 607 N.W.2d 372 (2000).
[484] http://www.michigan.gov/documents/sos/SOS258_Substance_Use_Evaluation_Form_404465_7.pdf
[485] M.C.L. 257.904; M.C.L. 257.301; M.C.L. 257.904a.
[486] **Coker v. Georgia,** 433 U.S. 584, 97 S.Ct. 2861, 53 L.Ed.2d 982 (1997).
[487] M.C.L. §257.904.
[488] Defendant had to place ad in newspaper with his mug shot and a caption of "DUI convicted." - **Lindsay v. State,** 606 So.2d 652, 17 Fla. L. Weekly D2159 (Fla. App. 4 Dist. 1992); Making the person on probation wear a pink bracelet that said "DUI Convict," **Ballenger v. State,** 210 Ga. App. 627, 436 S.E.2d 793 (1993); Defendant must attend AA meetings and have random urine screens, or serve more jail time - **State v. Lamis,** 139 Ohio App.3d 617, 744 N.E.2d 1260 (Ohio App. 8 Dist. 2000)
[489] M.C.L. 257625(7)(a)(ii).
[490] M.C.L. 257.303.

Chapter 19

[491] M.C.L. 324.80101 *et. seq.*
[492] M.C.L. 324.80176.
[493] M.C.L. 324.80176(3).
[494] M.C.L. 324.80176.
[495] M.C.L. 324.80176(3).
[496] M.C.L. 324.80176(3).
[497] P.A.1903, No. 61; M.C.L. 257.625.

[498] M.C.L. 324.80184.
[499] M.C.L. 324.80187.
[500] M.C.L. 324.80189.
[501] M.C.L. 324.80186; M.C.L. 324.80197a; MCR 6.302.
[502] M.C.L. 324.80147.
[503] M.C.L. 324.80176(4).
[504] M.C.L. 324.80176(5).
[505] M.C.L. 324.80181(1)(b).
[506] M.C.L. 324.80181(1)(b).
[507] M.C.L. 324.80186(1)(b)(i).
[508] M.C.L. 324.80186(1)(b)(ii).
[509] M.C.L. 324.80177(a).
[510] M.C.L. 324.80177(b).
[511] M.C.L. 324.80180(1).
[512] M.C.L. 324.80180(2)(a).
[513] M.C.L. 324.80180.
[514] 14 C.F.R. § 91.17(a) No person may act or attempt to act as a crew member of a civil aircraft – (1) Within 8 hours after the consumption of any alcoholic beverage; (2) While under the influence of alcohol; (3) While using any drug that affects the person's faculties in any way contrary to safety; or (4) While having .04 percent by weight or more alcohol in the blood.
[515] M.C.L. 259.185.

Chapter 20

[516] **People v. Rogers,** 438 Mich. 602, 475 N.W.2d 717 (1991).
[517] Department of State, *What Every Driver Must Know,* (Michigan Department of State, 2011), 123.
[518] M.C.L. 324.82128(1)(a).
[519] M.C.L. 324.82128(3).
[520] Department of State,124.
[521] M.C.L. 324.82128(1)(b).
[522] Department of State,124 and 125.
[523] M.C.L. 324.82128(1)(c).
[524] Department of State,125.
[525] M.C.L. 324.82127(5).
[526] M.C.L. 324.82127(4).
[527] Department of State,125.
[528] Department of State,123.
[529] Department of State,56.
[530] M.C.L. 324.82128(5).
[531] Michigan Department of Natural Resources, *Handbook of Michigan Off-Road Vehicle Laws,* (Kalkomey Enterprises, Inc. 2011), 40.
[532] Michigan Department of Natural Resources, 40.

[533] **People v. O'Neal**, 198 Mich. App. 118, 497 N.W.2d 535 (1993).
[534] M.C.L. 324.81134.
[535] M.C.L. 324.81134(4).
[536] M.C.L. 324.81134(5).
[537] M.C.L. 324.81134(6).
[538] M.C.L. 324.81134(8).
[539] M.C.L. 324.81134(7).
[540] Department of State,124 and 125.
[541] M.C.L. 324.81134(9).
[542] M.C.L. 324.81134(10).
[543] M.C.L. 324.81134(11).
[544] M.C.L. 324.81134(12).
[545] M.C.L. 324.81135(2).
[546] Department of State,123 and 124.
[547] M.C.L. 324.81134(3).

Chapter 21

[548] M.C.L. 257.625(1)(c).
[549] M.C.L. 257.625(9)(a)(ii).
[550] M.C.L. 257.625(9)(a)(iii).
[551] M.C.L. 257.319(8)(g) and §MCL 257.322(9).
[552] M.C.L. 257.319(8)(h).
[553] M.C.L. 257.904d(1)(c) and §MCL 257.319(8)(i).
[554] M.C.L. 257.625l(2).
[555] M.C.L. 257.319(8)(g).
[556] M.C.L. 257.625b(5).
[557] M.C.L. 257.625(7)(a)(i).
[558] M.C.L. 257.625(7)(c).
[559] M.C.L. 257.625(a)(ii).
[560] M.C.L. 257.625(7)(c).
[561] M.C.L. 257.625(2).
[562] M.C.L. 257.625(10)(a).
[563] M.C.L. 257.625(10)(b).
[564] M.C.L. 257.625(10)(c).

Notes

1. *United States v. Powell*, 469 U.S. 57, 65 (1984).
2. *Id.*
3. Leonard W. Levy, Essays on the Making of the Constitution 258, 269 (2d ed. 1987).
4. *Id.*
5. Albert W. Alschuler, *A Brief History of Criminal Jury in the United States*, 61 U. Chi. L. Rev. 867, 871 (1994).
6. *Id.* at 874.
7. James Alexander, A Brief Narrative of the Case and Trial of John Peter Zenger, Printer of the New York Weekly Journal (1963).
8. *Id.*
9. *Id.* at 78 (Chief Justice DeLancey stated that "the jury may find that Zenger printed and published those papers, and leave it to the Court to judge whether they are libelous; you know this is very common; it is the nature of a special verdict, where the jury leave the matter of law to the Court.").
10. *Id.*
11. Declaration of Independence, 1 Stat. 1 (1776).
12. USCA Const. amend. VI-Jury Trials.
13. *See* U.S. Const. art. III, § 2, cl. 3 ("The trial of all Crimes ... shall be by jury"); *id.* amend. VI ("In all criminal prosecutions, the accused shall enjoy the right to a speedy and public trial, by an impartial jury of the State and district wherein the crime shall have been committed[.]").
14. U.S. Const. amend. V, VI, VII.
15. Akhil Reed Amar, *The Bill of Rights as a Constitution*, 100 Yale L.J. 1131, 1183 (1991).
16. *See supra* note 4.
17. *See* Alan Scheflin & Jon Van Dyke, *Jury Nullification: The Contours of a Controversy*, Law & Contempt. Probs. 51, 57-58 (Autumn 1980) (discussing the acceptance of nullification by the Founders).
18. *See infra*, note 20 and accompanying text.
19. *See* Richard E. Ellis, The Jeffersonian Crisis: Court and Politics in the Young Republic 115 (1971) (citing an early New Hampshire case in which the justice very deferentially instructed the jury that "[a] clear head and an honest heart are [worth] more than all the law of the lawyers").
20. *Georgia v. Brailsford*, 3 U.S. 1 (1794).
21. *Id.* at 4.
22. *Id.*
23. *See generally* Andrew J. Parmenter, *Nullifying the Jury: 'The Judicial Oligarchy' Declares War on Jury Nullification*, 46 Washburn L.J. 379 (2007).
24. *Id.* at 385.
25. *Id.*
26. *Sparf v. United States*, 156 U.S. 51 (1895).
27. Parmenter, *supra* note 23, at 385.

28. *Id.* at 107.
29. Many states suddenly struck down the practice of informing juries that they could judge the law as well as the facts. *See, e.g., Pierson v. States*, 12 Ala. 149 (1847); *Pleasant v. State*, 13 Ark. 360 (1852); and *State v. Buckley*, 40 Conn. 246 (1873).
30. Clay S. Conrad, *Jury Nullification as a Defense Strategy*, 2 Tex F. on C.L. & C.R. 1, 15 (1997).
31. *Sparf*, 156 U.S. at 106.
32. Parmenter, *supra* note 23, at 393.
33. *Id.* at 394.
34. *Id.* at 393.
35. John T. Reed, Comment, *Penn, Zender, and O.J.: Jury Nullification — Justice of the 'Wacko Fringe's' Attempt to Further It's Anti-Government Agenda?*, 34 Duq. L. Rev. 1125, 1125 (1996).
36. Arie M. Rubenstein, *Verdicts of Conscience: Nullification and the Modern Jury Trial*, 106 Colum. L. Rev. 959, 962 (2006).
37. *Id.*
38. *Id.*
39. *California v. Simpson*, Case No. BA097211 (Los Angeles Cnty., Cal. Sup. Ct., Oct. 3, 1995) (unpublished).
40. *See* Irwin A. Horowitz, *Jury Nullification: Legal and Psychological Perspectives*, 66 Brook. L. Rev. 1207, 1211 (2001).
41. *Horning v. District of Columbia*, 254 U.S. 135, 138 (1920).
42. *Compare* U.S. Const. art. I (describing the role of Congress), *id.* art. II (describing the role of the president), and *Id.* art. III (describing the role of the judiciary).
43. *Id.*
44. Letter of Jefferson to L'Abbe Armond, July 19, 1789, in 3 Works of Thomas Jefferson 81, 82 (Wash. ed. 1854).
45. *See generally* Clay S. Conrad, Jury Nullification: The Evolution of a Doctrine 167-205 (1998).
46. *Id.* at 171-73.
47. Alan W. Scheflin, *Jury Nullification: The Right to Say No*, 45 S. Cal. L. Rev. 168, 170 (1972).
48. B. Michael Dann, *'Must Find the Defendant Guilty,' Jury Instructions Violate the Sixth Amendment*, 91 Judicature 12 (July-Aug. 2007).
49. Will Lester, *Many Would Use Own Judgment as Jurors*, The Commercial Appeal (Memphis), Oct. 24, 1995, at A5.
50. *Dann* at 14.
51. *Id.*
52. Benjamin Weiser, *Jury Nullification Advocate Is Indicted*, N.Y. Times, Feb. 25, 2011, http://www.nytimes.com/2011/02/26/nyregion/26jury.html?_r=2&hp& (last visited Nov. 2, 2012).
53. *Id.*
54. *Id.*
55. *Id.*

56. Paul Butler, *Racially Based Jury Nullification: Black Power in the Criminal Justice System*, 105 Yale L.J. 677 (1995).
57. *Id.* at 679.
58. *United States v. Thomas*, 116 F.3d 606, 614 (2d Cir. 1997).
59. *Id.*
60. *United States v. Trujilo*, 714 F.2d 102, 106 (11th Cir. 1983).
61. American Bar Association Standards for Criminal Justice, 4-7.7.
62. Model Rules of Prof'l Conduct R. 1.3, cmt. 1.
63. Paul Butler, *Jurors Need to Know That They Can Say No*, N.Y. Times, Dec. 20, 2011, http:/www.nytimes.com/2011/12/21/opinion/jurors-can-say-no.html?_r=1&emc=eta1 (last visited April 16, 2011).

About the Author

Patrick T. Barone is the principal and founding member of The Barone Defense Firm, whose practice is exclusively limited to zealously defending citizens accused of intoxicated driving. The Firm has offices throughout Michigan. Mr. Barone is the author of two books on DUI defense including the well respected two volume treatise *Defending Drinking Drivers* (James Publishing), a chapter in *Defending DUI Vehicular Homicide Cases,* 2012 ed. (*West/Aspatore Books*), and has served as the executive editor of the nationally circulated legal periodical *The DWI Journal: Law & Science* (Whitaker Newsletters, Inc.) and the author of a monthly DUI defense column for Michigan's *Criminal Defense Newsletter*. Mr. Barone is an adjunct professor at the Thomas M. Cooley Law School where he teaches *Drunk Driving Law and Practice*. He is a graduate of the Gerry Spence Trial Lawyer's College, and is on the faculty of the Michigan Trial Practice College. Mr. Barone frequently lectures at national and state seminars attended by lawyers, judges and scientists, and he has provided expert commentary in newspapers, on television and on radio. Mr. Barone has an "AV" (highest) rating from *Martindale-Hubbell,* has been listed as "Seriously Outstanding" by *SuperLawyers,* rated "Outstanding/10.0" by AVVO and since 2009 has been included in the highly selective *US News & World Report's America's Best Lawyers,* and The Barone Defense Firm has been included in their companion *American's Best Law Firms.*